1986

Corner House Publishers

SOCIAL SCIENCE REPRINTS

General Editor MAURICE FILLER

*I pray God
to bless you
Martha Wilson*

THE WOMEN

OF THE

AMERICAN REVOLUTION.

BY

ELIZABETH F. ELLET,

AUTHOR OF "THE CHARACTERS OF SCHILLER," "COUNTRY RAMBLES," ETC

VOL. II.

CORNER HOUSE PUBLISHERS

WILLIAMSTOWN, MASSACHUSETTS 01267

1980

REPRINTED 1980

BY

CORNER HOUSE PUBLISHERS

ISBN 0–87928–107–3

Printed in the United States of America

CONTENTS OF VOL. II.

vi

CONTENTS.

XXVI.

MARTHA WASHINGTON.

NONE who take an interest in the history of Washington can fail to desire some knowledge of her who shared his thoughts and plans, and was associated with him in the great events of his life. Few women have been called to move, in the drama of existence, amid scenes so varied and imposing; and few have sustained their part with so much dignity and discretion. In the shades of retirement, or the splendor of eminent station, she was the same unostentatious, magnanimous woman; through the gloom of adverse fortune she walked by the side of the Chief, ascending with him the difficult path Heaven had opened before him; and when standing with him on the summit, in the full light of his power and renown, the eyes of her spirit looked still upward, seeking in the smile of the Supreme a reward which earthly honors could not bestow.

Though the life of Mrs. Washington was a changeful one, and had its full measure of sorrow and joy, it affords little material for the biographer. She moved in woman's domestic sphere, to which pertain not actions that strike the public eye, but uncomplaining

endurance, and continual, unnoted self-sacrifice. The
best account of her is the memoir prepared for the
National Portrait Gallery, by her grandson, George
Washington Parke Custis, of Arlington, D. C. According to this, Martha Dandridge was descended from an
ancient family that migrated to the colony of Virginia,
and was born in the county of New Kent, in May,
1732. Her education was only a domestic one, such
as was given to females in those days, when there were
few seminaries of instruction, and private teachers
were generally employed. Her beauty and fascinating
manners, with her amiable qualities of character, gained
her distinction among the ladies who were accustomed
to resort to Williamsburg, at that time the seat of government.

When but seventeen, Miss Dandridge was married
to Colonel Daniel Parke Custis, of the same county.
Their residence—called the "White House,"—was on
the banks of the Pamunkey River, where Colonel Custis
became a highly successful planter. None of the children of this marriage survived the mother; Martha,
who arrived at womanhood, died at Mount Vernon, in
1770; and John perished eleven years later, at the age
of twenty-seven.

Mrs. Custis was early left a widow, in the full bloom
of beauty and "splendidly endowed with worldly benefits." As sole executrix, she managed with great ability
the extensive landed and pecuniary business of the
estate. Surrounded by the advantages of fortune and
position, and possessing such charms of person, it may

well be believed that suitors for her hand and heart were many and pressing.

"It was in 1758," says her biographer, "that an officer, attired in a military undress, and attended by a body servant, tall and militaire as his Chief, crossed the ferry called Williams's, over the Pamunkey, a branch of the York River. On the boat touching the southern, or New Kent side, the soldier's progress was arrested by one of those personages who give the beau ideal of the Virginia gentleman of the old regime—the very soul of kindness and hospitality." He would hear of no excuse on the officer's part for declining the invitation to stop at his house. In vain the Colonel pleaded important business at Williamsburg ; Mr. Chamberlayne insisted that his friend must dine with him at the very least. He promised, as a temptation, to introduce him to a young and charming widow, who chanced then to be an inmate of his dwelling. At last the soldier surrendered at discretion, resolving, however, to pursue his journey the same evening. They proceeded to the mansion. Mr. Chamberlayne presented Colonel Washington to his various guests, among whom was the beautiful Mrs. Custis. Tradition says that the two were favorably impressed with each other at the first interview. It may be supposed that the conversation turned upon scenes in which the whole community had a deep interest—scenes which the young hero, fresh from his early fields, could eloquently describe ; and we may fancy with what earnest and rapt interest the fair listener " to hear did seriously in-

1*

cline ;" or how "the heavenly rhetoric of her eyes" beamed unconscious admiration upon the manly speaker. The morning passed ; the sun sank low in the horizon. The hospitable host smiled as he saw the Colonel's faithful attendant, Bishop, true to his orders, holding his master's spirited steed at the gate. The veteran waited, and marvelled at the delay. "Ah, Bishop," says a fair writer describing the occurrence, "there was an urchin in the drawing-room more powerful than King George and all his governors ! Subtle as a sphynx, he had hidden the important despatches from the soldier's sight, shut up his ears from the summons of the tell-tale clock, and was playing such mad pranks with the bravest heart in Christendom, that it fluttered with the excess of a new-found happiness !"

Mr. Chamberlayne insisted that no guest ever left his house after sunset ; and his visitor was persuaded, without much difficulty, to remain. The next day was far advanced when the enamored soldier was on the road to Williamsburg. His business there being despatched, he hastened to the presence of the captivating widow.

A short time after the marriage, which took place about 1759, Colonel and Mrs. Washington fixed their residence at Mount Vernon. The mansion was at that period a very small building compared with its present extent. It did not receive many additions before Washington left it to repair to the first Congress, and thence to the command-in-chief of the armies of his country. He was accompanied to Cambridge by Mrs. Washington, who remained some time with him, and witnessed the siege and evacuation of Boston. She then returned to Virginia.

So prevalent at one time was the disaffection, as Mrs. Washington herself remarked, that on a visit to Philadelphia, upon her way to camp one season, few of the ladies of the city called upon her. A passage from Christopher Marshall's manuscript diary for the year 1775,* curiously illustrates the state of popular feeling at the breaking out of the war. Mrs. Washington arrived in the city on the twenty-first of November, on her journey to Cambridge. A ball was in preparation, to be given on the twenty-fourth; and it was expected that both she and the wife of Colonel Hancock would grace the entertainment with their presence. But from some threats thrown out, it was feared that a commotion would be made, which might result in disturbance of the peace of the city. A large and respectable committee was held at the Philosophical Hall, called together for the purpose of considering the propriety of allowing the ball to be given that evening; and after mature consideration, it was concluded that no such entertainment should take place, either then, or during the continuance of those melancholy times. A committee was appointed to inform the managers that they must proceed no further in the preparations; and also to wait upon ' Lady Washington,' and request her not to attend at the assembly to which she had been invited. The committee acted agreeably to directions; and

* This passage may be found, quoted from the MS., in a note in the Life and Correspondence of President Reed. Vol. II., p. 24.

reported that Lady Washington had received them with great politeness, thanked the committee for their kind care and regard in giving her timely notice, and assured them that their sentiments on this occasion were perfectly agreeable to her own.

It was not often that the interest taken by Mrs. Washington in political affairs was evinced by any public expression. The address already mentioned, which was read in the churches of Virginia, and published in the Philadelphia papers, June 1780, as "The Sentiments of an American Woman"—was attributed—it cannot be ascertained with what truth—to her pen.* She passed the winters with her husband. Mr. Custis states that it was the habit of the Commander-in-chief to despatch an aid-de-camp, at the close of each campaign, to escort Mrs. Washington to head-quarters. Her arrival at camp was an event much anticipated; the plain chariot, with the neat postillions in their scarlet and white liveries, was always welcomed with great joy by the army, and brought a cheering influence, which relieved the general gloom in seasons of disaster and despair. Her example was followed by the wives of other general officers.

It happened at one time while the ladies remained later than usual in the camp on the Hudson, that an alarm was given of the approach of the enemy from New York. The aids-de-camp proposed that the ladies should be sent away under an escort. To this Washington would not consent. "The presence of our

* Remembrancer, Vol. VIII.

wives," said he, "will the better encourage us to a brave defence." The night was dark ; and the words of command from the officers, the marching of the troops, the dragging of artillery into the yard, and the noise of removing the windows of the house—the house itself being filled with soldiers—all gave " dreadful note of preparation." The enemy, however, finding themselves mistaken in their hopes of a surprise, withdrew without coming to blows.

Lady Washington, as she was always called in the army, usually remained at head-quarters till the opening of the succeeding campaign, when she returned to Mount Vernon. She was accustomed afterwards to say that it had been her fortune to hear the first cannon at the opening, and the last at the closing, of all the campaigns of the Revolutionary war. How admirably her equanimity and cheerfulness were preserved, through the sternest periods of the struggle—and how inspiriting was the influence she diffused, is testified in many of the military journals. She was at Valley Forge in that dreadful winter of 1777–8; her presence and submission to privation strengthening the fortitude of those who might have complained, and giving hope and confidence to the desponding. She soothed the distresses of many sufferers, seeking out the poor and afflicted with benevolent kindness, extending relief wherever it was in her power, and with graceful deportment presiding in the Chief's humble dwelling.* In a letter to Mrs. Warren she says, " The General's apartment is very small; he has

* Thacher's Journal and other authorities.

had a log cabin built to dine in, which has made our quarters much more tolerable than they were at first." Their table was but scantily furnished ; but the soldiers fared still worse, sitting down at a board of rough planks, set with horn spoons and a few tumblers ; the food being often salt herrings and potatoes, without other vegetables, or tea, coffee, or sugar. Their continental money was no temptation to the farmers to sell them produce. The stone jug passed round was filled with water from the nearest spring; and rare was the privilege of toddy in which to drink the health of the nation. Yet here, forgetful of herself, the patriot wife anxiously watched the aspect of affairs, and was happy when the political horizon brightened. She writes to Mrs. Warren—"It has given me unspeakable pleasure to hear that General Burgoyne and his army are in safe quarters in your State. Would bountiful Providence aim a like stroke at General Howe, the measure of my happiness would be complete."*

The Marquis de Chastellux says of Mrs. Washington, whom he met at the house of General Reed in Philadelphia,—"She had just arrived from Virginia, and was going to stay with her husband, as she does at the end of every campaign. She is about forty, or five-and-forty, rather plump, but fresh, and of an agreeable countenance." In another passage, he notices the camp life shared by her: "The head-quarters at Newburgh consist of a single house, built in the Dutch fashion, and neither large nor commodious. The largest

* MS letter, March 7th, 1778.

room in it, which General Washington has converted into his dining room, is tolerably spacious, but it has seven doors and only one window. The chimney is against the wall; so that there is, in fact, but one vent for the smoke, and the fire is in the room itself. I found the company assembled in a small room which served as a parlor. At nine, supper was served, and when bedtime came, I found that the chamber to which the General conducted me was the very parlor spoken of, wherein he had made them place a camp-bed. We assembled at breakfast the next morning at ten, during which interval my bed was folded up; and my chamber became the sitting room for the whole afternoon; for American manners do not admit of a bed in the room in which company is received, especially where there are women. The smallness of the house, and the inconvenience to which I saw that General and Mrs. Washington had put themselves to receive me, made me apprehensive lest M. Rochambeau might arrive on the same day. The day I remained at head-quarters was passed either at table or in conversation."

The recollections of a veteran still living at Manchester, Massachusetts, at the age of ninety-two, bear testimony to the kindness of Mrs. Washington towards those in the humblest sphere. One little incident occurred when she came to spend the cold season with her husband in winter-quarters. There were but two frame-houses in the settlement, and neither had a finished upper story. The General was contented with his rough dwelling, but wished to prepare for his wife a more retired and comfortable apartment. He sent for the young mechanic, and desired him and one of his fellow-apprentices to fit up a room in the upper story for the accommodation of Lady Washington through the winter. She herself arrived before the work was commenced. "She came," says the narrator, "into the place—a portly-looking, agreeable woman of forty-five, and said to us: 'Now, young men, I care for nothing but comfort here; and should like you to fit me up a beauffet on one side of the room, and some shelves and places for hanging clothes on the other.' We went to work with all our might. Every morning about eleven Mrs. Washington came up stairs with a glass of spirits for each of us; and after she and the General had dined, we were called down to eat at their table. We worked very hard, nailing smooth boards over the rough and worm-eaten planks, and stopping the crevices in the walls made by time and hard usage. Then we consulted together how we could smoothe the uneven floor, and take out, or cover over some of the huge black knots. We studied to do every thing to please so pleasant a lady, and to make some return in our humble way for the kindness of the General. On the fourth day, when Mrs. Washington came up to see how we were getting along, we had finished the work, made the shelves, put up the pegs on the wall, built the beauffet, and converted the rough garret into a comfortable apartment. As she stood looking round, I said, 'Madam, we have endeavored to do the best we could; I hope we have suited you.' She replied, smiling, 'I am astonished! your work would do honor to an old master, and you are mere lads. I am not only satisfied, but highly gratified with what you have done for my comfort.' " As the old soldier repeated these words, the tears ran down his furrowed cheeks. The thrill of delight which had seventy years before penetrated his heart at the approving words of his General's lady, again animated his worn frame, sending back his thoughts to the very moment and scene.

At one time the head-quarters of the Commander-in-chief were at the house of Mrs. Berry, in New Jersey. While he remained here Mrs. Washington arrived. When the carriage stopped, and a female in a plain russet gown, with white handkerchief neatly folded over her neck, was seen, Mrs. Berry imagined her to be a domestic. But she was undeceived when the General went forward to receive her, assisted her from the carriage, and after the first greeting, began to inquire after his pet horses. A ball was given in honor of the arrival of "Lady Washington," at which her brave husband himself condescended to lead a minuet; it being the first occasion in a long time on which he had been known to dance.*

An anecdote illustrative of the heroic spirit of the lady whose house was the Chief's abode on this occasion, will not be here misplaced. Her husband was at Saratoga attending to some private business, when General Washington, with his officers and troops, went forth to battle. Mrs. Berry and the wives of the officers

* Communicated by a friend of Mrs. Berry.

who were with her, were busily occupied in preparing bandages and wrappings for the use of the army; every sheet and article of linen in the house having been torn up for that purpose. She was harassed with anxiety lest her husband should not return to assume his post before the departure of the troops. He did not arrive in time; and she had the mortification of seeing another appointed to the command of his men. Some-time after they were gone, she heard the welcome sound of his horse's feet. He rode up hastily, and stopped only long enough to change his wearied horse for another. As he galloped down the lane leading from the house, he heard his wife's voice calling, "Sidney, Sidney!" She was leaning from a window, her hand stretched towards him, as if eagerly soliciting his attention. He turned and rode within hearing; she wished but to give him her parting words. These were, "Remember, Sidney, to do your duty! I would rather hear that you were left a corpse on the field, than that you had played the part of a coward!"

Mrs. Wilson, a lady whose name is mentioned else-where in this book, has favored me with an account of Mrs. Washington's visit to her father's house at Union Farm, the last time she came to that part of New Jersey. She was escorted by Major Washington and ten dragoons. She remained a day and night at the house of Colonel Stewart, and spoke much with his daughter concerning house-keeping and her domestic affairs. Her conversation is described as agreeable, and her manners simple, easy, and dignified. Among other particulars, Mrs. Washington mentioned that she had a great deal of domestic cloth made in her house, and kept sixteen spinning wheels in constant operation. She showed Mrs. Wilson two dresses of cotton striped with silk, manufactured by her own domestics, and worn by herself; one weighing a pound and a half, the other rather less. The silk stripes in the fabric were made from the ravellings of brown silk stockings, and old crimson damask chair-covers. Her coachman, footman, and waiting-maid, were all habited in domestic cloth; though the coachman's cuffs and collars, being scarlet, must have been imported. In the practice of this economy and moderation, as in the simplicity of her dress, Mrs. Washington appeared desirous of affording an example to others in inferior station. As late as 1796, Mrs. Wilson, inquiring for pocket handkerchiefs at a celebrated fancy store in Philadelphia, was shown some pieces of lawn, of which Mrs. Washington had just purchased. The information was added, that she paid six shillings for handkerchiefs for her own use, but went as high as seven shillings for the General's.

The anniversary of the alliance with France was celebrated by an entertainment given in the camp near Middlebrook.* On this festive occasion Mrs. Washington, Mrs. Greene and Mrs. Knox, and the wives of several officers were present; and a circle of brilliants, the least of which, says the gallant journalist, was more valuable than the stone which the king of Portugal received for his Brazilian possessions. The ladies and gentlemen from a large circuit around the camp, attended the celebration. It was opened by a discharge of cannon; and dinner was prepared in a building used for an academy. There was dancing in the evening, and a grand display of fire-works. The ball was opened by General Washington. As this was a festival given by men who had not enriched themselves by the war, the illuminations were on a cheap scale, being entirely of their own manufacture; the seats were adorned with no armorial blazonry, but were the work of native, and rather unskillful artizans. "Instead of knights of different orders, such as pageants like the Mischianza could boast, there were but hardy soldiers; happy, however, in the consciousness that they had contributed to bring about the auspicious event they had met to celebrate."

Among the lively sallies of the belles of this entertainment, one is recorded, that caused no inconsiderable amusement. A young lady, when asked if the roaring of the British lion in his late speech had not somewhat depressed the spirit of the dance—replied: "No, it should rather enliven it; for I have heard that such animals always increase their howlings when frightened."

For Mrs. Washington a heavy cloud of sorrow hung over the conclusion of the glorious campaign of 1781. Her only child was seized with a fever while attending to his duties during the siege of Yorktown. He lived to behold the surrender of the British army, and expired in the arms of his mother, mourned for by Washington as a son. The Marquis de Chastellux visiting Mount Vernon not long after this sad event, says: "I had the pleasure of passing a day or two with Mrs. Washington, at the General's house in Virginia, where she appeared to me one of the best women in the world, and beloved by all about her. She has no family by the General, but was surrounded by her grandchildren and Mrs. Custis, her son's widow. The family were then in mourning for Mr. Custis, whose premature death was a subject of public and private regret."

After the close of 1783, General Washington had leisure for the superintendence of improvements in the building and grounds at Mount Vernon. This old mansion was always crowded with visitors. Social and rural pleasures winged the hours, and past dangers were pleasantly talked over. A letter never before published, of Mr. N. Webster, affords a passing glimpse of this period.

"When I was travelling to the south in the year 1785, I called on General Washington at Mount Vernon. At dinner the last course of dishes was a species of pancakes, which were handed round to each guest, accompanied with a bowl of sugar, and another of molasses for seasoning them, that each one might suit himself. When the dish came to me, I pushed by me the bowl of molasses, observing to the gentlemen present that I had enough of *that* in my own country. The General burst out with a loud laugh, a thing very unusual with him; 'Ah,' said he, 'there is nothing in that story about your eating molasses in New England!' There was a gentleman from Maryland at the table, and the General immediately told a story, stating that during the Revolution, a hogshead of molasses was stove in at

Westchester by the oversetting of a wagon; a body of Maryland troops being near, the soldiers ran hastily and saved all they could by filling their hats or caps with molasses.

"Near the close of the Revolutionary war, I think in 1782, I was at West Point, when the birth of a Dauphin in France was celebrated by the American troops at that place. The troops were arranged in a line along the hills on the west of the camp, on the point, and on the mountains on the east side of the Hudson. When the order was given to fire, there was a stream of firing all around the camp, rapidly passing from one end of the line to the other; while the roar of cannon reverberated from the hills, resounded among the mountains, and thousands of human voices made the atmosphere ring with a song prepared for the occasion. 'A Dauphin is born!' This was a splendid exhibition, closed with a handsome repast under a long arcade or bower formed with branches of trees. I have never seen any account of this celebration in print."

While the victorious general was thus merged in "the illustrious farmer of Mount Vernon," Mrs. Washington performed the duties of a Virginia housewife, which in those days were not merely nominal. She gave directions, it is said, in every department, so that, without bustle or confusion, the most splendid dinner appeared as if there had been no effort in the preparation. She presided at her abundant table with ease and elegance, and was indeed most truly great in her appropriate sphere of home. Much of her time was occupied in the care of the children of her lost son.

The period came when this rural Eden, which had bloomed and flourished under their care, was to be exchanged for new scenes. A few years of rest and tranquil happiness in the society of friends having rewarded the Chief's military toils, he was called by the voice of the nation to assume the duties of its Chief Magistrate. The call was obeyed. The establishment of the President and Mrs. Washington was formed at the seat of government. The levees had more of courtly ceremonial than has been known since; but it was necessary to maintain the dignity of office by forms that should inspire respect. Special regard was paid to the wives of men who had deserved much of their country. Mrs. Robert Morris was accustomed to sit at the right of the lady of the President, at the drawing-rooms; and the widows of Greene and Montgomery were always handed to and from their carriages by the President himself; the secretaries and gentlemen of his household performing those services for the other ladies. In this elevated station, Mrs. Washington, unspoiled by distinction, still leaned on the kindness of her friends, and cultivated cheerfulness as a duty. She was beloved as few are in a superior condition. Mrs. Warren says, in reply to one of her letters, "Your observation may be true, that many younger and gayer ladies consider your situation as enviable; yet I know not one who by general consent

would be more likely to obtain the suffrages of the sex,
even were they to canvass at elections for the elevated
station, than the lady who now holds the first rank in
the United States."*

On the retirement of Washington from public life, he
prepared to spend the remnant of his days in the retreat
his taste had adorned. It was a spectacle of wonder to
Europeans, to see this great man calmly resigning the
power which had been committed to his hands, and
returning with delight to his agricultural pursuits. His
wife could justly claim her share in the admiration;
for she quitted without regret the elevated scenes in
which she had shone so conspicuous, to enter with the
same active interest as before upon her domestic employments. Her advanced age did not impair her
ability or her inclination to the discharge of house-
wifely duties. But she was not long permitted to enjoy
the happiness she had anticipated. It was hers too soon
to join in the grief of a mourning nation for the death
of Washington.

Visits of condolence were paid to the bereaved lady
by the President and others; and from all quarters came
tributes of sympathy and sorrow. She continued to
receive the visitors who came to Mount Vernon, and
gave the same attention to her domestic concerns.
But in less than two years after her husband's death,
she was attacked by a fever that proved fatal. When
aware that the hour of her dissolution was approaching,
she called her grandchildren to her bedside; discoursed

* Manuscript letter

to them on their respective duties; spoke of the happy
influences of religion; and then, surrounded by her
weeping family, resigned her life into the hands of her
Creator, in the seventy-first year of her age. Her
death took place on the 22d of May, 1802. Her remains rest in the same vault with those of Washington,
in the family tomb at Mount Vernon.

Those who read the record of her worth, dwell with
interest on the loveliness of her character. To a superior mind she joined those amiable qualities and Chris-
tain virtues which best adorn the female sex, and a
gentle dignity that inspired respect without creating
enmity. Her features are familiar to all, from the por-
traits of her, taken at different ages, published in Sparks'
Life of Washington, and the National Portrait Gallery.
These have been copied into different publications.

2

XXVII.

~~~~~~~~

ABIGAIL ADAMS.

THE Letters of Mrs. Adams are well known to American readers. Her history and character have been so well unfolded in these and in the memoir by her grandson, that an extended sketch of her would be superfluous. Only a brief notice, therefore, is here required.

Abigail Smith was descended from the genuine stock of the Puritan settlers of Massachusetts. Her father, the Reverend William Smith, was for more than forty years minister of the Congregational Church at Weymouth. The ancestors of her mother, Elizabeth Quincy, were persons distinguished in the sacred office, and first in honor among the leaders of the church. From this ancestry, it may be inferred that her earliest associations were among those whose tastes and habits were marked by the love of literature. She was the second of three daughters, and was born at Weymouth, Nov. 11th, 1744. Not being sent to any school, on account of the delicate state of her health, the knowledge she evinced in after life was the result of her reading and observation, rather than of what is commonly called education.. The lessons that most deeply impressed her mind were received from Mrs. Quincy, her grandmother, whose beneficial influence she frequently acknowledges. Her marriage took place, October 25th, 1764. She passed quietly the ten years that succeeded, devoting herself to domestic life, and the care of her young family. In 1775 she was called to pass through scenes of great distress, amid the horrors of war and the ravages of pestilence.

She sympathized deeply in the sufferings of those around her. "My hand and heart," she says, "still tremble at this domestic fury and fierce civil strife. I feel for the unhappy wretches, who know not where to fly for succor; I feel still more for my bleeding countrymen, who are hazarding their lives and their limbs !" To the agonized hearts of thousands of women went the roar of the cannon booming over those hills! Many a bosom joined in breathing that prayer—" Almighty God ! cover the heads of our countrymen, and be a shield to our dear friends."

When the neighborhood was no longer the field of military action, she occupied herself with the management of the household and farm. Mr. Adams was appointed joint commissioner at the court of France, and embarked in February, 1778, with his eldest son, John Quincy. During the years in which Mrs. Adams was deprived of his society, she devoted herself to the various duties devolving on her, submitting with patience to the difficulties of the times. In all her anxieties, her calm and lofty spirit never deserted her; nor did she regret the sacrifice of her own feelings for the good of the community. After the return of peace, Mr. Adams was appointed the first representative of the nation at the British court and his wife departed to join him; moving from this time amidst new scenes and new characters, but preserving, in the variety and splendor of life in the luxurious cities of the old world, the simplicity and singleness of heart which had adorned her seclusion at home. In the prime of life, with a mind free from prejudice, her record of the impressions she received is instructive as well as interesting. She resided for a time in France, and visited the Netherlands, enjoying all she saw, with that delicate perception of beauty which belongs to a poetic spirit. When the official duties of Mr. Adams called him to the court of St. James, the unaffected republican simplicity, and exquisite union of frankness and refinement in her manners, charmed the proud circles of the English aristocracy. As was to be expected, neither she nor her husband were exempted from annoyances growing out of the late controversy. She writes to Mrs. Warren: "Whoever in Europe is known to have adopted republican principles must expect to have all the engines of every court and courtier in the world displayed against him."*

The aspect of independence she maintained, considering what was due to her country, did not tend to propitiate the pride of royalty; yet notwithstanding the drawbacks that sometimes troubled her, her resi-

* Unpublished letter

dence in London seems to have been an agreeable one. Her letters to her sisters are a faithful transcript of her feelings. She observed with mingled pleasure and pain the contrast between the condition of her own country and that of the prosperous kingdoms she visited. Writing to Mrs. Shaw she says,—"When I reflect on the advantages which the people of America possess over the most polished of other nations, the ease with which property is obtained, the plenty which is so equally distributed,—their personal liberty and security of life and property, I feel grateful to Heaven who marked out my lot in that happy land; at the same time I deprecate that restless spirit, and that baneful ambition and thirst for power, which will finally make us as wretched as our neighbors."*

When Mr. Adams, having returned with his family to the United States, became Vice President, his wife appeared, as in other situations—the pure-hearted patriot —the accomplished woman—the worthy partner of his cares and honors. He was called to the Presidency, and the widest field was opened for the exercise of her talents. Her letter written on the day that decided the people's choice, shows a sense of the solemn responsibility he had assumed, with a spirit of reliance upon Divine guidance, and forgetfulness of all thoughts of pride in higher sentiments—honorable to the heart of a Daughter of America. Well might the husband thus addressed bear the testimony he does in one of his letters, in the midst of the perils of war: "A soul as pure, as benevolent, as

* Unpublished letter, 1787.

virtuous, and pious as yours, has nothing to fear, but every thing to hope and expect from the last of human evils.'

In her elevated position, the grace and elegance of Mrs. Adams, with her charms of conversation, were rendered more attractive by her frank sincerity. Her close observation, discrimination of character, and clear judgment, gave her an influence which failed not to be acknowledged. Her husband ever appreciated her worth, and was sustained in spirit by her buoyant cheerfulness and affectionate sympathy, in the multiplicity of his cares and labors. It was hers, too, to disarm the demon of party spirit, to calm agitations, heal the rankling wounds of pride, and pluck the root of bitterness away.

After the retirement of her husband, Mrs. Adams continued to take a deep interest in public affairs, and communicated to her friends her opinions both of men and measures. Writing to Mrs. Warren, March 9th, 1807, she says : " If we were to count our years by the revolutions we have witnessed, we might number them with the Antediluvians. So rapid have been the changes that the mind, though fleet in its progress, has been outstripped by them, and we are left like statues gazing at what we can neither fathom nor comprehend. You inquire, what does Mr. Adams think of Napoleon ? If you had asked Mrs. Adams, she would have replied to you in the words of Pope,

> ' If plagues and earthquakes break not heaven's design,
>   Why then a Borgia or a *Napoline* ?' "*

* Manuscript letter.

Her health was much impaired; and from this time she remained in her rural seclusion at Quincy. With faculties unimpaired in old age, her serenity and benign cheerfulness continued to the last; the shadows of a life full of changes never deepened into gloom; she was still a minister of blessing to all within her influence, and in the settled calm of Christian contentment awaited the change that was to terminate her connection with the things of earth. To this she was summoned on the twenty-eighth of October, 1818.

Her character is a worthy subject of contemplation for her countrywomen. With intellectual gifts of the highest order she combined sensibility, tact, and much practical knowledge of life. Thus was she qualified for eminent usefulness in her distinguished position as the companion of one great statesman, and the guide of another. Few may rise to such pre-eminence; but many can emulate the firmness that sustained her in all vicissitudes, and can imitate her Christian virtues. These are pictured in her Letters, the publication of which was the first attempt to give tradition a palpable form, by laying open the thoughts and feelings of one who had borne an important part in our nation's early history.

THE mother of Abigail Adams, it is said, took her last illness from a soldier who had served in her daughter's family, and whom she visited at Braintree, he having returned sick from the army.

She was the daughter of the Hon. John Quincy, of Braintree, and died in 1775, at the age of fifty-three. Without the least tincture of what is called pride of family, she possessed a true dignity of character, with great kindness of heart; and her efforts to relieve those in need extended to all objects of distress within her reach. Prudent and industrious in her own domestic management, she was attentive to provide employment for her poor neighbors; and was mild, frank and friendly in her intercourse with the parishioners, who regarded her with unbounded esteem and affection.

Another of her three celebrated daughters—Elizabeth —was remarkable in character and influence. She was born in 1750, and married the Rev. John Shaw of Haverhill. Her second husband was the Rev. Stephen Peabody, of Atkinson. Like her sister, she possessed superior powers of conversation, with a fine person, and polished and courtly manners. Her reading was extensive, and when speaking to youthful listeners on some improving topic, she would frequently recite passages from Shakspeare, Dryden, and the other English poets. Attentive to her domestic duties, and economical from Christian principle, to purity of heart and highly cultivated intellectual powers she united the most winning feminine grace. Her house at Haverhill was the centre of an elegant little circle of society for many years after the Revolution, and resorted to by the most cultivated residents of Boston and its vicinity. In Atkinson her gentle and friendly deportment won the lasting regard of the parishioners. She loved to instruct

the ignorant, feed the poor, and comfort the afflicted;
and the young were particularly the objects of her
solicitude. Thus dispensing light and joy wherever she
moved, she passed a useful, and therefore a happy life,
which terminated at the age of sixty-six.

Mrs. Peabody formed an early and enduring friendship with Mrs. Warren, for whose character and intellect her letters express the highest respect. Her correspondence contains frequent remarks upon the prospects of the country, and the movements of the army.
"Lost to virtue," she says to John Adams—"lost to
humanity must that person be, who can view without
emotion the complicated distress of this injured land.
Evil tidings molest our habitations, and wound our
peace. Oh, my brother! oppression is enough to make
a wise people mad."

On her road to Plymouth to visit Mrs. Warren, her
MS. journal mentions that she stopped at the house of
Dr. Hall, where she dined on salt bacon and eggs.
Three of the daughters were grown, and appeared
sensible as well as pretty. "But," she says, "in order
to discover whether their sensibility reached further
than their faces, I sat down after dinner, while they
were quilting a very nice homespun bedquilt, and read
in a book I had brought with me several detached
pieces—"Virtue and Constancy rewarded," "Zulima
the Coquette, etc." This little memorandum throws light
not only on the writer's character, but the manners
of the time. The result appeared satisfactory; the

2*

young ladies being so well pleased with the reading that they begged their visitor to continue it.

The eldest daughter, Mary, was married in 1762, to Richard Cranch, afterwards Judge of the Court of Common Pleas in Massachusetts. In 1775, the family removed from Boston to Quincy, then a part of Braintree, where they continued to reside till 1811. In October of that year both Mr. and Mrs. Cranch died, and were buried on the same day. The life of Mrs. Cranch was spent in deeds of charity and kindness. She was remarkable for her cheerfulness and fortitude, with earnestness in the discharge of her Christian duties. The Hon. Judge William Cranch, of Washington, is her son.

In those portions of the country which were, at different periods, the scene of military operations, the energy, heroism, and magnanimity of woman were called by necessity into continual exercise. But there were other women whose more homely heroism was not without its effect; whose unacknowledged influence extended widely into the future. Their sphere of action limited to the bosom of their own families, the influence wrought quietly and unmarked, yet sent forth an impulse and an energy, like the life-blood propelled from the heart, through our whole national system. The mothers, who through years of adverse fortune were true to American principles, and who kept them pure in their homes in the season of prosperity, although no brilliant acts illustrate their simple history, rendered real service to the country. Their duties during the war, or after the return of peace, were fulfilled in a spirit of self-sacrifice, without the wish or expectation of reward. The noblest reward, however, was theirs: the sons in whose minds they had nursed the germs of patriotism and virtue, rose up to call them blessed.

Our country offers abundant examples of men who have attained the highest eminence, ascribing all to early maternal influence and training. For the mother of HENRY CLAY, that great man—the pride and honor of his country—has ever expressed feelings of profound affection and veneration. Though her life afforded no incidents of striking or romantic interest, she was what expresses the perfection of female character—an excellent mother. She was the youngest of two daughters, who were the only children of George and Elizabeth Hudson. Her name also was Elizabeth. She was born in the county of Hanover, in Virginia, in 1750. Her early education was such as was attainable at that period in the colony. In her fifteenth year she was married to John Clay, a preacher of the Baptist denomination, and became the mother of eight children. Mr. Clay died during the war of the Revolution. Some years afterwards, Mrs. Clay contracted a second marriage with Mr. Henry Watkins; and in course of time eight children more were added to her family. The cares devolving upon her, in the charge of so many children, and the superintendence of domestic concerns, of course occupied her time to the exclusion of participation in matters of public interest. She must, however, have borne her share in the agitations and dangers of the time, in behalf of those who claimed her maternal solicitude and guidance.

Her son, 'Henry, was separated from her when only thirteen years of age, having before that period been occasionally absent from home for months in going to school. In 1792, his step-father removed, with his mother and family, from Hanover County to Woodford County in Kentucky, leaving him at Richmond, in Virginia. He did not again see his mother till the fall of 1797, when he himself emigrated to Kentucky. His estimable and beloved parent died in 1827, having survived most of her children, of whom there are now but four remaining—two by her first, and two by her last marriage.

She was from her youth a member of the Baptist Church, and eminent in piety. Her distinguishing traits of character were energy and industry ; and she was most faithful in the performance of all her domestic duties.

XXVIII.

~~~~~~~

MARTHA WILSON.

ONE of the representatives of those times, in which America must ever feel pride, is yet living at the Lakelands, Lake of Otsego, near Cooperstown, New York. She not only retains an accurate and vivid recollection of scenes in the stormy and fearful infancy of the nation on whose vigorous manhood she is permitted to look, but has kept pace in intellectual cultivation, with the advancement of modern days. The grasp of mind that apprehends and appreciates the progress of her country's prosperity and power, gives a deeper interest to her thrilling recital of incidents belonging to its struggle for life. I am particularly favored in having received from her various anecdotes of persons with whom she was intimately acquainted at that period, her reminiscences of whom would form a most valuable contribution to the domestic history of the Revolution.

The subject of this brief sketch is a daughter of the late Colonel Charles Stewart of New Jersey. She was born December 20th, 1758, at Sidney, the residence of her maternal grandfather, Judge Johnston, in the township of Kingwood, and county of Hunterdon, in that State. This old mansion was at that time one of the most stately and aristocratic of the colonial residences in this section of West Jersey. Constructed while the border settlements of the province were still subject to treacherous visits from the Indian, its square and massive walls and heavy portals had reference as well to protection and defence as to " the pride of life ;" and for many years, in its earlier days, it was not only the stronghold of the wealthy proprietor, his family and dependants, but the refuge in alarm, for miles around, to the settlers whose humbler abodes were more assailable by the rifle and firebrand of the red man. " The big stone house," as it was designated in the common parlance of the people, was thus long a place of note as a refuge from danger ; and not less, in later times, as one for a redress of wrongs, and the punishment of crime ; Judge Johnston having been, for more than thirty years previous to the Revolution, the chief magistrate of that section of the colony, holding a court regularly, on Monday of every week, in one of the halls of his dwelling.

It stood in that region of undulating hill country, between the high mountains of North and the flat sands of South Jersey, of the beauty of which those who fly across the State by railroad at the present day can form no conception : where blue hills and tufted woodlands, winding streams and verdant valleys, often present to the eye in their varied forms and combinations, a perfection of picturesque and rural beauty,

which, while it seldom fails to attract the admiration of
the passing traveller, fastens upon the heart of the resident with an enduring charm. Finely situated on an
elevated terrace, at the confluence of the Capulong and
a branch of the Raritan, overhung by extensive and
park-like woods, with encircling waters and clusters of
grove-covered islets behind, and wide-spread valleys in
front, it was regarded in olden times as one of the
choicest residences in the State. As the birthplace
and home in childhood of the subject of this record, it
has attractions of association and memory which cause
her affections to revert warmly to it after a pilgrimage,
amid other scenes, of well nigh a century.

The old house was accidentally burned down some
fifty years ago, and a new, though less imposing, dwelling erected on the same site, by a branch of the Coxe
family. This, in its turn, became the resort, for many
years, of a circle greatly distinguished for beauty, wit,
and cultivated talent; but now, for a long time, vicissitudes of fortune, neglect, desertion, and decay, have
accomplished in it their accustomed work; and stripped
of its embellishments of taste, despoiled of much of its
fine woods, and its majestic single trees, it presents little indication of its former fortunes, and is fallen in its
uses to the purposes of a common farm.

Previous to the Revolution, Colonel Stewart resided
chiefly at Landsdown, a beautiful property in Kingwood, immediately adjoining the estate of his father-in-
law at Sidney. It was here that the later years of the
childhood of his daughter were spent; and here, at the

early age of thirteen, she was bereaved of her mother—
a woman of strong and polished intellect, of a refined
and poetical taste, and said to have been the best read
female in the province. Till within a short time of
Mrs. Stewart's death, the education of her daughter
had been exclusively at home. She had been but a
brief period at a boarding-school, when summoned to
the dying bed of the mother; and it is no slight proof
of the mental attainments and maturity of character
which she already possessed, that her father, in his bereavement, found her society too necessary to his happiness, and the maternal care which she was called to
exercise over her sisters and brothers of a more tender
age, too essential to their welfare, to permit her again to
resume her place at school. It is chiefly, therefore, to
the self-cultivation of an inquiring and philosophic
mind, and to association at home and in society, with
the intelligent and the wise, that are to be ascribed the
rich stores of general information and wide-spread
practical knowledge, for which, from early womanhood
to the passing day, she has been so highly distinguished,
and so justly and extensively honored.

The hospitality of Colonel Stewart was unbounded.
His friend Chief Justice Smith of New Jersey has
expressed this trait of character in the epitaph upon
his tomb—" The friend and the stranger were almost
compelled to come in." His house was the resort of
the choice spirits in intellect and public influence, of the
times; and it was at his table and fireside that his
daughter, called at the early age we have mentioned

to the responsible position of female head of his family,
from 1771 to 1776, imbibed even in childhood from
him and his compeers the principles of patriotism and
the love of freedom which entitle her name and character to a prominent place among the Women of the
Revolution.   Colonel Stewart himself had been trained
from infancy in the spirit of 1688.   His grandfather,
Charles Stewart, of Gortlee, a cadet of the Stewarts of
Garlies, was an officer of dragoons in the army of
William III., and acquitted himself gallantly, at the side
of his monarch, in the battle of the Boyne.   The
demesne which he afterwards possessed, in the north of
Ireland, was the reward of his valor; but, in transmitting
to his son and his son's son the untrammelled spirit of
a Scotch Puritan, who had periled his life in the cause
of civil and religious liberty, he conferred upon them
a better and more enduring heritage.

It was the proud and honorable independence of the
same indomitable principles, that led his descendant in
early youth, ere he had fully attained his majority, to
self exile in the new world.   Energy of character and
enlarged enterprise soon secured to him here both
private fortune and public influence; and the first
breath of the spirit of " '76" which passed over the land,
kindled within his bosom a flame of zeal for the freedom
and honor of his adopted country, which no discouragement could dampen, and which neither toil, nor danger,
nor disaster could extinguish.

His daughter well recollects having been told by him,
on his return from the first general meeting of the

patriots of New Jersey for a declaration of rights, an incident relating to himself, highly characteristic of the times. Many of the most distinguished royalists were his personal and intimate friends; and when it became evident that a crisis in public feeling was about to occur, when disregarded remonstrance would be converted into open resistance, great efforts were made by some of those holding office under the crown, to win him to their side. Tempting promises of ministerial favor and advancement were made to induce him at least to withhold his influence from the cause of the people, even if he would not take part in support of the king; and this with increased importunity till the very opening of the meeting. But when it was seen to have been in vain—when he immediately rose and was one of the first, if not the very first, with the Stocktons, the Pattersons, and the Frelinghuysens of the day, in the spirit, at least, of the Declaration of 1776, boldly to pledge his "life, his fortune, and his sacred honor" in defence of the rights of freemen against the aggressions of the throne—the Attorney General, approaching and extending his hand, said to him, in saddened tones, as if foretelling a speedy doom—"Farewell, my friend Charles!—when the halter is about your neck, send for me!—I'll do what I can to save you!"

It was thus that the familiar confidence of the patriot father cherished and strengthened, in the bosom of his daughter, sympathies and principles corresponding with his own; while in the accelerated movements of the

Revolution, he successively and rapidly became a
member of the first Provincial Congress of New Jersey,
Colonel of the First Regiment of minute-men of that
State; Colonel of the Second Regiment of the line;
and eventually, one of the staff of Washington, as
Commissary General of Issues, by Commission of the
Congress of 1776.

In January of this year, Miss Stewart, at the age of
seventeen, gave her hand in marriage to Robert Wilson,
a young Irishman of the Barony of Innishowen, who,
after being educated and trained for mercantile life in
one of the first houses of his native land, had emigrated
to America a few years before, and amassed a considerable fortune.   In her husband she made choice of one
not less congenial in political sentiments and feeling
than in intellectual culture and in winning manners.
The first intelligence of the battle of Lexington had
fired his warm blood into immediate personal action in
the cause; and he was one of the volunteers who, with
his friend Colonel Reed, accompanied General Washington from Philadelphia to the camp at Cambridge.
A brief journal kept by him at this time shows that for
six months he was at head-quarters, as muster-master-
general, honored by the confidence of the Commander-
in-chief, and often a guest at his table.   He shared largely
in the exposures of the camp, and distinguished himself
for daring intrepidity, in two or three instances, in the
skirmishes and cannonading which occurred at times
between the forces.   But his health failing, he was obliged

to forego the prospect of a military appointment pledged to him; and resigning his position sought the milder climate of the Jerseys.

Among the officers in the British army were several near relatives of Mr. Wilson ; and it is a fact illustrative of the times, that a young cousin-german, who not long before the commencement of hostilities had visited the family of their common friend and relative, Colonel Stewart, at Kingwood, was now at Boston, in the gallant discharge of his duty in the enemy's ranks. He was afterwards wounded at the battle of Germantown, and visited by Colonel Stewart under a flag of truce.

It was on his return to Jersey that Mr. Wilson's marriage took place. Shortly afterwards, he, with his bride, became a resident of Hackettstown, near which he possessed a valuable property. During the year 1777, he was again in public service, as Assistant Commissary General of Purchases ; but, finding the duties of the station too arduous for his health, he resigned his appointment and entered into mercantile pursuits in Philadelphia. In these he was very extensively and successfully engaged—greatly honored and beloved—till his death, in 1779, at the early age of twenty-eight. His wife had accompanied him to Philadelphia, and was established in much elegance there ; but on her widowhood thus in her twentieth year, she returned to her residence at Hackettstown, where she remained till near the close of the war.

During the whole Revolution, the situation of Mrs. Wilson was as favorable, if not more so, for observation and a knowledge of important movements and events, than that of any other lady in her native State. Her father, at the head of an important department, in the staff of the Commander-in-chief, became generally, and almost from necessity, familiarly acquainted with the principal officers of the army ; and head-quarters being most of the time within twenty or thirty miles of her residence, she not only had constant intercourse in person and by letter with him, but frequently and repeatedly entertained at her house many of his military friends. Among these, with numerous others of less distinction, were Washington, La Fayette, Hamilton, Wayne, Greene, Gates, Maxwell, Lincoln, Henry Lee, Stevens, Walter Stewart, Ethan Allen, Pulaski, Butler, Morgan, Sinclair, Woodward, Varnum, Paul Jones, Cochrane, Craik, &c.

With General Washington she was on terms of friendship. She first met him in Philadelphia, in 1775, when he was preparing to join the army at Cambridge. He afterwards visited her at different times at her residence in Hackettstown ; on the last occasion a year after her husband's death, and a short time after the execution of Major André. His approach, with Mrs. Washington and his staff, under the escort of a troop of horse, was privately announced to Mrs. Wilson in time to have dinner in readiness for a party of thirty or forty persons. To one whose patriotism was so decided, it must have been a pleasure indeed, thus to welcome to her roof and table the leading spirits of the land. The party did not leave till after luncheon on the second day ;

and knowing that they could not reach their destination till late at night, ample provision was made from her larder and wine cellar, to furnish all needed refreshment by the way.

Before these distinguished guests took their departure, a large concourse of people from the adjacent country and the towns in the vicinity had crowded round the house to catch a glimpse of the idolized Chief. A few members of the legislature and the prominent gentlemen of the neighborhood were admitted and formally introduced. Among these was Dr. Kennedy, the family physician, whose salutation, as Mrs. Wilson well recollects, was: "I am happy indeed to meet the man whom under God, I deem the saviour of our country." As it was impossible for the multitude to obtain entrance, a little stratagem was devised by one of the gentlemen, by which those without could be gratified without subjecting the General to the annoyance of a mere exhibition of himself. Knowing his admiration of a fine horse, he ordered an animal remarkable for its beauty to be brought into the street, and then invited him out to inspect it. Thus an opportunity was afforded to the whole assemblage to gaze upon and salute him with their cheers.

Mrs. Wilson relates the following anecdote in connection with another of the visits of Washington to her:

One Mrs. Crafts, a native of Germany, who had emigrated and settled in New Jersey, through the industry of herself and husband had become the owner of a fine farm near Hackettstown, and was in comfortable and easy circumstances. She was an excellent neighbor; and though an ardent tory, was universally respected for her many kind and good qualities. On the morning of General Washington's departure, as on the visit before described, Mrs. Wilson's house was surrounded by a throng of persons eager to obtain a glance at him. In this state of things, Mrs. Crafts, tory as she was, repaired to the spot and sent a message to Mrs. Wilson in her parlor, requesting from her the privilege of seeing the General. A reply was sent, saying that General Washington was at the time surrounded by a crowd of officers; but if Mrs. Crafts would station herself in the hall till he passed through, her desire would be gratified. She accordingly took her post there, and patiently waited his appearance. When, at length, she obtained a full view of his majestic form and noble countenance, raising both hands, she burst into tears, uttering in her native tongue an exclamation expressive of intense astonishment and emotion! Mrs. Crafts never afterwards ranked herself on the tory side. "The august and commanding presence of the father of his country," as Mrs. Wilson remarks, "having alone inspired her with such profound veneration for the man as to produce an abiding respect for the cause of which he was leader."

Mrs. Washington was several times the guest of Mrs. Wilson, both at her own house and that of her father. These visits were made when on her way to and from the camp.   That mentioned in the sketch of " Martha Washington," was at the Union Farm, the residence of Colonel Stewart.

The hospitality which Mrs. Wilson had the privilege thus repeatedly to extend to these illustrious guests, was not forgotten by them, but most kindly acknowledged, and returned by very marked attentions to her daughter and only child, on her entrance into society in Philadelphia during the Presidency of Washington.   In personal calls and invitations to her private parties, Mrs. Washington distinguished her by courtesies rarely shown to persons of her age.   The merest accident has placed before me, without the knowledge or agency of any one interested, the letter of a lady to a friend, in which the appearance and dress of this daughter at a drawing-room at the President's is described.   I insert it as illustrative of the costume on such an occasion, now more than half a century ago.   She says, " Miss Wilson looked beautifully last night.   She was in full dress, yet in elegant simplicity.   She wore book muslin over white mantua, trimmed with broad lace round the neck ; half sleeves of the same, also trimmed with lace ; with white satin sash and slippers ; her hair elegantly dressed in curls, without flowers, feathers, or jewelry. Mrs. Moylan told me she was the handsomest person at the drawing-room, and more admired than any one there."

Mrs. Wilson herself was favored with more than ordinary advantages of feature and person.   In youth she is said to have been remarkably handsome.   Even at the age of thirty-eight, the period of life at which

the likeness engraved for this volume was taken, a lady
of Philadelphia thus writes of her during a visit there:
"I wish you could see dear Mrs. Wilson. She is the
genteelest, easiest, prettiest person I have seen in the
city. And I am far, I can assure you, from being alone in
this sentiment. I hear many others constantly express the same opinion. She looked charmingly this
evening in a Brunswick robe of striped muslin, trimmed with spotted lawn; a beautiful handkerchief grace-
fully arranged on her neck; her hair becomingly craped
and thrown into curls under a very elegant white bonnet, with green-leafed band, worn on one side. She
says she is almost worn out with a round of visiting
among the Chews, Conynghams, and Moylans, Mrs.
General Stewart, &c., &c.; but she does not look so.
I do not wonder that all who know this good lady should
so love her. I am sure no one could know her intimately
and not do so."

It was not alone for friends and acquaintances, and
persons of distinction and known rank, that Mrs. Wilson
kept open house in the Revolution. Such was the liberality of her patriotism, that her gates on the public road
bore inconspicuous characters the inscription, " Hospitality within to all American officers, and refreshment for
their soldiers." An invitation not likely to prove a
mere form of words on the regular route of communication between the northern and southern posts of
the army. Not satisfied with having given even this
assurance of welcome, instances have occurred in
which the stranger of respectability, who had taken

quarters at the public-house of the village, has been transferred at her solicitation to the comforts and elegance of her table and fireside.

On one occasion it was reported to her that a gentleman had been taken ill at the tavern. Knowing, if this were true, that he must suffer there from the poorness of the accommodations, and want of proper attention, a male friend was sent to make inquiry; and learning that this was the case, she had him brought by her servants immediately to her dwelling, and the best medical aid and nursing secured. He proved to be a surgeon in the army,* of high respectability, several of whose friends, male and female, hastened to visit him; and during a critical illness, and long convalescence, shared with him the hospitality of the benevolent hostess, and formed with her an enduring friendship.

From the commencement of the struggle for freedom till its close, Mrs. Wilson was occasionally a personal witness and participator in scenes and incidents of more than ordinary interest. She was in Philadelphia on the day of the Declaration of Independence, and made one of a party—embracing the elite of the beauty, wealth, and fashion of the city and neighborhood—entertained at a brilliant fête, given in honor of the event, on board the frigate Washington, at anchor in the Delaware, by Captain Reid, the Commander. The magnificent brocade which she wore on the occasion, with its hooped petticoat, flowing train, laces, gimp, and flowers, remained in its wardrobe unaltered long after the commencement of the present century, and till the dif-

* Dr. Crosby, of New York.

ficulty of transporting it in its ample folds and stately
dimensions led to its separation into pieces, and thus
prepared the way for it to become a victim to the modern
taste for turning the antique dresses of grandmammas
into eiderdown bed-spreads, and drawing-room chair-
covers.

Within the month after, she became a witness to a
scene—the legitimate result of that Declaration—the
mustering of her neighbors and fellow citizens in Jersey
under the banner of her uncle, Colonel Philip Johnston
of Sidney, and the girding on of their arms for the
bloody conflict in which, on Long Island, they were so
speedily engaged. Colonel Johnston, when a mere youth,
a student of college at Princeton, had abandoned his
books for the sword, in the French war of 1755, and
with such bravery and success as to return to his home
with military reputation and honors. He was now appointed by the Congress of New Jersey to the command of its first volunteer regiment; and in a few
days a thousand strong arms and brave hearts were
gathered round him, in readiness to march against
the invading foe. Mrs. Wilson was present in his
house at the final leave-taking of his youthful wife and
infant daughters. He was a fine-looking officer—tall
and athletic, and of great physical power. He was
said to have had a premonition of his fate. This impression, it was thought, added to his own, if not to the
common grief of his family. He was seen in his closet
in earnest prayer just before taking his departure. The
final embrace of his family was deeply affecting, and

is well pictured in the frontispiece of Glover's Leonidas,
where the husband and the father, departing for Ther-
mopylæ, overcome by the grief of his wife hanging
upon his bosom, and that of his children clinging in his
embrace, looks to Heaven in strong appeal for aid,
while

> " Down the hero's cheek—
> Down rolls the manly sorrow."

Colonel Johnston fell a victim on the altar of his
country a few days afterwards, in the fatal conflict of
the 27th August, 1776. General Sullivan, in whose
division he served, bore the strongest testimony to his
intrepidity and heroism. " By the well-directed fire of
his troops," he wrote, " the enemy were several times
repulsed, and lanes made through them, till a ball in the
breast put an end to the life of as gallant an officer as
ever commanded a battalion."

The robbery of her father's house by a company of
bandit tories was, however, the most alarming and
exciting scene, illustrative of the times of the Revolution,
through which Mrs. Wilson passed. This occurred in
June, 1783. Deprived, by the marriage of his daughter
in 1776, of the maternal care which she had exercised
over his younger children, Colonel Stewart, on his appointment to the staff of the Commander-in-chief, had placed
them at school, and broken up his establishment in
Kingwood. But when the triumph at Yorktown gave
assurance of peace, in the hope of a speedy return to
the enjoyments of private life, he gathered his two sons

and two daughters to a home again, under the management, for a second time, of their elder and now widowed
sister: not at Landsdown, his former dwelling, however,
but at the "Union," in the adjoining township of Leba-
non.   Like Sidney, this old residence was, in that day,
one of the great houses of upper Jersey; and the surrounding farm, comprising a thousand acres of land
under fine cultivation, was noted throughout the State.
The dwelling consisted of three separate houses, built at
different periods—one of brick, one of wood, and the
other of stone—without regard to any harmony of style
or architecture.   They were so situated as to form the
connecting sides of a quadrangular court-yard, into
which the porches and a piazza opened.   With a farm
house and numerous out-buildings clustering round, the
whole presented the aspect of a hamlet, rather than of a
single abode, in the midst of the landscape spreading
widely on the east, the west and the south.   Immediately
in the rear, on the north, stretches the chain of rugged
hills, which separate the head waters of the Raritan
from those of the Muskenetcong, a tributary of the
Delaware; and within a quarter of a mile of the house
was the mouth of the wild ravine of the "Spruce Run,"
the only pass through them for miles on either hand.
This gorge, filled with interlacing trees and closely-set
thickets bordering the rapid waters of the stream,
afforded, in the days of Indian warfare, a choice place
of ambush; and on the occasion referred to, was selected
by the tory robbers, as the securest approach to the
scene of their depredations, and a safe place of conceal-

ment, for the day preceding their descent upon "the Union." It was the Sabbath. Spies in advance, whom the servants at the dairy recollected to have seen moving stealthily about in the early dusk, reported to their accomplices, as was afterwards learned, the retirement for the night of the workmen to their quarters, and the departure of the overseer also to his home, after having been to Mrs. Wilson, as accustomed, for instructions for the following day. These could scarce have had time to fall asleep, when the family, with some female friend, on a visit, enjoying the cool of the evening in the porch of the principal building, were startled by the sudden exclamation, in a suppressed but authoritative tone: "Surround the house! Close in !" While from either side some twenty or thirty men, disguised with paint and charcoal, and armed with various weapons, rushed upon them. Silence was enjoined on pain of death, and inquiry made for Colonel Stewart. They evidently supposed him to be at home, and his capture if not assassination, was doubtless a chief object in their plans. But he had been summoned away by express, and accompanied by General Lincoln, had left for Philadelphia, with a large amount of public funds at a late hour the day before. Being assured of this, the ring-leaders approached Mr. Charles Stewart, the eldest son of the Colonel, and a son-in-law, the late Judge Wilson of Landsdown, both young men some twenty years of age and the only gentlemen of the party, saying, " you are our prisoners ;" and demanded their purses and watches. Young Wilson, somewhat recovered from the first surprise,

and his Irish blood inflamed by the indignity, replied,
"I would like to know who the d——l you are, first!"
when he instantly received a severe stroke across the
head with a sword or sabre, laying open his forehead
from temple to temple. A pistol was immediately
afterwards placed at the breast of young Stewart,
because he hesitated, after delivering his purse, to yield
up his watch, the dying gift of his mother. Mrs.
Wilson in alarm for her brother rushed forward, promising, if life and further bloodshed were spared, the
money and every thing valuable in the house should be
delivered up. Upon this she was ordered with her
brother, to show two of the gang to her father's apart-
ments. Here, besides a considerable amount in specie,
they secured four thousand dollars in current bills,
while another package containing the same amount,
being placed among some wearing apparel, escaped their
notice. In addition to this money, a large amount of
silver plate, a quantity of valuable linen, every article
of gentlemen's apparel in the house, three watches,
Colonel Stewart's sword and a pair of superb pistols,
with heavy mountings of solid silver beautifully and
elaborately wrought, a present of friendship from Baron
Steuben, were among the booty secured.

The pistols thus lost, brought from Europe by the
Baron, had been carried by him through the war. The
circumstances under which they were presented to
Colonel Stewart are honorable alike to the generous
spirit both of himself and friend, and deserve a record.

After the capture of Yorktown, the superior officers

of the American army, together with their allies, vied
with each other in acts of civility and attention to the
captive Britons.   Entertainments were given to them
by all the Major Generals except the Baron Steuben.
He was above prejudice or meanness, but poverty prevented him from displaying that liberality which had
been shown by others.   Such was his situation, when
calling on Colonel Stewart, and informing him of his
intention to entertain Lord Cornwallis, he requested that
he would furnish him the money necessary for this purpose, as the price of his favorite charger.   "'Tis a good
beast," said the Baron, "and has proved a faithful servant through all the dangers of the war: but, though
painful to my heart, we must part."   Colonel Stewart
immediately tendering his purse, recommended the sale
or pledge of his watch should the sum it contained prove
insufficient.   "My dear friend," replied the Baron, "'tis
already sold.   Poor North was sick and wanted neces-
saries.   He is a brave fellow and possesses the best of
hearts.   The trifle it brought is set apart for his use.
So, say no more—my horse must go."   To the purchase,
however, Colonel Stewart would not listen ; and having
pressed upon the Baron the means requisite for his purpose, received from him in acknowledgment of his
friendship the pistols above referred to.   It was to
expenditures of this kind, it is probable, that the gen-
erous-hearted soldier and patriot alluded, when as he
first met his daughter after this decisive crisis in the
Revolution, he exclaimed—"Well, Martha, my dear, I
come to you a thousand dollars out of pocket by the

surrender of Yorktown. But I care not. Thank God! the struggle is over and my country is free!"

Three hours were spent by the leaders of the banditti in ransacking the dwelling under the forced guidance of Mrs. Wilson and her brother. The others, relieving each other in standing guard outside, and over the rest of the family, refreshed themselves abundantly from the store-rooms and cellars which the servants were compelled to throw open to them. Mrs. Wilson at last ventured the request that they would leave, as her brother-in-law, Mr. Wilson, ill from loss of blood, required her attention. During the whole time she had been treated with great deference and respect; so much so as to have been asked by the leaders as they passed over the house, to point out what belonged to her personally, that it might be left in her possession. On preparing to depart, they took the whole family to an upper room, and extorting a promise from Mrs. Wilson that no one should attempt to leave it within two hours, fastened them in. The staircases were then closely barricaded with tables, chairs and every kind of furniture, the windows and doors firmly fastened, the lights all extinguished, the front door locked, and the key thrown among the grass and shrubbery in the court-yard. The jingling of the plate in the bags in which it was carried off, could be heard for some time, and marked the rapidity of their flight when once started with their booty. The gentlemen, not regarding Mrs. Wilson's promise as of any binding force, insisted upon an immediate alarm of the workmen and neighborhood. But the difficulty of making a way out was such that they were long in accomplishing it. By daybreak, however, some three hundred were in pursuit of the plunderers. Some of them were taken on suspicion, but could not be fully identified on account of the paint and disguises they had worn. The ring-leaders, Caleb and Isaac Sweezey, and one Horton, all tories of the neighborhood, made their escape to New York, and though known, were not heard of till after the evacuation of the city by the British, when it was ascertained that they had purchased a vessel with the proceeds of this robbery, and sailed for Nova Scotia.

Till the death of Colonel Stewart, in 1800, Mrs. Wilson continued at the head of his family—the wise, benevolent, energetic and universally admired manager of a house proverbial in her native State, and extensively out of it, for generous and never changing hospitality.   Among the many guests entertained at the Union, General Maxwell was a constant visitor. Mrs. Wilson expresses her regret that justice has not yet been done, in a full biography, to this valued friend. "As a soldier and patriot," is her testimony, "he had few superiors; and in integrity, strength of mind, and kindness of heart—but few equals." She saw him first in 1775, at a review of his regiment, the second raised in New Jersey, Lord Stirling being the commander of the first. Her father was intimately acquainted with him; he was ever a welcome guest, and after the war, spent much of his time at their fireside.*

* It is unquestionably true that injustice has been done to this

For a period of near fifteen years after the death of Colonel Stewart, much of the time of his daughter became necessarily devoted, as his sole administratrix, to the settlement of a large and widely scattered landed estate, including the disputed proprietorship of a portion of the valley of Wyoming, which the business habits and energy of her father had scarce disenthralled at his death from the effects of unavoidable neglect and inattention during the discharge of his official duties in the Revolution. The strength of mind, clearness of judgment, practical knowledge, and firmness of purpose and character, witnessed in her by much of the finest talent at the

officer—his merits and services never having been properly represented before the public. In early life he was an officer in the Colonial service; fought on the field of the Monongahela and in other battles; and continuing in the army after the commencement of the Revolutionary war, was one of the most prominent patriots in New Jersey. He was at the storming of Quebec, and distinguished himself in the battles of Brandywine, Germantown, Monmouth, &c., &c. In numerous letters and journals of the day, testimony is borne to his high character and services. Less than two years before the close of the war, he resigned his commission in displeasure at the appointment over him of an inferior officer. His death took place, probably in 1796, at the house of Colonel Stewart. He had escorted the young ladies on a visit, from which the whole party had returned early in the evening in fine spirits. The Colonel and the General had sat down to their usual evening amusement of backgammon, when Maxwell was suddenly taken ill. Supposing it to be a headache, which he had never experienced before, he rose to retire to his room: But the attack was fatal, and he expired about one o'clock the same night. Expresses were sent for his brothers, one of whom was an officer in the Revolution; but they did not arrive until some hours after his death. His remains rest in the Presbyterian church-yard, at Greenwich, Warren County, New Jersey.

bar and on the bench, not only of New Jersey, but of the adjoining States, in the legal investigations of claims, and titles, and references, and arbitrations, were such as to secure to her, in general estimation, a degree of respect for talent and ability not often accorded to her sex.

Though thus for a long time placed in circumstances which tasked heavily the energies both of body and of mind, she was ever prompt and true to the discharge of the gentler and more feminine duties of life, to all who had any possible claim upon her kindness and regard. Not long after she had been called to the management of her father's estate, two orphan sons of her brother were left in their childhood to her guardianship and maternal care. Delicacy to Mrs. Wilson and to her correspondents yet living, has forbidden an inquiry for any letters from her pen, illustrating her character; but a series written by her to one of these adopted sons* while a boy in school and college, shows so strikingly the fidelity with which she discharged her trust, and at the same time so clearly exhibits her own principles and views of character and life, that I cannot forego the privilege granted me of making one or two extracts.

After pointing out some grammatical errors in a letter just received, she thus writes:

"*February 16th*, 1811.

"It is not from any pleasure in finding fault that I

* The Rev. C. S. Stewart—of the U. S. Navy—the distinguished missionary, and author of " A RESIDENCE IN THE SANDWICH ISLANDS "—" VISIT TO THE SOUTH SEAS," etc.

point out these errors ; but from the sincere desire that you should be as perfect as possible in every branch of education. Next to your being an honest and virtuous man, I wish to see you the accomplished gentleman. You have no better friend on earth than myself : regard, therefore, my advice. Solomon says, ' A wise man will take counsel from a friend, but a fool will despise it.' Prove yourself to be the former by putting in practice all I say in reference to your mind, manners and morals. Let your example to your brother, as the eldest, ever be such as to induce him to look to you as a polar-star by which he may safely guide his own conduct.

" Your desire to attend the birth-night ball, is neither improper nor unnatural at your age. It is always a gratification to my heart to promote, or be the means of promoting your innocent enjoyment, and that which is esteemed pleasure in youth, when the indulgence is not incompatible with your interest and honor, and not contrary to the rules of the institution to which you belong. But I would by no means have you forfeit a character for obedience and good order, with your tutors, for the trifling gratification of a dance ; and let it never be forgotten by you that the reputation established by a boy at school and college, whether it be of merit or demerit, will follow him through life. As to your dress and manners, avoid as you would a pestilence those of a fop. Be plain and simple in your apparel and modest and unassuming in your address—respectful and courteous to all, but especially to the aged. The wise and the well-bred will ever mete to you a just reward ;

for nothing affords more pleasure to the good and truly great, while nothing certainly is more prepossessing than a modest youth.

"You say that you have received much attention from the first families in ——. Whatever company you do keep, should ever be the first—that is, the wisest and the best; but for the present, the less time you spend in society of any kind the better. Close attention to your studies, in the acquisition of a solid and polished education, will yield you a larger profit. Be particular in the intimacies formed with your schoolmates. Boys of good family and good breeding are always to be preferred as companions, if their principles and conduct are praiseworthy. But where this is not the case, those morally good, though destitute of such advantages, are to be chosen as more worthy of your regard and friendship.

"I again commend you to the care of Heaven. May the Almighty guide and shield you—preserving you from temptation and delivering you when tempted."

In a letter written shortly afterwards, she says:

"B — has read to me a paragraph from a letter just received, in which it is stated that you are one of the most studious and best scholars in ——. If you knew how gratifying to my heart this intelligence is, it would, I am sure, inspire you with the love of honest fame. Go on, my dear boy, as you have begun, and you will attain all that is most desirable and most valuable in this world—the character and position of a good and wise man, useful, beloved, and honored in your generation. True, there is no near male friend in your family to extend a fostering hand to you and lead you onward to fame and fortune. Let not this circumstance, however, discourage you, but rather let it stimulate you to fresh industry and exertion. A faithful use of the means in your power will insure to you the desired result. But ever remember that in this more even will depend on your moral conduct as a man and gentleman than on your mental accomplishments. There is much even in external manner—more than many wise people think; and a gentlemanlike deportment, accompanied by honest candor, strict integrity, and undeviating truth will secure more respect and esteem for you in youth, as well as in after age, than any degree of talent, however brilliant, possibly can without them."

When, some three years afterwards, the same relative had commenced his collegiate course, she thus writes, under the date of May 31st, 1814:

" I am happy to learn that you have received so much kindness from so many friends. Be mindful of their civilities and ever prove yourself worthy of them. I confess I have been greatly gratified in hearing from many quarters such flattering reports of your good conduct and success in study. Press forward, my dear son, in the ways of wisdom—they are ways of pleasantness, and their end is peace. Industry is the handmaid of good fortune; and always keep it in mind, that persevering assiduity will surely accomplish for you all that is desirable in this world. Under this conviction, which is certainly a truth, let no trivial obstacle you may occasionally meet discourage your efforts or impede

your progress. You have gained considerable distinction in your career thus far;—never rest satisfied
short of the first honors of the institution you have now
entered.

"Your advantages for the study of composition and
oratory have not been, I fear, as good heretofore as I
could have wished. Let these important branches now
engage much of your attention ; you cannot excel in
either of the leading professions without them. If you
would become a wise man, a variety of reading from
the best authors, both ancient and modern, must also
be added to your attainments in college studies. Acquire, too, a habit of observation on men and manners,
without which you can never secure the knowledge of
the world essential to success in practical life. Political
knowledge, also, is absolutely indispensable to the
attainment in our country of a conspicuous and influential position, at which I trust you will aim ; pay attention,
therefore, to the passing events of the day and to the
information to be derived from the best conducted public
prints. Man can do much for himself as respects his
own improvement, unless self-love so blinds him that he
cannot see his own imperfections and weaknesses.
Some of the most finished characters, in all ages, of
which the world can boast, are those who found the
greatest difficulty in controlling their natural propensi-
ties, but whose persevering efforts caused even bad
habits to give place to the most graceful accomplishments. Above all, my dear son, take care of your
morals. All I ever say to you proceeds from the sin-

cerest affection and the deepest anxiety for your success
and happiness in life. Keep yourself for the future, as
you have for the past, as far as possible from unprinci-
pled young men, many of whom you will every where
find around you. Treat your tutors and professors
with the respect to which they are entitled, and conform
promptly and strictly to the discipline and usages of the
college. If ever tempted to a different course, resist
the evil. The exercise of a little self-denial for the time
will be followed by the pleasure of having achieved the
greatest of triumphs—a triumph over one's self.

"I cheer myself daily with thoughts of your constant
improvement in every thing calculated to be useful and
honorable to yourself, and gratifying to your friends.
May God ever bless and keep you."

One additional extract from a letter to the same individual, written while he was still in college, under the
date of March 20th, 1815, presents briefly, but clearly,
the sentiments and feelings of Mrs. Wilson, on the most
important of all subjects—that of personal and experi-
mental piety.

"Your last letter," she writes, "gave me more pleasure than any one I have ever received from you. I
cannot be too thankful to that great and good Being
who, in infinite mercy, hath opened your eyes to see
yourself spiritually as you are—a guilty sinner, in need
of a better righteousness than your own, to appear
acceptably in His sight. Believers, even as others, are
by nature dead in trespasses and sins; but by faith in
the Son of God—derived from him alone—they arise

to newness of life, and become heirs of eternal glory.
The blessed assurance is, 'Because I live, ye shall live
also.' Live in life, and live for ever.

"I doubt not that your views of the world, and the
things pertaining to it, as well as of yourself, are different from what they ever were before. You see and
feel that to the renewed soul, all things, in comparison
with 'Christ and Him crucified,' are of small consideration. Since God has been pleased to impress your
soul with a sense of His divine perfections, of the
depravity of your nature, and of the riches of His
grace, be watchful, my dear son, and continue instant
in prayer. Confident that the life of a sincere Christian
will ever be your highest honor, on this subject regard
neither the smiles nor frowns of the world—neither its
fashions nor its favors. I have often thought of you
with much satisfaction, in the belief that you would
prove yourself worthy of my warmest and sincerest
affection; but the possession of the finest talents, such
as would command the applause of a vain world, attended with the most brilliant success, could never give
me half the happiness of an assurance that you were
truly a pious man. I could write much upon this interesting and sublime subject, but the necessity of preparing several letters for the present mail, obliges me to
close with my blessing."

Mrs. Wilson herself became interested in the subject
of personal and practical piety in early youth, and made
a profession of her faith, at the time, in the Presbyterian
church of Bethlehem, New Jersey, of which her grand-

father, Judge Johnston, was the founder and chief patron through life. Her example as a Christian has ever been in harmony with the leading traits of her character—consistent, energetic, decisive—abounding in charities, and full of good works. In religion, as in intellectual advancement, she has kept pace in spirit and active zeal with the enlarged benevolence and expanding enterprise of the passing age; and though now in her ninetieth year, not only by her subscriptions and her prayers, but often by her personal presence and aid, still cheers the ladies of her neighborhood in their associations for purposes of local and general benevolence and piety.

The marriage of her only daughter and child in 1802, to the late John M. Bowers, Esq., of Bowerstown, county of Otsego, New York, led Mrs. Wilson, in 1808, to change her home from Flemington, New Jersey, to Cooperstown, New York, in which village for a long period afterwards, she, at different times occupied her own dwelling; but now for many years she has lived exclusively at the Lakelands, the beautiful residence of her daughter, in the immediate vicinity of that place. Here, respected and honored by all who know her, and reposing in the affections of a devoted household, with the blessings of unnumbered poor—the widow, the orphan, the destitute and friendless of every name—descending like dews of Hermon on her head, she cheerfully awaits the change when the "corruptible shall put on incorruption, and the mortal put on IMMORTALITY."

XXIX.

REBECCA MOTTE.

FORT MOTTE, the scene of the occurrence which so
strikingly displayed the patriotism of one of South Carolina's daughters, stood on the south side of the Congaree
river.   The height commands a beautiful view, several
miles in extent, of sloping fields, sprinkled with young
pines, and green with broom grass or the corn or cotton
crops; of sheltered valleys and wooded hills, with the
dark pine ridge defined against the sky.   The steep
overlooks the swamp land through which the river
flows; and that may be seen to a great distance, winding,
like a bright thread, between the sombre forests.

After the abandonment of Camden to the Americans,
Lord Rawdon, anxious to maintain his posts, directed
his first effort to relieve Fort Motte, at the time invested
by Marion and Lee.*   This fort, which commanded
the river, was the principal depôt of the convoys from
Charleston to Camden and the upper districts.   It was
occupied by a garrison under the command of Captain
M'Pherson, of one hundred and sixty-five men, having
been increased by a small detachment of dragoons from

* Ramsay's History of South Carolina: Moultrie's Memoirs: Lee's
Memoirs of the War in the Southern Department, &c.

REBECCA MOTTE.

Rebecca Motte

Charleston, a few hours before the appearance of the
Americans. The large new mansion-house belonging
to Mrs. Motte, which had been selected for the establishment of the post, was surrounded by a deep trench,
along the interior margin of which was raised a strong
and lofty parapet. Opposite, and northward, upon
another hill, was an old farm-house, to which Mrs.
Motte had removed when dismissed from her mansion.
On this height Lieutenant Colonel Lee had taken position with his force; while Marion occupied the eastern
declivity of the ridge on which the fort stood; the
valley running between the two hills permitting the
Americans to approach it within four hundred yards.

M'Pherson was unprovided with artillery, but hoped
to be relieved by the arrival of Lord Rawdon to dislodge the assailants before they could push their preparations to maturity. He therefore replied to the
summons to surrender—which came on the 20th May,
about a year after the victorious British had taken
possession of Charleston—that he should hold out to the
last moment in his power.

The besiegers had carried on their approaches rapidly,
by relays of working parties; and aware of the advance
of Rawdon with all his force, had every motive for
perseverance. In the night a courier arrived from
General Greene, to advise them of Rawdon's retreat
from Camden, and urge redoubled activity; and Marion
persevered through the hours of darkness in pressing
the completion of their works. The following night
Lord Rawdon encamped on the highest ground in the

country opposite Fort Motte; and the despairing garrison saw with joy the illumination of his fires; while
the Americans were convinced that no time was to be lost.

The large house in the centre of the encircling trench,
left but a few yards of ground within the British works
uncovered; burning the mansion, therefore, must compel the surrender of the garrison. This expedient was
reluctantly resolved upon by Marion and Lee, who,
unwilling under any circumstances to destroy private
property, felt the duty to be much more painful in the
present case. It was the summer residence of the
owner, whose deceased husband had been a firm friend
to his country, and whose daughter (Mrs. Pinckney)
was the wife of a gallant officer, then a prisoner in the
hands of the British. Lee had made Mrs. Motte's
dwelling his quarters, at her pressing invitation, and
with his officers had shared her liberal hospitality. Not
satisfied with polite attention to the officers, while they
were entertained at her luxurious table, she had attended
with active benevolence to the sick and wounded,
soothed the infirm with kind sympathy, and animated
the desponding to hope. It was thus not without deep
regret that the commanders determined on the sacrifice,
and the Lieutenant Colonel found himself compelled to
inform Mrs. Motte of the unavoidable necessity of the
destruction of her property.

The smile with which the communication was received, gave instant relief to the embarrassed officer.
Mrs. Motte not only assented, but declared that she
was "gratified with the opportunity of contributing to

the good of her country, and should view the ap
proaching scene with delight." Shortly after, seeing
by accident the bow and arrows which had been prepared to carry combustible matter, she sent for Lee,
and presenting him with a bow and its apparatus, which
had been imported from India, requested his substitution of them, as better adapted for the object than
those provided.

Every thing was now prepared for the concluding
scene. The lines were manned, and an additional force
stationed at the battery, to meet a desperate assault, if
such should be made. The American entrenchments
being within arrow shot, M'Pherson was once more
summoned, and again more confidently—for help was
at hand—asserted his determination to resist to the
last.

The scorching rays of the noon day sun had prepared
the shingle roof for the conflagration. The return of
the flag was immediately followed by the shooting of the
arrows, to which balls of blazing rosin and brimstone
were attached. Simms tells us the bow was put into
the hands of Nathan Savage, a private in Marion's
brigade. The first struck, and set fire; also the second
and third, in different quarters of the roof. M'Pherson
immediately ordered men to repair to the loft of the
house, and check the flames by knocking off the shingles;
but they were soon driven down by the fire of the six
pounder ; and no other effort to stop the burning being
practicable, the commandant hung out the white flag,
and surrendered the garrison at discretion.

If ever a situation in real life afforded a fit subject for poetry, by filling the mind with a sense of moral grandeur—it was that of Mrs. Motte contemplating the spectacle of her home in flames, and rejoicing in the triumph secured to her countrymen—the benefit to her native land, by her surrender of her own interest to the public service. I have stood upon the spot, and felt that it was indeed classic ground, and consecrated by memories which should thrill the heart of every American. But the beauty of such memories would be marred by the least attempt at ornament ; and the simple narrative of that memorable occurrence has more effect to stir the feelings than could a tale artistically framed and glowing with the richest hues of imagination.

After the captors had taken possession, M'Pherson and his officers accompanied them to Mrs. Motte's dwelling, where they sat down together to a sumptuous dinner. Again, in the softened picture, our heroine is the principal figure. She showed herself prepared, not only to give up her splendid mansion to ensure victory to the American arms, but to do her part towards soothing the agitation of the conflict just ended. Her dignified, courteous, and affable deportment adorned the hospitality of her table ; she did the honors with that unaffected politeness which wins esteem as well as admiration ; and by her conversation, marked with ease, vivacity and good sense, and the engaging kindness of her manners, endeavored to obliterate the recollection of the loss she had been called upon to sustain, and at

the same time to remove from the minds of the prisoners
the sense of their misfortune.

To the effect of this grace and gentle kindness, is
doubtless due much of the generosity exercised by the
victors towards those who, according to strict rule, had
no right to expect mercy. While at the table, " it was
whispered in Marion's ear that Colonel Lee's men were
even then engaged in hanging certain of the tory
prisoners. Marion instantly hurried from the table,
seized his sword, and running with all haste, reached
the place of execution in time to rescue one poor wretch
from the gallows. Two were already beyond rescue or
recovery. With drawn sword, and a degree of indignation in his countenance that spoke more than words,
Marion threatened to kill the first man that made any
further attempt in such diabolical proceedings."*

Other incidents in the life of Mrs. Motte, illustrate
the same rare energy and firmness of character she
evinced on this occasion, with the same disinterested
devotion to the American cause. When an attack upon
Charleston was apprehended, and every man able to
render service was summoned to aid in throwing up
intrenchments for the defence of the city, Mrs. Motte,
who had lost her husband at an early period of the war,
and had no son to perform his duty to the country,
despatched a messenger to her plantation, and ordered
down to Charleston every male slave capable of work.
Providing each, at her own expense, with proper implements, and a soldier's rations, she placed them at the

* Simms' Life of Marion, p. 239.

4

disposal of the officer in command. The value of this unexpected aid was enhanced by the spirit which prompted the patriotic offer.

At different times it was her lot to encounter the presence of the enemy. Surprised by the British at one of her country residences on the Santee, her son-in-law, General Pinckney, who happened to be with her at the time, barely escaped capture by taking refuge in the swamps. It was to avoid such annoyances that she removed to "Buckhead," afterwards called Fort Motte, the neighborhood of which in time became the scene of active operations.

When the British took possession of Charleston, the house in which she resided—still one of the finest in the city—was selected as the head-quarters of Colonels Tarleton and Balfour. From this abode she determined not to be driven ; and presided daily at the head of her own table, with a company of thirty British officers. The duties forced upon her were discharged with dignity and grace, while she always replied with becoming spirit to the discourteous taunts frequently uttered in her presence, against her "rebel countrymen." In many scenes of danger and disaster was her fortitude put to the test; yet through all, this noble-spirited woman regarded not her own advantage, hesitating at no sacrifice of her convenience or interest, to promote the general good.

One portion of her history—illustrating her singular energy, resolution, and strength of principle—should be recorded. During the struggle, her husband had become deeply involved by securities undertaken for his friends. The distracted state of the country—the pursuits of business being for a long time suspended,—plunged many into embarrassment; and after the termination of the war, it was found impossible to satisfy these claims. The widow, however, considered the honor of her deceased husband involved in the responsibilities he had assumed. She determined to devote the remainder of her life to·the honorable task of paying the debts. Her friends and connections, whose acquaintance with her affairs gave weight to their judgment, warned her of the apparent hopelessness of such an effort. But, steadfast in the principles that governed all her conduct, she persevered; induced a friend to purchase for her, on credit, a valuable body of rice-land, then an uncleared swamp—on the Santee—built houses for the negroes, who constituted nearly all her available property—even that being encumbered with claims—and took up her own abode on the new plantation. Living in an humble dwelling—and relinquishing many of her habitual comforts—she devoted herself with such zeal, untiring industry, and indomitable resolution to the attainment of her object, that her success triumphed over every difficulty, and exceeded the expectations of all who had discouraged her. She not only paid her husband's debts to the full, but secured for her children and descendants a handsome and unincumbered estate. Such an example of perseverance under adverse circumstances, for the accomplishment of a high and noble purpose, exhibits in yet brighter colors the heroism that shone in her country's days of peril!

In the retirement of Mrs. Motte's life after the war, her virtues and usefulness were best appreciated by those who knew her intimately, or lived in her house. By them her society and conversation were felt to be a valued privilege. She was accustomed to amuse and instruct her domestic circle with various interesting anecdotes of persons and events; the recollection of which, however, at this distant period, is too vague to be relied on for a record. The few particulars here mentioned were received from her descendants.

She was the daughter of Robert Brewton, an English gentleman, who emigrated to South Carolina, and settled in Charleston before the war. Her mother was a native of Ireland, and married Mr. Brewton after her removal to this country, leaving at her death three children—Miles, Frances, and Rebecca. Miles Brewton took part with the first abettors of resistance to British oppression; and their consultations were held at his house in Charleston. Early in the war he was drowned on his way to England with his family, whom he intended to leave there, while he should return to take part with the patriots.

Rebecca Brewton was born on the 28th June, 1738.* She married Jacob Motte† in 1758, and was the

* The dates are taken from the family Bible, recorded in Mrs. Motte's own hand-writing.

† A celebrated writer informs me that the name is **French**, and was originally spelled *Mothé*.

mother of six children, only three of whom lived to maturity. General Thomas Pinckney married in succession the two elder daughters.* The third surviving daughter was married to the late Colonel William Alston, of Charleston. By the children of these, whose families are among the most distinguished in the State, the memory of their ancestor is cherished with pride and affection. Her fame is, indeed, a rich inheritance; for of one like her the land of her birth may well be proud!

Mrs. Motte died in 1815, at her plantation on the Santee. The portrait from which the engraving is taken is said to be an excellent likeness.

~~~~~~~~~~

SOME facts related to Major Garden by Mrs. Brewton, who was an inmate of Mrs. Motte's family at the time of the destruction of her house, are interesting in this connection. She stated that Mrs. Motte and her family had been allowed to occupy an apartment in the mansion while the American forces were at a distance; but when the troops drew near, were ordered to remove immediately. As they were going, Mrs. Brewton took up the quiver of arrows, and said to her friend that she would take those with her, to prevent their being destroyed by the soldiers. She was passing the gate with

* It was the wife of Thomas Pinckney who dressed his wounds after the battle of Camden, with her own hands, and fainted when the task was over.

the quiver in her hands, when M'Pherson asked what she had there, at the same time drawing forth a shaft, and applying the point to his finger. She sportively bade him be careful, "for the arrows were poisoned;" and the ladies then passed on to the farm-house where they were to take up their abode.

On several occasions Mrs. Brewton incurred the enmity of the British officers by her lively sallies, which were sometimes pointed with severity. Before the siege of Fort Motte, a tory ensign had frequently amused himself, and provoked the ladies, by taunts levelled against the whigs, sometimes giving the names of the prominent commanders to pine saplings, while he struck off their heads with his weapon. After the surrender, Mrs. Brewton was cruel enough, meeting this young man on the spot where he had uttered these bravadoes, to request, sportively, another exhibition of his prowess, and regret that the loss of his sword did not permit him to gratify her.

Not long after this, Mrs. Brewton obtained permission to go to Charleston. An officer in the city inquiring the news from the country, she answered "that all nature smiled, for every thing was *Greene*, down to Monk's Corner." This *bon mot* was noticed by an order for her immediate departure; she was obliged to leave the city at a late hour, but permitted to return the following day. Her ready wit procured her still further ill-will. An officer going into the country offered to take charge of letters to her friends. She replied, "I should like to write, but have no idea of hav-

ing my letters read at the head of Marion's brigade."
The officer returned in a few days on parole, having
been taken prisoner by Marion, and called to pay his
thanks, as he said, to her for having communicated the
intelligence of his movements.

The society of this sprightly and fascinating widow
appears to have been much sought by the more cultivated among the British, who enjoyed her brilliant
conversation, while they winced under her sarcasm.
One day when walking in Broad street, wearing deep
mourning, according to the custom of the whig ladies,
she was joined by an English officer. They were passing the house of Governor Rutledge, then occupied by
Colonel Moncrief, when taking a piece of crape that
had been accidentally torn from the flounce of her
dress, she tied it to the front railing, expressing at the
same time her sorrow for the Governor's absence, and
her opinion that his house, as well as his friends, ought
to wear mourning. It was but a few hours after this
act of daring, that the patriotic lady was arrested and
sent to Philadelphia.

XXX.

~~~~~~

SUSANNAH ELLIOTT.

THE presentation of a pair of colors, by the wife of
Colonel Barnard Elliott, is mentioned in several historical works. They were presented to the second
South Carolina regiment of infantry, commanded by
Colonel Moultrie,—on the third day after the attack on
Fort Moultrie, Sullivan's Island, which took place June
28th, 1776. These colors were very elegant, and both
richly embroidered by Mrs. Elliott's own hand. One
was of fine blue, the other of red silk. They were presented with these words : " Your gallant behavior in
defence of liberty and your country, entitles you to the
highest honors ; accept these two standards as a reward
justly due to your regiment ; and I make not the least
doubt, under Heaven's protection, you will stand by
them as long as they can wave in the air of liberty."*

The colors having been received from the lady's
hands by the Colonel and Lieutenant Colonel, she was
thanked for the gift—and a promise was made by the
Colonel in the name of the soldiers—that they should be

* Moultrie's Memoirs ; Ramsay's History of South Carolina; McCall's
History of Georgia.

honorably supported, and never tarnished by the second regiment.   Never was pledge more nobly fulfilled. Three years afterwards, they were planted on the British lines at Savannah.   Two officers, who bore them, lost their lives ; and just before the retreat was ordered, the gallant Sergeant Jasper, in planting them on the works, received a mortal wound and fell into the ditch.   One of the standards was brought off in the retreat ; and Jasper succeeded in regaining the American camp.   In his last moments he said to Major Horry, who had called to see him—" Tell Mrs. Elliott I lost my life supporting the colors she presented to our regiment."   The colors were afterwards taken at the fall of Charleston, and were deposited in the Tower of London.

The maiden name of Mrs. Barnard Elliott was Susannah Smith.   She was a native of South Carolina, and the daughter of Benjamin Smith, for many years Speaker of the Assembly of the province.   Left young an orphan and an heiress, she was brought up by her aunt, Mrs. Rebecca Motte, with whom she lived till her marriage.   Mrs. Daniel Hall used to say she was "one of the most busy among the Revolutionary women, and always active among the soldiers."   It is known that her husband raised and maintained a regiment at his own expense.   Among the papers in the possession of the family is a letter from General Greene to Mrs. Elliott, expressive of high respect and regard, offering her a safe escort through the camp, and to any part of the country to which she might desire to travel.

While at her plantation called "The Hut," she had

4*

three American gentlemen as guests in the house. Surprised one day by the sudden approach of the British, she hurried them into a closet, and opening a secret door, disclosed a large opening back of the chimney, known only to herself, and contrived for a hiding-place. Two entered; but the third determined to trust to the fleetness of his horse, and his knowledge of the woods. In leaping a fence he was overtaken, and cut down within sight of the house.

This was searched thoroughly for the others; but no threats could induce Mrs. Elliott to reveal their place of retreat. The officers then demanded her silver; and pointing to some mounds of earth not far off, asked if the plate was buried there. Mrs. Elliott replied that those mounds were the graves of British soldiers who had died at her house. Not believing her, they ordered two of the soldiers to dig and see. The coffin in one of the graves was soon disinterred; and on opening it the truth was at once made manifest. After the men had taken their departure, Mrs. Elliott released her two guests. The silver had been put in a trunk and buried in the marsh by a faithful servant, who after the close of the war came to Mrs. Elliott's son, requested assistance to dig for it, and brought it out safe, though perfectly blackened.

Mrs. Elliott was beautiful in person, with a countenance inexpressibly soft and sweet. Her portrait is in the possession of the family, defaced by the act of a British soldier—a small sword having been run through one eye. Her descendants reside in Charleston, and in other parts of the State.

A Revolutionary *jeu d'esprit* sent me by a friend in Charleston, containing allusions to some of the prominent whig ladies, mentions the name of Mrs. Elliott. It is a letter from Major Barry to "Mrs. G." and was found copied in the hand-writing of Bishop Smith. It appears to be a burlesque dedication of a poem, which unfortunately has not descended to posterity. It is somewhat curious to observe how the writer, with playful sarcasm, characterises women of the opposite party, while seeking one who might fitly matronize his offspring.

"The feathers which bedeck the head of Mrs. Ferguson for a moment attracted my attention, but right fearful was I lest the critics and poetasters of this age might infer a light foundation from so airy a superstructure ; which most sorrowful event might at once over-throw both the patronized and patronizer.

"Mrs. Savage and Mrs. Parsons called vociferously for notice ; but their zeal so shook the dagger and the bowl in their hands, that I deemed them unfit for the calm dignity of the tragic scene. Too much mildness, on the other hand, superseded the veteran Mrs. Pinckney, when I beheld her smiling, sliding, gliding advance to meet the commissioners of sequestration. As for Mrs. Charles Elliott, she is only allied to such exalted spirits by the zeal of party—perhaps in her case the too exuberant emanation of a delicate and susceptible

mind.   And as the banners in the hand of Mrs. Barnard
Elliott waved but for a moment, flimsy as the words
that presented them, so slight a triumph could not
entitle her to fame so pre-eminent as this.   'Tis in you
alone, madam, we view united every concomitant for
this most eminent distinction—qualities which receive
addition, if addition they can have, from the veteran
and rooted honors of that exalted character, the General
—a character allied to you by all the warm as well as
tender ties.   It is with pleasure I ever view the *Wharf
and Bridge*, those works of his hands, which stand, like
the boasted independence of your country, the crumb-
ling monuments of his august repute.   With what
rapture do I behold him, in the obscure recesses of St.
Augustine, attracting the notice of all mankind, and, as
he traverses the promised land, planting deep in Hebrew
ground the roots of everlasting fame, etc."

Although not active in political affairs, the patriotic
feeling and secluded, yet picturesque life of SABINA
ELLIOTT, passed in the exercise of the domestic and
Christian virtues, was not without its influence.   By
the early death of her parents, she was left in her eighth
year, the eldest of several daughters, dependent on their
relatives ; and was brought up by an aunt.   Her personal
beauty was remarkable ; and when she was about fourteen, arrested the attention of William Elliott, a wealthy
widower, who had been twice married, but had no
children.   He saw her accidentally in the street, dressed

in coarse apparel, and carrying a pitcher of water into the house; and deeply impressed by her appearance, sought an early introduction to the aunt, and soon after married the object of his admiration. He then procured masters for her and her sisters, whom he took home and educated. All, except one, married from his house.

When Mrs. Elliott was about twenty-eight, the sad event took place which cast a blight on her life. Her husband riding one day over his rice fields, on a low horse he commonly used, struck with his whip a dog lying by the roadside. The animal sprang upon him and tore his cheek. It was discovered soon after to be mad; and Mr. Elliott calmly made preparations to meet his terrible and inevitable fate. So fearful was he that in the paroxysms of the disease he might injure some of his family, that he strictly commanded two of his stoutest men servants to bind him hand and foot upon the first symptom. At the end of forty days he died of hydrophobia.

The grief caused by this misfortune, and the loss of three children, permanently impaired Mrs. Elliott's health. Two daughters remained to her; the eldest married Daniel Huger; Ann, the youngest, was united, at the close of the war, to Colonel Lewis Morris, aid-de-camp to General Greene, and eldest son of Lewis Morris, of Morrisania, one of the signers of the Declaration of Independence.

Mrs. Elliott employed herself constantly in useful domestic occupations; and was remarkable for industry and economy of time. She superintended the manufacture of the wool and cotton worn by her slaves, to whom she was most kind and indulgent; and made salt on her plantation during the war. Some of the stockings knit by her are still extant—having the date, 1776, knit in the threads.

Garden relates a pleasant anecdote of her wit. A British officer having ordered the plundering of her poultry houses, she afterwards observed, straying about the premises, an old muscovy drake, which had escaped the general search. She had him caught, and mounting a servant on horseback, ordered him to follow and deliver the bird to the officer with her compliments; as she concluded that in the hurry of departure, it had been left altogether by accident.

She took particular delight in improving the family seat, Accabee, seven miles from Charleston. This place, mentioned in history, was noted during the war as a place of refuge; being unmolested because its mistress had no male relative to be obnoxious to the British. The mansion was of brick, solidly built; with a piazza in front, and a garden and lawn extending to the Ashley river. The grounds were covered with grass, on which the sheep owned by Mrs. Elliott might be seen lying under the magnificent live oaks decorated with the floating, silvery moss so beautiful in the low country. The graceful fringe tree and magnolia grandi-flora, with other ornamental trees, grew in clumps in front and on either side. In the rear, a portico looked on an avenue of flowering locusts, nearly a mile in length. A circular stairs ascended from the spacious

hall to Mrs. Elliott's study.   This beautiful country seat
—now in ruins—was the usual residence of Mrs. Elliott
in the spring months ; the summers being spent at
Johnson's Fort, on John's Island.   It was there that
she died.

~~~~~~~~~~

ANN ELLIOTT, the wife of Lewis Morris, was born
at Accabee.   In Charleston, while the city was occupied by the British, she wore a bonnet decorated with
thirteen small plumes, as a token of her attachment to
republican principles ; and for her patriotic spirit, was
called "the beautiful rebel."   Kosciusko was her ad-
mirer and correspondent.   An English officer—the
second son of a noble family—who was billeted upon
her mother, became so enamored of her that he sought
the good offices of one of her female friends to inter-
cede in his behalf ; and even offered, if she would
favor him, to join the Americans.   Miss Elliott bade her
friend say to him in reply, that to her former want of
esteem, was added scorn for a man capable of betraying
his sovereign for selfish interest.   She had before declined the gift of a splendid English saddle-horse, of
which he wished her acceptance.   She would not
attend church, as she had been accustomed, in Charleston, while prayers were offered there for the success of
the British arms ; preferring to join in the service read
at her mother's house, where petitions were put up for
the downfall of the invaders.

At one time, while Colonel Morris, to whom she was

then engaged, was on a visit to her at Accabee, the attention of the family was drawn to the windows by an unusual noise, and they perceived that the house was surrounded by the Black Dragoons, in search of the young officer, who had no time to escape. Ann went to one of the windows, opened it, and presenting herself to the view of the dragoons, demanded what they wanted. " We want the —— rebel!" was the reply. " Go and look for him in the American army!" answered the young girl. "How dare you disturb a family under the protection of both armies?" Her firmness and resolution conquered; and the enemy departed without further molestation.

Colonel and Mrs. Morris owned, among other possessions, a cotton plantation on the Edisto River, about four miles from Charleston, called the Round O, which is mentioned in Lee's Southern War. They had also a residence upon Sullivan's Island. In September of one year there was so severe a gale that several houses were blown down. The house of Colonel Morris, which stood on a narrow part of the island, was undermined by the advance of the tide. There was only time to remove the family to a neighbor's, when the house fell, overthrown by the assault of wind and waves.

Mrs. Lewis Morris was one of the belles distinguished at the levees of the first President. Her residence during the last years of her life, was in Morrisania. She died in New York the 29th of April, 1848, at the age of eighty-six.

THE incident of Jane Elliott's first acquaintance with her husband might adorn a chapter in the romance of the real. She was the only child of Charles Elliott, of St. Paul's parish—a staunch whig in principle, who exhibited his devotion to the cause by equipping a considerable body of troops at his own expense ; but fell a victim to disease ere the war had been waged in Carolina. His daughter having imbibed his opinions, endeavored to serve the cause he had espoused, by the bestowal of a portion of her wealth for the relief of the wounded American soldiers, and to contribute to the establishment of hospitals for that purpose. Not satisfied with this substantial aid, Miss Elliott gave her personal supervision to certain wards in the hospital, which she visited to attend to the sufferers. It was on one of these ministering visits that she first saw Colonel Washington, who had been wounded and taken prisoner in the cavalry charge at Eutaw Springs, and sent to Charleston for surgical aid, and for safe keeping. The interest with which the young girl heard the story of his perils, the sympathy given to his misfortunes, and the gratitude and admiration of the brave young soldier, may all be imagined, as leading to the reciprocal sentiment that soon grew up between them. Miss Elliott was then in the early bloom of youth, and surpassingly beautiful. Her manners were dignified, yet gentle and winning ; her perceptions quick, and her nature frank and generous. Homage had been paid to her charms by the conquerors, from which she turned to succor the defenders of her country. Major Barry, whose pen seems to have celebrated the charms of many rebel fair ones, addressed a poem " to Jane Elliott playing the guitar," which was lately found in the ruins of Accabee by a daughter of Mrs. Lewis Morris. These lines may serve as a specimen :

> " Sweet harmonist ! whom nature triply arms
> With virtue, beauty, music's powerful charms,—
> Say, why combin'd, when each resistless power
> Might mark its conquest to the fleeting hour ?"

Colonel Washington was a gallant officer, imbued with the chivalric feeling of that period, ardent in patriotism, and covered with the brilliant renown of a successful soldier. It was not strange that two so congenial should love each other, and become bound by a mutual pledge to unite their fortunes; but the marriage did not take place till the spring of 1782. With the return of peace the soldier exchanged the fatigues of the camp for the quiet avocations of the planter, establishing himself at the family-seat of his wife, at Sandy Hill, South Carolina. They had two children ; one of whom, a daughter, is yet living. Mrs. Washington survived her husband about twenty years, and died in 1830, at the age of sixty-six.

ANNA, the wife of Charles Elliott, was a patriot by inheritance, being the daughter of Thomas Ferguson, one of the bravest and most zealous among the friends of liberty. It was said of her that she " appeared to consecrate every thought and every hour of existence to the interests of America." She received under her hospitable roof the sick and wounded, and gave them her personal attention and sympathy; she divided of her substance among those who needed aid ; she was the advocate and friend of such as were unjustly persecuted. The prisoners she visited at regular intervals received hope and strength from her presence, and were beguiled into forgetfulness of their sufferings by her conversation. To the afflicted she was indeed an angel of blessing; and even the enemies of her country were influenced by the remarkable power of fascination she possessed, which few, even the most harsh and unbending, could resist. This was acknowledged in the most satisfactory way—the granting of privileges and favors by many British officers. What she would not have condescended to ask for herself, she solicited for the benefit of her countrymen. Major Garden says: " I do not know an officer who did not owe to her some essential increase of comfort." Yet her efforts in the cause of justice and clemency were not always successful ; she is said to have drawn up the petition addressed to Lord Rawdon, and signed by the ladies of Charleston, in behalf of the gallant and unfortunate Colonel Isaac Hayne.

The following anecdote of Mrs. Elliott has been mentioned. An officer of the royal army, noted for his cruelty and relentless persecution of those opposed to his political views, was one day walking with her in a garden where was a great variety of flowers. " What is this, madam ?" he asked, pointing to the chamomile.

" The rebel flower," she replied.   " And why is it called
the rebel flower ?" asked the officer.   " Because," answered Mrs. Elliott, " it always flourishes most when
trampled upon."

One day an officer, in the house of Mrs. Elliott in
Charleston, pointed out to her a young French officer
of the legion of Pulaski, passing by.   " There, Mrs.
Elliott," he cried, " is one of your illustrious allies ! He
has a fine form and martial appearance.   What a pity
the hero is minus his *sword !*"   She answered promptly
and with spirit, "Had two thousand such men been here
to aid in the defence of our city, I should not at this
moment, sir, have been subjected to the insolence of
your observation."

Her impulsive and feeling nature is shown by another
anecdote.   When her father was arrested and put on
board a transport ship to be sent into exile, Mrs. Elliott,
who had received the intelligence in the country, hastened to Charleston and solicited permission to bid him
farewell.   Her request was granted.   She went on
board the vessel in which he was a prisoner, but had
scarcely entered the cabin, when, oppressed with grief,
she fainted, and was laid upon a couch.   The captain,
in alarm, recommended a variety of remedies, and at
last said " A cordial would revive her ; we have some fine
French liqueur."   On hearing this, Mrs. Elliott sprang
from her couch in sudden excitement.   " The French !"
she exclaimed ; " who speaks of the French ? God
bless the nation !"   Then turning to her father, she
trove by her touching eloquence, to sustain him under

his misfortunes, and inspire him with hope for the future. " Let not oppression shake your fortitude," she said, " nor the hope of gentler treatment cause you for a moment to swerve from strict duty. Better times are in store for us; the bravery of the Americans, and the friendly aid of France, will yet achieve the deliverance of our country from oppression. We shall meet again, my father, and meet with joy."

The historian Ramsay bears heart-warm testimony to the patriotism of the Carolinian women, who gloried in being called " rebels ;" and did their utmost to support the fortitude of their relatives.

The wife of Isaac Holmes, one of the patriots sent into exile at St. Augustine, sustained his firmness by her own resolution, to the moment when the guard separated him from his family. Bidding him have no fears for those he left, her parting injunction was, " Waver not in your principles, but be true to your country."

When the sons of Rebecca Edwards were arrested as objects of retaliation, she encouraged them to persevere in devotion to the cause they had espoused. Should they fall a sacrifice, a mother's blessing, and the approbation of their countrymen, would go with them to the last; but if fear of death ever prevailed on them to purchase safety by submission, they must forget she was their parent, for it would to her be misery to look on them again.

THE sufferings of the sick and wounded American prisoners after the fall of Charleston, appealed to female benevolence also among the loyalists. Though attached to the royal cause, Mrs. SARAH HOPTON and her daughters were indefatigable in their attentions to the sufferers, whom many feared to visit in consequence of the prevalence of a contagious fever in the hospitals. The English were well supplied with necessary stores; the Americans were destitute, and therefore experienced their kindness and bounty. Their servants were continually employed in carrying them nourishment and articles needed; and in some cases, they paid the hire of nurses, where personal services were indispensable. They soothed the death-bed of many with the consolations of religion, prayed with those who were in danger, and joined with the convalescent in returning thanks. These kind offices were rendered to men of whose political principles and acts they disapproved, while great bitterness of feeling existed between the opposing parties; but no prejudice could make these Christian women insensible to the claims of humanity.

The lessons of piety and charity—the great lessons of life—taught by Mrs. Hopton to her daughters, were afterwards neither forgotten nor neglected. They were prominent in promoting the diffusion of religious education, and devoted to such objects their energies and wealth. Two of them aided in the establishment of a charity school for the education of female orphans. Mrs. Gregorie, the eldest daughter, appropriated a fund to aid in the support of this school, with many other bequests to different religious associations.

XXXI.

BEHETHLAND FOOTE BUTLER.

THE influence of women, so powerful an agent during the progress of the Revolutionary war, was essential after its close in restoring a healthful tone and vigor to society. The exercise of the higher qualities of character was then no less demanded than in the troublous times of violent popular excitement. Energy, industry, and perseverance were necessary to the fulfilment of daily duties, which were to form the character and shape the destinies of the youth of the Republic. It was the part of women to reclaim what the ravages of war had laid waste; to weed from the soil the rank growth it had nourished; to carry out in practice the principles for which patriots had shed their blood, and to lay a moral foundation on which the structure of a nation's true greatness might be built. How faithfully the honorable yet difficult task was performed, may be best seen from the characters of those who were prepared for usefulness under this training. And it is not a little remarkable how indifferent were those to whom this mighty trust was committed, to views of personal ambition or interest. The spirit of Mary Washington was among them. No distinction was in their eyes worthy to be coveted, except that of eminent usefulness ; they thought not of the fame or power to be won by service to the Republic, but in their simplicity and singleness of heart believed a patriot's best reward the consciousness of having done his duty. Such were the matrons of the nation's early day. Had they been otherwise, America would not have been what now she is.

It is pleasant to dwell upon the character of one of these matrons, whose influence, exerted in the privacy of the domestic circle, has borne rich fruit in those who owe their distinction to her training. But few incidents of her early personal history can be obtained ; her life, like that of most women, has been too quiet and secluded to furnish material for the chronicler of mere events ; but in view of the part she has borne in the great work appointed by Providence to American women, and the example afforded, its lesson should not be lost.

Behethland Moore was born on the 24th December, 1764, in Fauquier County, Virginia. Her father, Captain Frank Moore, commanded as lieutenant one of the Virginia troops at Braddock's defeat. Her mother was Frances Foote, of whose family many still reside in that part of the State. About 1768, five years after the marriage of her parents, they removed to South Carolina, and settled on Little River, in Laurens District, where Captain Moore died two years afterwards. His widow contracted a second marriage with Captain

Samuel Savage, who in 1774 removed to Edgefield District, and fixed his residence on Saluda River, just above Saluda Old Town. Here Miss Moore and her two brothers, William and George, lived with her mother and stepfather. Her education was attended to with more care than was usually bestowed on the tuition of young girls. She was sent to school in Camden, and placed under the charge of a female teacher who enjoyed in that day a very high reputation, receiving instruction in various useful and ornamental branches.

While she was at this school, Count Pulaski, with the forces under his command, passed through Camden on his way to join the American army at Charleston. Miss Moore and her young companions took great pleasure in looking at the soldiers as they passed through the streets; though they were frequently rebuked for this indulgence of a natural curiosity. In 1781, she returned home. The small-pox was making fearful ravages through the country ; and to secure her against the dangers of the disease in its more violent form, Miss Moore was sent to the neighborhood of Ninety-Six, where she was innoculated by a British surgeon. While awaiting the effects of the operation, being placed as a boarder in the house of James Maysons, General Greene laid siege to Ninety-Six. The wife of Colonel Cruger, the commander of the garrison, had lodgings in the same house with Miss Moore, and was well acquainted with the American General. The approach of Lord Rawdon rendered it necessary to attempt carrying the place by storm. Greene determined on this ; but with

5

characteristic humanity and delicacy, gave notice of his intention to Mrs. Cruger, and detached a sergeant and guard of eight men to protect the house in which she resided, from dangers that might be apprehended in the heat of the assault. When the cannonading commenced, Mrs. Cruger was engaged in sewing up guineas in a girdle; an occupation which she continued in spite of the alarm occasioned by the successive reports. Miss Moore, as may be supposed, had her share in the uneasiness caused by the military preparations. She returned home the day before Lord Rawdon's troops passed along the road, not far from the dwelling of her parents. The terrors of war were brought to their very door; for it was here that a sanguinary skirmish took place between Rawdon's men and a body of Colonel Washington's cavalry sent to impede their progress. Soon after, one of the royalist officers came to the house, where there were none but women; and advised the family to take care of their property. The caution was not unnecessary; for they were presently intruded upon by several British soldiers. In their search for plunder, they rolled down from above stairs some apples that had been gathered and stored for the use of the family. The soldiers below began picking them up as they fell on the floor; Miss Moore commanded them to desist, and gathering some of the fruit in her apron, offered it to a non-commissioned officer who stood by. Struck with the cool courage and determination of so young a girl, he made some remark expressive of his admiration, and ordered the soldiers instantly to desist

from their rude trespass. He then asked if her father
did not own some sheep; to which she replied in the affir-
mative. " The men are killing them, then, in the lot,"
said the officer. Miss Moore hastened thither, followed by her informant. Two men were in the act of
slaughtering one of the sheep; but at the officer's bidding, with the threat of reporting them to the commander, were compelled to let them go. This incident,
though trifling, exhibits the same spirit which in other
instances impelled to heroic actions. The determination to interfere, though at no little personal hazard, for
the protection of her father's property, required a degree
of courage in one of her age, which can be estimated
only when we consider the ferocity of the marauders
who then made it their business to pillage private
families.

On another occasion a band of tories came to the
house of Captain Savage, and were taking off a negro
boy who had been the personal attendant of Miss
Moore's father in the Indian war. With no thought
of the risk to herself, she hastened after them to rescue
him from their hands. The men, however, merely
wanted him to show them where the horses were.
When they returned driving the latter, one of them
ordered another servant to catch one for him. Miss
Moore commanded him not to obey such an order; it
was repeated ; and the tory swore he would beat the
servant for his disobedience. As he was about to put
his threat in execution, the young girl threw herself
between them, and the grumbling assailant was forced

to forego the intended violence. It must be remembered that the intrepid maiden thus braved the ruthless band entirely on a point of honor—knowing that the horses would be taken, but resolved not to permit a servant belonging to her family to wait upon a tory.

While she resided at home, it became necessary to convey intelligence of danger to Captain Wallace, who was in command of a small force on the other side of the Saluda. There was difficulty in doing this, as no male messenger could be procured. Miss Moore, at that time but fifteen years old, volunteered to undertake the service. Accompanied by her little brother, and a friend named Fanny Smith, she went up the river in a canoe in the middle of the night; gave the warning to Captain Wallace, and through him to Colonel Henry Lee, who had crossed the Island Ford on the retreat ordered by General Greene.

The next morning a young American officer, who had been below on some reconnoitering service, rode up to the house to make a few inquiries. These were answered by the young lady, who, it is said, was somewhat struck with the appearance of the handsome man in dragoon uniform. This was the first occasion on which she saw her future husband. It appears that the pleasing impression at first sight was reciprocal; and that the fair girl's image accompanied Captain William Butler into his next battle-field; for it was not long before the courtship took place. This did not meet the full approbation of the stepfather; but love seldom yields to the discouragement of obstacles; and the

lover's perseverance was crowned with success. The
marriage took place in 1784. The young people took
possession of a small farm which Captain Butler had
inherited from his father, near Mount Willing. Fourteen years afterwards they removed to an estate on one
of the branches of Saluda River, where they continued
to live till the husband's death in 1821.

General Butler was almost constantly engaged in
public service, and was necessarily absent from home
a great part of his time. In Congress from 1801 to
1814, and commanding the South Carolina forces in
Charleston as Major General during 1814 and 1815,
the whole care not only of his family, but of his plantation and business, devolved upon Mrs. Butler. Never
were such varied responsibilities more worthily met and
discharged. It was in this situation that the sterling
qualities of her character were developed, and shone
with brightest lustre. She had the care of a large
family, the support of which was derived mainly from
the produce of a small farm; and the energy with
which she devoted herself to the charge, evinced a wonderful fertility in resources, commanding the admiration
of all who knew her. She undertook the superintendence of her children's education, and especially of its
most important part—that moral training which always
gives tone to character in after life. Abundant occasions were afforded, in many trying scenes, for the exercise of the unfaltering fortitude and prompt judgment which have been her most remarkable character-
istics. One who has enjoyed an intimate acquaintance

with her, says he has never known her, in many years, to perform an act, or utter a word, which calm and deliberate judgment could disapprove. Amid trials and difficulties, sustained by high principle, integrity and independence, her character has impressed itself upon those who know her as rare and remarkable, commanding universal respect ; while her gentle virtues endear her to all within the circle of her acquaintance. With a singular power of command and stern energy, she combines the softest and most womanly qualities. In her it may be seen that a superior mind, rigidly disciplined, may belong to a woman without the development of any harsh or unfeminine lineaments ; and that a heart the most tender and affectionate may prompt to all the generous charities of life, without being allied to weakness. It is this union of benignity with force of intellect and firmness of resolution, which has given her the ascendancy she possesses over others—an attribute difficult to define, yet which is felt instinctively, as the most peculiar and imposing of natural gifts.

The best testimony that could be borne to the excellence of this noble mother, and of her system of education, is afforded by the career of her sons, several of whom have attained distinction in public service. Their acknowledgment of indebtedness to her for this eminence speaks more than volumes of eulogy. The family consisted of seven sons and one daughter. The eldest, James, was sheriff in his native district, and a Colonel in the militia of the State. He died in 1821. George, a Major in the army, which he left in 1815 for the

bar, was one of the most prominent men in the State;
and died at the age of thirty-three. The Hon. William
Butler studied medicine, and was for several years in
the navy. The fourth son, who practised law, died in
1828. The eminent talents and public career of Andrew Pickens Butler, for many years a distinguished
member of the Judiciary of South Carolina, and now
United States Senator, are too well known to need illus-
tration. It may suffice to say that in domestic life, and
in the social circle, he commands the same esteem as in
public station. He appears to have inherited the cheerfulness of disposition still retained by his mother, and
which contributes more than any other quality to shed
around home the sunshine of happiness. The late
Colonel Pierce Mason Butler was celebrated for heroic
and generous qualities. A hero in the best sense of the
the term was this "American Douglas." He commanded the regiment of his native State in the Florida war;
and subsequently received the highest testimony of the
people's confidence, in his election to the Chief Magis-
tracy of South Carolina. He fell at the head of the
Palmetto regiment in Mexico. Few of our prominent
men have left any single condensed expression that has
become classic by fixing itself in popular remembrance;
some of Colonel Butler's are, however, thus embalmed.
In his letter to General Worth, on the day of the battle
of Churubusco, he claims a position for his command in
the front of the action. "*South Carolina,*" he says,
"*is entitled to a place in the picture.*" And his motto
for his regiment—"*Our State expects us to do our duty,*

but to make no show of it"—is an expression strongly characteristic not only of him, but of the noble-minded mother by whose precepts, discipline, and example his character was formed. To her judicious care, and the high example of their father, her sons owe the large share they have exhibited of the old Greek feeling that they were born for their country.

The parting of Mrs. Butler with her gallant son, on his departure for Mexico, was cheered by no expectation of meeting again—his health being greatly impaired. She gave him her last embrace with tearless eyes, though with an agonized heart. Chosen as he was by the unanimous and spontaneous call of the State to lead her forces, he could not refuse to accept the trust; nor would his mother allow the exhibition of her sorrow to impede him in the performance of his duty.

The youngest son, Leontine, died at the age of twenty-five. The only daughter, Emmala E., was the wife of Hon. Waddy Thompson, late Minister to Mexico.

A single anecdote of domestic management may serve to illustrate Mrs. Butler's power over the minds trained by her, and her habit of making use of slight occurrences to mould the character. The children of the late Colonel Butler attended school in the village of Edgefield, where she resides. One day when it rained violently, the children having been provided with cloaks and umbrellas sent for the purpose, her grandson, eleven years of age, observed that a little girl, the child of humble parents, had no such protection. He gave her his arm and the shelter of his umbrella, and conducted her home amid the jeers and laughter of his young companions. The amount of moral courage required for this simple act of courtesy and kindness, can be estimated when we consider the sensitiveness to ridicule in a boy of such early age. His grandmother's expression of approval was sufficient reward, and she lost not the opportunity of exhorting the generous child never to be ashamed of an honorable action, however humble the object.

It may perhaps be seen, even in this brief and inadequate sketch, how in the incidents of Mrs. Butler's early life, were developed the high mental and moral qualities which marked her in after years, illustrated in her actions, and sending forth so many streams of blessing. In her children, whom she reared to usefulness, and whose devotion to her has never faltered, her recompense has been found. Admired and beloved by her descendants and friends—the object of the high regard and respect of a large circle of acquaintance—she has yet the consciousness of being able to contribute to the enjoyment and improvement of those around her. It is but recently she has been called to mourn the death of her only daughter, worthy of her in her elevated principles, her gentle yet lofty spirit, and her grace and benignity of nature. The death of the brother whom she loved—Colonel Butler—it is said, was the blow which consigned her to an untimely grave. The memory of her amiable and noble qualities, and her deep and unaffected piety, is warmly cherished in the hearts of her kindred and friends.

5*

XXXII.

~~~~~~~~~~

HANNAH CALDWELL.

FEW occurrences in the history of ancient or modern warfare have so strongly influenced the public feeling —have excited so universal a sentiment of horror, or such deep resentment towards the authors of the crime—as the deliberate and barbarous murder of Mrs. Caldwell. It was perpetrated not only as an act of vengeance upon an individual, but with the design of striking terror into the country, and compelling the inhabitants to submission. So far, however, from producing this effect, it but roused the indignation of the whole community, filling all with one spirit—one desire to avenge the deed, and drive the invaders from their soil. It animated the brave with new energy, inspired the timid to feats of heroism, and determined the irresolute to throng to the standard of liberty. One of the journals of the day says: "The Caldwell tragedy has raised the resolution of the country to the highest pitch. They are ready almost to swear everlasting enmity to the name of a Briton."

The Rev. James Caldwell, pastor of the First Presbyterian church in Elizabethtown, New Jersey, was

descended of a Huguenot family, and born in Virginia.
He married in 1763, Hannah, the daughter of John
Ogden of Newark. Her mother was Miss Sayre, a
descendant of the Pilgrims. Her brothers were all
staunch whigs, with the exception of Jonathan, who
subsequently held the offices of Surgeon General in the
British army, and Judge of Newfoundland.

Shortly after the settlement of Mr. Caldwell at Elizabethtown, the war broke out; and inheriting from his
ancestors a feeling of opposition to tyranny, he warmly
espoused the cause of his country. He acted as chaplain
of those portions of the American army that successively
occupied New Jersey; joined Colonel Dayton's regiment,
and accompanied the Jersey brigade to the northern
lines. He was stationed some time at Johnstown,
New York, and was afterwards appointed assistant
commissary to the army; stood high in the confidence
of Washington; and by his eloquent and patriotic
appeals, contributed greatly, in times of despondency,
to excite and sustain the drooping spirits of the soldiers.
All the influence commanded by his character and talents
—his energy, and his unbounded popularity in the community—was devoted to the cause of American freedom.

This zeal and activity did not fail to render him
obnoxious to the enemy, and no effort was spared to do
him injury. A price was set upon his head; and it
is said that while preaching the gospel of peace to
his people, he was often forced to lay his loaded pistols
by his side in the pulpit. On account of the predatory
incursions of the British, he was compelled to leave

his home. for a temporary residence at Springfield, New Jersey. The parsonage thus deserted, and the church in which he preached, were used as a hospital for the sick and wounded of the American army. Its bell sounded the alarm through the town on the approach of the enemy;* the weary soldiers often slept upon its floor, and ate their hurried and scanty meals from the seats of the pews; so that worshippers on the Sabbath were not unfrequently compelled to stand through the service. Even of this shelter the British and tories, who cherished implacable enmity towards the pastor of the church, determined to deprive the soldiers; it was burnt, with the parsonage, on the night of January 25th, 1780.

Finding the situation at Springfield inconvenient, and the distance too great from his church, Mr. Caldwell again removed to "Connecticut Farms," four miles from Elizabethtown. It was during his residence at this place that the British troops from New York, under the command of the Hessian General Knyphausen, landed at Elizabethtown, before daylight, on the seventh of June.

Their march into the interior was marked by cruelty and devastation. Several houses were fired, and the inhabitants left destitute of provisions or shelter. When informed of the enemy's approach, Mr. Caldwell put his elder children into a baggage waggon in his possession as commissary, and sent them to some of his friends for protection. Three of the younger ones—Josiah

* See Notes concerning Elizabethtown, by Rev. Dr. Murray.

Flint, Elias Boudinot, and Maria, an infant about eight
months old, remained with their mother in the house.*
Mr. Caldwell had no fears for the safety of his wife and
young family; for he believed it impossible that resentment could be extended to a mother watching over her
little ones. He had that morning taken an early breakfast, intending to join the force collecting to oppose
the enemy. Having in vain endeavored to persuade
his wife to go with him, he returned to make a last
effort to induce her to change her determination; but
she remained firm. She handed him a cup of coffee,
which he drank as he sat on horseback. Seeing the
gleam of British arms at a distance, he put spurs to
his horse, and in a few moments was out of sight.

Mrs. Caldwell herself felt no alarm. She had hid
several articles of value in a bucket and let it down
into the well; and had filled her pockets with silver
and jewelry. She saw that the house was put in
order, and then dressed herself with care, that should
the enemy enter her dwelling, she might, to use her own
expression—"receive them as a lady." She then took
the infant in her arms, retired to her chamber, the
window of which commanded a view of the road,
towards which the end of the house stood—and seated
herself upon the bed. The alarm was given that the
soldiers were at hand. But she felt confidence that no

* The nurse also remained, and a little girl named Abigail Lenning-
ton, a soldier's daughter, whom Mr. Caldwell had taken into his family.
She is still living at Elizabethtown. Immediately after the tragedy,
she with the nurse, gave deposition as to the facts before a magistrate.

one could have the heart to do injury to the helpless inmates of her house. Again and again she said— "They will respect a mother." She had just nursed the infant and given it to the nurse, who was in the room. The girl, Abigail, was standing by the window. A soldier* left the road, and crossing a space of ground diagonally to reach the house, came to the window of the room, put his gun close to it, and fired. Two balls entered the breast of Mrs. Caldwell; she fell back on the bed, and in a moment expired.†

After the murder, Mrs. Caldwell's dress was cut open, and her pockets were rifled by the soldiers. Her remains were conveyed to a house on the other side of the road ; the dwelling was then fired and reduced to ashes with all the furniture. The ruthless soldiers went on in their work of destruction, pillaging and setting fire to the houses, piling beds and clothing in the street and destroying them, till the village was laid waste.

Let it be imagined what were the feelings of the husband, when the terrible news was communicated to him. It is said that he overheard some soldiers in a house where he stopped, speaking of the occurrence ; and by questioning them, learned the truth. La Fayette, on his last visit to America, informed one of the family, that Mr. Caldwell was with him that morning on the heights near Springfield, and saw, by the aid of

---

* He wore a red coat, and is generally supposed to have been a British soldier. Some have attributed the act to a refugee.

† The little girl received in her face some of the glass when the two balls entered, both of which took such deadly effect.

a spy-glass, the smoke ascending from the burning houses. "Thank God," he exclaimed, "the fire is not in the direction of my house." He was fatally mistaken!

Mr. Josiah F. Caldwell, one of the sons—the sixth of the nine children who were thus bereaved of a mother —relates what he remembers of the event. He was at the time six years of age. About sunrise, when it was announced that the British were coming, he went into the street and joined the people who were driving their cattle to Springfield. There he saw his father with a field-piece—a six pounder, which had formerly been used as an alarm piece. Thence the little boy proceeded to Bottle Hill, and found his second sister, Hannah, at the house of Mr. Sayre; and a day or two after, both the children set off on foot for Connecticut Farms, to see their mother. On their way, they were met by the nurse, Katy, with the two youngest children, in a chair belonging to Mr. Caldwell; she informed the young orphans of their mother's death, and insisted that they should return with her to Bottle Hill. The sister yielded, and was taken into the carriage; the little brother refused to go till he had taken a last look at his beloved parent, and pursued his way to the Farms. On his arrival he was conducted to the house where his mother's remains were laid. His father, who had arrived a short time before, was standing beside the bed on which reposed the lifeless form of this victim of political hatred. What a meeting for the heart-stricken mourner, and the child scarce able to comprehend his irreparable loss!

Some attempts were made by the royalist party to escape the odium of this sanguinary transaction, by pretending that Mrs. Caldwell had been killed by a chance shot.* The actual evidence, however, sets the fact beyond question that one of the enemy was the murderer; and there is too much reason to believe that the deed was deliberately ordered by those high in command. A letter to General Knyphausen, published in the New Jersey Journal, in reproaching him for the outrages of his army, unhesitatingly casts the blame of the murder on him, as committed designedly by one of his men: and the various rumors that went abroad amidst the popular excitement on the subject, and were mentioned in the papers of the day, show that such was the prevalent opinion.†

* Rivington's Royal Gazette, 1780.

† The Hon. Samuel L. Southard, alluding to Mrs. Caldwell's death, in connection with a memorial presented to the U. S. Senate for the church and property destroyed, says " her children were baptized to piety and patriotism in a mother's blood." Mr. Caldwell himself presented an address to the public,* showing that the murder of his wife had been a deliberate act, committed at the instigation of those in authority. " Mrs. Caldwell," he says, " was of so sweet a temper, and so prudent, benevolent and soft in her mnnners, that I verily believe she had not upon earth one personal enemy; and whatever rancor the enemy felt against myself for my public conduct and political character, I have no reason to believe there was any person among them under the influence of any personal difference, or private revenge. I cannot therefore esteem it the private action of an individual. No officer interfered to preserve the corpse from being stripped or burnt, nor to relieve the babes left thus desolate among them. Many officers, indeed, showed their abhorrence of the murder, and their tenderness

* Pennsylvania Journal, October 4, 1780.

The children were left at different places, till Mr. Caldwell bought a small farm at Turkey, now called New Providence, where he collected his family together, under the care of the faithful nurse, Katy. The remains of Mrs. Caldwell were interred in the burial-ground of the Presbyterian Church at Elizabethtown ; and the congregation placed above the grave a neat freestone slab, on which is an inscription recording her bright virtues, and her melancholy fate. The memory of this martyr to American liberty will long be revered by the inhabitants of the land with whose soil her shed blood has mingled !

Her personal appearance is described as conveying the abiding impression of benevolence, serenity, and peculiar sweetness of disposition. She was about the medium height, with dark gray eyes, auburn hair, and complexion of singular fairness ; of pleasing countenance, and quiet, gentle, and winning manners.

The tragedy was not yet complete. On the 24th of November, 1781, Mr. Caldwell went to Elizabethtown Point for a Miss Murray, who came under the protection of a flag of truce from New York, where she had shown great kindness to some of the sick soldiers. Mr.

for the babes ; why did they not set a sentinel over the corpse, till the neighboring women could have been called ? They knew she was a lady of amiable character and reputable family ; yet she was left half the day stripped in part, and tumbled about by the rude soldiery ; and at last was removed from the house before it was burnt, by the aid of those who were not of the army. From this I conclude the army knew the will of their superiors ; and that those who had benevolence dared not show it to this devoted lady."

Caldwell conducted her to his gig, and then went back into the boat for her bundle containing some articles of clothing. As he came on shore he was challenged by the American sentinel, who demanded what " contra- band goods" he had there. Unwilling then to dispute the matter, he turned back to leave the bundle with the officer ; and at that moment was shot by a man named Morgan, who had just been relieved from duty as a sentinel. This man is supposed to have been bribed by British gold to the deed. Mr. Caldwell fell, pierced by two balls ; and his body was borne to Mrs. Noel's house in Elizabethtown. Morgan, who fired upon him, was afterwards tried, found guilty of murder, and executed. The remains of Mr. Caldwell were laid in the same grave-yard with those of his wife ; and the " Caldwell monument," at the inauguration ceremonies of which Dr. Miller and Hon. William L. Dayton de- livered their eloquent addresses in 1846, was erected to their memory.

Mrs. Noel, the steadfast friend of the family, took the children under her protection, assembled their friends, and consulted upon measures to be taken for the care of them. All lived to become eminent and useful mem- bers of society. The eldest son, John Edwards, was taken by La Fayette to France, where he was edu- cated ; and in after years was foremost in New York in benevolent enterprises, and editor of one of the first religious periodicals in the country. The fifth son, Elias Boudinot, was taken by the Hon. Elias Boudinot, President of the first Congress ; and was afterwards Clerk of the United States Supreme Court, and one of the originators of the Colonization Society. Mrs. Noel adopted the youngest child—a daughter—who is still living in New York.

The Rev. Dr. Murray of Elizabethtown, who has thoroughly investigated the subject, has prepared an accurate account of the death of the devoted patriot and pastor, which will shortly be given to the public.

~~~~~~~~~~~~~

ON the 28th of February, 1779, a party of British troops from New York landed at Elizabethtown Point, for the purpose of capturing the Governor of New Jersey, and surprising the force stationed in the village under General Maxwell. One detachment marched at night to " Liberty Hall," the residence of Governor Livingston, and forced an entrance; but failed of their object—for it happened that he had left home some hours previously. Disappointed in the expectation of securing his prisoner, the British officer demanded the Governor's papers. Miss Livingston assented to the demand; but appealing to him as a gentleman, requested that a box standing in the parlor, which she claimed as containing her private property, should be secured from molestation. A guard was accordingly stationed over it, while the library was thrown open to the soldiers, who filled their foraging bags with worthless law papers and departed. The box, which had been sedulously guarded, contained all the Governor's correspondence with Congress, with the Commander-in-chief, and the

State officers; the young lady's stratagem thus preserving what would have proved a most valuable prize to the plunderers.*

A repartee made by one of Lord Dorchester's aids to Miss Susan Livingston, has been celebrated. When the British were evacuating New York, she expressed a wish to him that their departure might be hastened, " for among your incarcerated belles, the *scarlet* fever must rage till you are gone." Major Upham, the aid, replied that he feared, if freed from the prevailing malady— "they would be tormented by a worse—the *blue* devils."

All the letters of Livingston to his daughters show the sympathy that existed between them, and his confidence in the strength of their republican principles. His opinions and wishes on all subjects are openly expressed to them. In a letter to the Earl of Stirling, he says he has entrusted to his daughter Catharine his despatches to his correspondents in Spain. He writes at one time to her, noticing the favor shown to the British captives—"I know there are a number of flirts in Philadelphia, who will triumph in our over-complaisance to the red-coat prisoners lately arrived in that metropolis. I hope none of my connections will imitate them, either in the dress of their heads, or the still more tory feelings of their hearts."

Catharine, the second daughter, afterwards married Matthew Ridley, of Baltimore. He was at Nantes in 1778, in the American commission business.† She took

---

* Life of Livingston, by Theodore Sedgwick.

† The following copy of an order sent to Nantes, rather curiously

a deep interest in public affairs. Her friend, Lady Catharine Alexander, writes from Valley Forge, after the cheering news of the alliance with France—" We have nothing here but rejoicings; every one looks happy and seems proud of the share he has had in humbling the pride of Britain, and of establishing the name of of America as a nation." The following note, addressed to her by Washington from the same place, has never before been published.*

shows the precariousness of transportation in those times. It is extracted from a MS. letter of John Jay, dated Madrid, Jan. 21st, 1782, which expresses a hope that one of the parcels may meet its destination:

"Be pleased to send for Miss Kitty W. Livingston, to the care of Hon. R. Morris, Esq., at Philadelphia, by the first three good vessels bound there, the three following parcels, viz :

"*No.* 1 *to contain—*

2 White embroidered patterns for shoes.

4 Pair silk stockings.

A pattern for a negligeé of light pink colored silk, with a set of ribbons suitable to it.

6 Pair of kid gloves.

6 Yards of catgut, and cap-wire in proportion.

6 Yards of white silk gauze.

"*No.* 2 *to contain—*

"The same as above, except that the silk for the negligeé must not be pink-colored, but of any other color that Mrs. Johnson may think fashionable and pretty. The shoes and ribbons may be adapted to it.

"*No.* 3 *to contain—*

"The same as above, except that the silk for the negligeé must be of a different color from the other two, and the shoes and ribbons of a proper color to be worn with it."

* The MS. correspondence of Miss Catharine Livingston, including this note, is in the possession of Mr. Theodore Sedgwick.

"General Washington having been informed lately of the honor done him by Miss Kitty Livingston in wishing for a lock of his hair, takes the liberty of inclosing one, accompanied by his most respectful compliments.

"*Camp, Valley Forge*, 18*th Mar.*, 1778."

The wife of William Livingston was Susannah, the daughter of Philip French, and grand-daughter, by the mother's side, of Anthony Brockholst, Lieutenant Governor, under Andross, of the Colony of New York, and subsequently its chief magistrate. Simple and unpretending in manners, she was endowed with a strong intellect and a warm and tender heart. The letters of her husband show his high respect as well as love for her. When the British troops made the memorable incursion into New Jersey by Elizabethtown, the Governor, being absent from his family, suffered intense anxiety on their account. But while the neighboring villages were seen in flames, the enemy respected "Liberty Hall," and treated its inmates with courtesy. A correspondent of Rivington's Gazette accounts for this by saying that one of the British officers received a rose from Miss Susan Livingston on his visit to the house, as a memento of a promise of protection. An anecdote connected with this invasion has been traditionally preserved, which, if proved authentic, would furnish curious evidence as to the agency concerned in the murder of Mrs. Caldwell. After a day of alarm, the flames of Springfield and Connecticut Farms being in

view, and soldiers continually passing the house, Mrs
Livingston and her daughters were at a late hour surprised by the entrance of several British officers, who
announced their intention of lodging there.   Their
presence was felt to be a protection, and the ladies
retired. About midnight the officers left the house,
called away by some startling news ; and not long afterwards a band of straggling soldiers, intoxicated, rushed
with oaths and threats into the hall.   " The maid servant—all the males in the establishment having taken
refuge in the woods early in the day to avoid being
made prisoners—fastened herself in the kitchen; and
the ladies crowding together like frightened deer, locked
themselves in another apartment.   Their place of retreat
was soon discovered by the ruffians; and afraid to exas-
perate them by refusing to come out, one of Governor
Livingston's daughters opened the door.   A drunken
soldier seized her by the arm.   She grasped the villain's
collar, and at the very moment a flash of lightning illu-
mining the hall and falling full upon her white dress—
he staggered back, exclaiming, with an oath—'It's Mrs.
Caldwell, that we killed to-day!'   One of the party was
at length recognized, and the house by his intervention
finally cleared of the assailants.*"

The influence of Mrs. Livingston over her husband,
in spite of his unyielding and irritable temper, is repeatedly noticed by his biographer.   This influence was
secured by her strong good sense, her sympathy, and
unselfish tenderness.   She shared his thoughts in time

* Life of Livingston, p. 353.

of war, and his joy when allowed to relinquish his wandering life, and return to his home; to enter once more his deserted library, and superintend his long neglected garden. In his simple and rural occupations she was his constant and faithful companion; and his letters evince the solicitude with which he watched over her health, with the warm affection he cherished for her through years of absence and absorbing occupation. She died on the 17th of July, 1789.

SARAH, LADY STIRLING, was the sister of Governor Livingston. She accompanied the Earl, her husband, who was Major General in the American army, to the camp. While the Earl was in the camp at White Plains, she paid a visit to New York—then in possession of the British—with her youngest daughter, Lady Catharine Alexander, to visit her eldest daughter, whose husband, Robert Watts, had remained quietly in the city, taking no active part on either side. The letters of both mother and daughter descriptive of this visit are interesting as showing the situation and temper of those Americans who had continued in the city during its occupation by the enemy. Lady Catharine, who writes —August, 1778—from Parsippany, the place where Governor Livingston's family had taken refuge after an invasion of Elizabethtown, is sanguine in her hope of soon seeing her relatives as zealous patriots as herself. Mr. Watts, she says, is among the number of those who are heartily sick of the tyranny witnessed;

and "as to Mary, her political principles are perfectly *re-bellious*. * * The sentiments of a great number have undergone a thorough change since they have been with the British army; as they have many opportunities of seeing flagrant acts of injustice and cruelty of which they could not have believed their friends capable. This convinces them that if they conquer, we must live in abject slavery." Lady Stirling exhibits her disinterested patriotism by refusing to avail herself of the permission sent from Sir Henry Clinton, to take anything she pleased out of the city; fearing "there would be a handle made of it," if she accepted the offer. "The last time I saw him (Mr. Elliott,) he told me I must take a box of tea; but I stuck to my text."

Lady Catharine afterwards became the wife of the Hon. William Duer. A letter of condolence from Washington to the Countess of Stirling—upon her husband's death—has been preserved in the Historical Collections of New Jersey.

6

XXXIII.

~~~~~

DEBORAH SAMSON.

WHEN the lapse of years shall have invested the period of the Revolution with the coloring of poesy, and the novelist shall seek his materials in the romance of American history, the heroism and deeds of the subject of this notice will perhaps afford the ground-work of a tragedy or a novel. Something of the latter sort has already been constructed upon this foundation; a production, half tale, half biography, entitled "The Female Review," published in Massachusetts about the commencement of the present century. I have not been able to find a copy; but have been told that it was not in any measure reliable, and that the heroine had repeatedly expressed her displeasure at the representation of herself, which she "did not at all recognize." The following facts respecting her, I received from a lady who knew her personally,* and has often listened with thrilling interest to the animated description given by herself of her exploits and adventures.

---

* A niece of Captain Tisdale, upon whom Robert attended in the army for some months.

Though not comparable, certainly, to the "prophet-
ess" in whom France triumphed—

> " The maid with helméd head,
> Like a war-goddess, fair and terrible—"

for the dignity with which the zeal of a chivalrous and
superstitious age, and the wonderful success of her mission invested her—it cannot be denied that this romantic girl exhibited something of the same spirit with the
lowly herdsmaid, who, amidst the round of her humble
duties, felt herself inspired with resolution to go forth
and do battle in her country's cause, exchanging her
peasant's garb for the mail, and the helmet, and the
sword.   There is something moving and interesting in
the aspect of the enthusiasm fostered in her secret soul,
struggling with obstructions and depressions, and at
length impelling her to the actual accomplishment of
what she had pondered in day-dreams; while the ignorance and error mingled with this enthusiasm, should
increase our sympathy without diminishing the share
of admiration we would bestow, had it been evinced in
a more becoming manner.

Several instances are mentioned in the history of the
war, in which female courage was displayed by actions
pertaining to the stronger sex.   The resolution of Congress is on record, in which honorable mention is made
of the services of Margaret Corbin.*   The story of the

* " Resolved—That Margaret Corbin, wounded and disabled at the
attack on Fort Washington, while she heroically filled the post of her
husband, who was killed by her side serving a piece of artillery, do

gunner's wife, who took her husband's place when he was killed at the battle of Monmouth, and did such execution that after the engagement she was rewarded by a commission,* has been often related. And many examples were there of matrons, who, having suffered incredibly from the spoliations of the enemy, lost patience, and fought manfully for the last loaf of bread, or the last bed-quilt for their children. In the case before us, the isolation from ordinary domestic and social ties favored the impulse that prompted to a course so extraordinary.

Deborah Samson was the youngest child of poor parents, who lived in the county of Plymouth, Massachusetts. Their poverty, rendered hopeless by pernicious habits, was the least of the evils suffered by the unfortunate children. Charity interposed to rescue them from the effects of evil example; they were removed from their parents, and placed in different families, where a prospect was afforded of their receiving proper care and instruction to fit them for maintaining themselves when arrived at a suitable age. Deborah found a home in the house of a respectable farmer, whose wife, a well-disposed woman, bestowed upon her as much attention as is common in such cases. The friendless and destitute girl was kindly treated, and provided with comfortable food and clothing; but had

receive during her natural life, or continuance of said disability, one-half the monthly pay drawn by a soldier in service of these States; and that she now receive out of public stores, one suit of clothes, or value thereof in money." July, 1779.

* History of Schoharie County.

no advantages of education. Her keen feeling of this deprivation, and the efforts she made to repair the deficiency, show her possession of a mind naturally superior, and that judicious training might have fitted her to promote in no insignificant degree the good of society. There was none to teach her; but she seized every opportunity for acquiring knowledge. She borrowed books from the children who passed the house in which she lived on their way to and from school, and persevered with untiring exertion in her private studies, till she had learned to read tolerably well; but attempted no other branch of scholarship, until, on the completion of her eighteenth year, the law released her from her indentures.

Her first arrangement on becoming the mistress of her own movements, was to secure herself the advantages of instruction. The only way in which she could do this was by engaging to work in the family of a farmer one half the time, in payment for her board and lodging, and attending the common district school in the neighborhood. Her improvement was rapid beyond example. In a few months she had acquired more knowledge than many of her schoolmates had done in years; and was by them regarded as quite a prodigy of industry and attainment.

Meantime, the Revolutionary struggle had commenced. The gloom that had accompanied the outburst of the storm, hung over the whole land; the news of the carnage on the plains of Lexington—the sound of the cannon at Bunker's Hill, had reached every dwelling, and vibrated on the heart of every patriot in New England. The zeal which had urged the men to quit their homes for the battle-field, found its way to a female bosom; Deborah felt as if she would shrink from no effort or sacrifice in the cause which awakened all her enthusiasm. She entered with the most lively interest into every plan for the relief of the army, and bitterly regretted that as a woman she could do no more, and that she had not the privilege of a man, of shedding her blood for her country.

There is no reason to believe that any consideration foreign to the purest patriotism, impelled her to the resolution of assuming male attire, and enlisting in the army. She could have been actuated by no desire of gaining applause; for the private manner in which she quitted her home and associates, entrusting no one with her design, subjected her to surmises of a painful nature; and the careful preservation of her secret during the period of her military service, exonerates her from the least suspicion of having been urged to the step by an imprudent attachment. It is very likely that her youthful imagination was kindled by the rumor of brave deeds, and that her visions of "the camp's stir and crowd and ceaseless 'larum" were colored richly by the hues of fancy. Curiosity to see and partake of this varied war-life, the restlessness of "a heart unsouled and solitary"—the consuming of energies which had no object to work upon, may have contributed to the forming of her determination. It must be borne in mind, too, that she was restrained by no consideration that could interfere with the project. Alone in the world, there were few to inquire what had become of her, and still fewer to care for her fate. She felt herself accountable to no human being.

By keeping the district school for a summer term, she had amassed the sum of twelve dollars. She purchased a quantity of coarse fustian, and working at intervals when she could be secure from observation, made up a suit of men's clothing; each article, as it was finished, being hid in a stack of hay. Having completed her preparations, she announced her intention of going where she could obtain better wages for her labor. Her new clothes, and such articles as she wished to take with her, were tied in a bundle. The lonely girl departed; but went not far, probably only to the shelter of the nearest wood, before putting on the disguise she was so eager to assume. Although not beautiful, her features were animated and pleasing, and her figure, tall for a woman, was finely proportioned. As a man, she might have been called handsome; her general appearance was extremely prepossessing, and her manner calculated to inspire confidence.

She now pursued her way to the American army, where she presented herself, in October, 1778, as a young man anxious to join his efforts to those of his country-men in their endeavors to oppose the common enemy. Her acquaintances, meanwhile, supposed her engaged in service at a distance. Rumors of her elopement with a British soldier, and even of her death, were afterwards current in the neighborhood where she had resided; but none were sufficiently interested to make such search for her as might have led to a discovery.

Distrusting her own constancy, and resolute to continue in the service, notwithstanding any change of her inclination, she enlisted for the whole term of the war. She was received and enrolled in the army by the name of Robert Shirtliffe. She was one of the first volunteers in the company of Captain Nathan Thayer of Medway, Massachusetts; and as the young recruit appeared to have no home or connections, the Captain gave her a home in his family until his company should be full, when they were to join the main army.

We now find her performing the duties and enduring the fatigues of military life. During the seven weeks she passed in the family of Captain Thayer, she had time both for experience and reflection; but in after years her constant declaration was that she never for one moment repented or regretted the step she had taken. Accustomed to labor from childhood, upon the farm and in out-door employment, she had acquired unusual vigor of constitution; her frame was robust, and of masculine strength; and having thus gained a degree of hardihood, she was enabled to acquire great expertness and precision in the manual exercise, and to undergo what a female delicately nurtured would have found it impossible to endure. Soon after they had joined the company, the recruits were supplied with uniforms by a kind of lottery. That drawn by Robert did not fit; but taking needle and scissors, he soon altered it to suit him. To Mrs. Thayer's expression of surprise at finding a young man so expert in using the implements of feminine industry, the answer was—that his mother having no girl, he had been often obliged to practice the seamstress's art.

While in the house of Captain Thayer, a young girl visiting his wife was much in the society of Deborah, or as she was then called, Robert. Coquettish by nature, and perhaps priding herself on the conquest of the "blooming soldier," she suffered her growing partiality to be perceived. Robert on his part felt a curiosity to learn by new experience how soon a maiden's fancy might be won; and had no scruples in paying attentions to one so volatile and fond of flirtation, with whom it was not likely the impression would be lasting. This little piece of romance gave some uneasiness to the worthy Mrs. Thayer, who could not help observing that the liking of her fair visitor for Robert was not fully reciprocated. She took an opportunity of remonstrating with the young soldier, and showed what unhappiness might be the consequence of such folly, and how unworthy it was of a brave man to trifle with a girl's feelings. The caution was taken in good part and it is not known that the "love passage" was continued, though Robert received at parting some tokens of remembrance, which were treasured as relics in after years.

For three years our heroine appeared in the character of a soldier, being part of the time employed as a waiter in the family of Colonel Patterson. During this time, and in both situations, her exemplary conduct, and the

6*

fidelity with which her duties were performed, gained the approbation and confidence of the officers. She was a volunteer in several hazardous enterprizes, and was twice wounded, the first time by a sword cut on the left side of the head. Many were the adventures she passed through; as she herself would often say, volumes might be filled with them. Sometimes placed unavoidably in circumstances in which she feared detection, she nevertheless escaped without the least suspicion being awakened among her comrades. The soldiers were in the habit of calling her " Molly," in playful allusion to her want of a beard; but not one of them ever dreamed that the gallant youth fighting by their side was in reality a female.

About four months after her first wound she received another severe one, being shot through the shoulder. Her first emotion when the ball entered she described to be a sickening terror at the probability that her sex would be discovered. She felt that death on the battle-field were preferable to the shame that would overwhelm her, and ardently prayed that the wound might close her earthly campaign. But, strange as it may seem, she escaped this time also unsuspected; and soon recovering her strength, was able again to take her place at the post of duty, and in the deadly conflict. Her immunity was not, however, destined long to continue—she was seized with a brain fever, then prevalent among the soldiers. For the few days that reason struggled against the disease, her sufferings were indescribable; and most terrible of all was the dread lest consciousness should desert her, and the secret she had guarded so carefully be revealed to those around her. She was carried to the hospital, and there could only ascribe her escape to the number of patients, and the negligent manner in which they were attended. Her case was considered a hopeless one, and she perhaps received less attention on this account. One day the physician of the hospital, inquiring—"How is Robert?" received from the nurse in attendance the answer—"Poor Bob is gone." The doctor went to the bed, and taking the hand of the youth supposed dead, found that the pulse was still feebly beating; attempting to place his hand on the heart, he perceived that a bandage was fastened tightly round the breast. This was removed, and to his utter astonishment he discovered a female patient where he had least expected one!

This gentleman was Dr. Binney, of Philadelphia. With a prudence, delicacy and generosity ever afterwards warmly appreciated by the unfortunate sufferer, he said not a word of his discovery, but paid her every attention, and provided every comfort her perilous condition required. As soon as she could be removed with safety, he had her taken to his own house, where she could receive better care. His family wondered not a little at the unusual interest manifested for the poor invalid soldier.

Here occurred another of those romances in real life which in strangeness surpass fiction. The doctor had a young and lovely niece, an heiress to considerable property, whose compassionate feelings led her to join her uncle in bestowing kindness on the friendless youth. Many censured the uncle's imprudence in permitting them to be so much in each other's society, and to take drives so frequently together. The doctor laughed to himself at the warnings and hints he received, and thought how foolish the censorious would feel when the truth should come out. His knowledge, meanwhile, was buried in his own bosom, nor shared even with the members of his family. The niece was allowed to be as much with the invalid as suited her pleasure. Her gentle heart was touched by the misfortunes she had contributed to alleviate ; the pale and melancholy soldier, for whose fate no one seemed to care, who had no possession in the world save his sword, who had suffered so much in the cause of liberty, became dear to her. She saw his gratitude for the benefits and kindness received, yet knew by intuition that he would never dare aspire to the hand of one so gifted by fortune. In the confiding abandonment of woman's love, the fair girl made known her attachment, and offered to provide for the education of its object before marriage. Deborah often declared that the moment in which she learned that she had unwittingly gained the love of a being so guileless, was fraught with the keenest anguish she ever experienced. In return for the hospitality and tender care that had been lavished upon her, she had inflicted pain upon one she would have died to shield. Her former entanglement had caused no uneasiness, but this was a heart of a different mould ; no way of amends seemed open, except confession of her real character, and to that, though impelled by remorse and self-reproach, she could not bring herself. She merely said to the generous girl, that they would meet again; and though ardently desiring the possession of an education, that she could not avail herself of the noble offer. Before her departure the young lady pressed on her acceptance several articles of needful clothing, such as in those times many of the soldiers received from fair hands. All these were afterwards lost by the upsetting of a boat, except the shirt and vest Robert had on-at the time, which are still preserved as relics in the family.

Her health being now nearly restored, the physician had a long conference with the commanding officer of the company in which Robert had served, and this was followed by an order to the youth to carry a letter to General Washington.

Her worst fears were now confirmed. From the time of her removal into the doctor's family, she had cherished a misgiving, which sometimes amounted almost to certainty, that he had discovered her deception. In conversation with him she anxiously watched his countenance, but not a word or look indicated suspicion, and she had again flattered herself that she was safe from detection. When the order came for her to deliver a letter into the hands of the Commander-in-chief, she could no longer deceive herself.

There remained no course but simple obedience. When she presented herself for admission at the headquarters of Washington, she trembled as she had never done before the enemy's fire. Her heart sank within her; she strove in vain to collect and compose herself, and overpowered with dread and uncertainty, was ushered into the presence of the Chief. He noticed her extreme agitation, and supposing it to proceed from diffidence, kindly endeavored to re-assure her. He then bade her retire with an attendant, who was directed to offer her some refreshment, while he read the communication of which she had been the bearer.

Within a short time she was again summoned into the presence of Washington. He said not a word, but handed her in silence a discharge from the service, putting into her hand at the same time a note containing a few brief words of advice, and a sum of money sufficient to bear her expenses to some place where she might find a home. The delicacy and forbearance thus observed affected her sensibly. "How thankful"—she has often said, "was I to that great and good man who so kindly spared my feelings! He saw me ready to sink with shame; one word from him at that moment would have crushed me to the earth. But he spoke no word—and I blessed him for it."

After the termination of the war, she married Benjamin Gannett, of Sharon. When Washington was President, she received a letter inviting Robert Shirtliffe, or rather Mrs. Gannett, to visit the seat of government. Congress was then in session, and during her stay at the capital, a bill was passed granting her a pension in addition to certain lands, which she was to receive as an acknowledgment for her services to the country in a military capacity. She was invited to the houses of

several of the officers, and to parties given in the city;
attentions which manifested the high estimation in
which she was there held.

In 1805 she was living in comfortable circumstances,
the wife of a respectable farmer, and the mother of three
fine, intelligent children, the eldest of whom was a youth
of nineteen.   The Dedham Register, dated December,
1820, states that during the late session of the court,
Mrs. Gannett had presented for renewal her claims for
services rendered the country as a *Revolutionary soldier*.
She was at that time about sixty-two; and is described
as possessing a clear understanding and general knowledge of passing events, as being fluent in speech,
delivering her sentiments in correct language, with
deliberate and measured accent; easy in her deportment, affable in her manners, and robust and masculine
in her appearance.   She was recognized on her appearance in court by many persons belonging to the county,
who were ready to testify to her services.   A brief
notice added of the life of this extraordinary woman,
was copied into many of the papers of the day, and appears in Niles' "Principles and Acts of the Revolution."

It is but a few years since she passed from the stage
of human life.   The career to which her patriotism
urged her, cannot be commended as an example; but
her exemplary conduct after the first step will go far to
plead her excuse.

XXXIV.

~~~~~~~~

MARGARET GASTON.

The name of Mrs. Gaston is associated with that of her distinguished son, to whose education she devoted herself with assiduous care, and whose eminent character was most appropriately praised when described as "the maturity of his mother's efforts." He himself always esteemed the possession of such a parent the greatest blessing of his existence, and attributes the part he acted in life to her watchful tenderness and judicious training. No honors are too high to be accorded to matrons who, like her, have formed the characters which shed lustre on the nation.

Margaret Sharpe was born in the county of Cumberland, England, about 1755.* Her parents desiring her to have every advantage of education in the Catholic faith, to which they were attached, she was sent to France when young, and brought up in a convent. She often recurred in after life to the happy days passed there. Her two brothers were extensively engaged in commerce in this country, and she came out to visit

* See Life of Judge Gaston. I am indebted for these particulars respecting Mrs. Gaston to her accomplished grand-daughter, Mrs. Susan G. Donaldson.

them. It was during her sojourn in North Carolina that she met Dr. Alexander Gaston, a native of Ireland, of Huguenot ancestry, to whom she was married at Newbern, in the twentieth year of her age. He had attended the expedition which captured the Havana, as surgeon in the British army; but being attacked by the epidemic, and suffering from the exhaustion of a warm climate, had resigned his post, to make his home in the North American provinces.

The happy married life of these two young persons was destined to be of brief duration. Dr. Gaston was one of the most zealous patriots in North Carolina—being a member of the committee of safety for the district where he resided, and serving in the army at various periods of the war; and his devotion to the cause of freedom, while it secured the confidence of the whigs, gained him the implacable enmity of the opposite party. On the 20th of August, 1781, a body of tories entered Newbern, being some miles in advance of the regular troops, who had marched with a view of taking possession of the town. The Americans, taken by surprise, were forced to give way after an ineffectual resistance. Gaston, unwilling to surrender to the foe, hurried his wife and children from their home, hoping to escape across the river, and thus retire to a plantation eight or ten miles distant. He reached the wharf with his family, and seized a light scow for the purpose of crossing the river. But before his wife and children had stepped on board, the tories, eager for his blood, came galloping in pursuit. There was no resource but to

push off from the shore, where his wife and little ones
stood—the wife alarmed only for him against whom the
rage of their enemies was directed.   Throwing herself
in agony at their feet, she implored his life, but in vain!
Their cruelty sacrificed him in the midst of her cries
for mercy—and the musket which found his heart was
levelled over her shoulder!

Even the indulgence of grief was denied to the bereaved wife; for she was compelled to exert herself to
protect the remains of her murdered husband.   Loud
were the threats of the inhuman tories that the "rebel
should not have even the rest of the grave;" and she
kept watch in her lonely dwelling beside the beloved
and lifeless form, till it was deposited in the earth.   She
was now left alone in a foreign land—both her brothers
and her eldest son having died before the event.   Her
son William, three years of age, and an infant daughter,
remained the sole objects of her care and love.   Many
women possessing her acute sensibility would have been
overwhelmed in such a situation; but severe trials
served only to develop the admirable energy of her
character.   Every movement of her being guided by
religion, she was strong in its support, and devoted herself
to the duties that devolved upon her, with a firmness
and constancy by which all who knew her saw that she
lived above time and above the world.

> " — Her footsteps seemed to touch the earth
> Only to mark the track that leads to Heaven."

Though still young when left a widow, she never laid
aside the habiliments of sorrow; and the anniversary of

her husband's murder was kept as a day of fasting and prayer. The great object of her life was the instruction of her son, and imbuing his mind with the high principles, the noble integrity, and Christian faith, which shone conspicuous in herself. Her income being small, she practised economy to enable her to gratify her dearest wish, and procure for him a complete education; while her maternal tenderness did not dispense with implicit obedience, and strict admonitions, or yet stricter discipline, were employed to correct the faults of childhood and youth. One slight anecdote may give an idea of her method of education. When her son was seven or eight years of age, being remarkable for his aptitude and cleverness, a little schoolmate as much noted for his dullness said to him—"William, what is the reason you are always head of the class, and I am always foot?"—"There *is* a reason," replied the boy; but if I tell you, you must promise to keep it a secret, and do as I do. Whenever I take up my book to study I first say a little prayer my mother taught me, that I may be able to learn my lessons." He tried to teach the words of the petition to the dull boy, who could not remember them. The same night Mrs. Gaston observed William writing behind the door; and as she permitted nothing her children did to be concealed from her, he was obliged to confess having been writing out the prayer for little Tommy, that he might be able to get his lessons.

When this cherished son, after several years absence, returned from Princeton College, where he had borne away the first honors of the institution from able and diligent competitors, her reception of him was characteristic.   He was greeted not with the common effusion of a mother's joy and pride ; but she laid her hands upon his head as he knelt before her, and exclaimed—" My God, I thank Thee !" ere she allowed herself the happiness of embracing this only son of a widow.   Her satisfaction in his success was enhanced by the knowledge that he preserved unsullied what was of far greater moment in her eyes—his youthful piety.   During his absence her house and furniture had been destroyed by fire ; yet her letters to him breathe no word even of regret for a calamity which, with her slender resources, must have been severely felt.

William Gaston married a distant relative in whose education his mother had taken a maternal interest.   In the house of these her affectionate children she passed the autumn of her days, regarded by all who approached her with feelings of the deepest respect, with which a portion of awe was blended among youthful spirits ; for she had very strict ideas as to the conduct of the young, and the deference due to age.   Her daughter, when a young lady, could venture but stolen glances in a mirror ; nor did she or any of her juvenile companions ever allow their shoulders the support of the back of the chair in Mrs. Gaston's presence.   Those who spoke of her invariably named her as the most dignified as well as most devout woman they had ever seen.   Her calm grey eyes, which were of surpassing beauty, could sternly reprove misconduct, while ever ready to soften

into kindness towards the distressed.   Her upright
carriage of person, and scrupulous neatness in dress,
were always remarkable. She kept primitive hours,
taking tea at four o'clock in summer; her arrangements
were marked by unsurpassed order, and in her domestic
management, economy and hospitality were so well
blended, that at any time she was ready to welcome a
guest to her neatly arranged table, without additions
which the pride of life teaches us to deem indispensable.
She survived the husband of her youth thirty-one years,
in which time she never made a visit, save to the
suffering poor, yet her life, though secluded, was not
one of inactivity. Her attendance on the sick and
indigent was unwearied, and the poor sailors who came
to Newbern, frequently experienced her kind offices.

During the last seven years of her life, after her son's
marriage, she seemed more constantly engaged in
preparation for her final change. A room in her house
was used as a Catholic place of worship, whenever a
priest visited that section of the State. She was to be
found at all hours with her Bible or some other book of
devotion in her hands; her thoughts were ever fixed
on things above; while the fidelity with which her high
mission had been fulfilled was rewarded even in this
world—the gratitude, love, and usefulness of her children forming the crowning joy and honor of a life
devoted to good. Her character is well appreciated
throughout North Carolina, and the memory of her
excellence is not likely soon to pass away. Her remains
rest in the burial ground at Newbern.

XXV.

FLORA M‘DONALD.

"MASSACHUSETTS has her Lady Arabella, Virginia her Pocahontas, North Carolina her Flora M‘Donald," says the eloquent author of the "Sketches" of that State. The residence of this celebrated heroine on the banks of Cape Fear River, and the part she took in the American Revolution, link her name as inseparably with the history of North Carolina, as it is with that of her own Scotland.*

During those events which succeeded the rising in favor of the Pretender, Charles Edward—the rebellion of 1745 —and led to the emigration of the colony of Highlanders who settled among the sandy forests on the Cape Fear, Flora M‘Donald first makes her appearance—a young and blooming maiden. After the battle of Culloden, which destroyed the power of the Highland "lairds," Prince Charles Edward sought concealment in the mountains of Rosshire, where he escaped capture by the generous self-

---

* The reader is referred to the Sketches of North Carolina, by Rev. William Henry Foote; see also "Memorials" of that State, by J. Seawell Jones; and an article on Pichot's History of Charles Edward, in the North American Review, Jan. 1847.

sacrifice of the chivalrous Mackenzie. Landing on the island of South Uist, he found a temporary shelter at Ormaclet with Laird M'Donald ; but being traced thither by the keen scent of his pursuers, it seemed that a miracle alone could save him from the net so closely drawn. After many projects for his escape had been proposed, and laid aside, the wife of the laird suggested the plan of disguising him in female attire, and passing him for a travelling waiting-maid; but it was difficult to find a lady willing to undertake the enterprise. Two who were appealed to, declined it from fear of the consequences. In this emergency she turned to the young and beautiful Flora M'Donald, the daughter of a petty laird in the same island, whose mother, after her father's death, had married an adherent of the government, Captain M'Donald, of Armadale, in the Isle of Skye. This stepfather was then in command of a company of the clan M'Donald, in the service of King George, and searching for the Prince. Flora had come to visit her relations, on her return from Edinburgh, where she had just completed her education. She was a simple, kind-hearted girl, possessed of strong natural sense, and a resolution firm to accomplish whatever she decided to undertake. She had never seen the Prince; but to the proposition made to her, and her kinswoman's question, " Will you expose yourself to this danger, to aid the Prince's escape from his enemies ?" she replied at once, " I am willing to put my life in jeopardy to save his Royal Highness from the dangers that beset him." In this heroic determination, she was actuated not so much

by attachment to the house of Stuart, as by a generous wish to succor the distressed.

O'Neill, an officer to whom Lady M'Donald entrusted
the business, and MacEachen, accompanied Flora to
Carradale, a rocky, wild, sequestered place, where the
royal fugitive had his place of concealment in a damp
and unwholesome cavern. They found him alone,
broiling a small fish upon the coals, for his solitary
repast. Startled at their approach, he made ready to
defend his life; but soon discovered that the new
comers were his friends, and entered with delight into
their plan for his escape. The preparations for leaving
the island being completed, the maiden secured a pass-
port from her step-father for herself and companions,
including a stout Irishwoman, whom she called Betsey
Burke, pretending she had engaged her as an assistant
in spinning for her mother in Armadale. On the 28th
of June, 1746, the party set out from Uist in an open
boat for the Isle of Skye. A violent storm overtook
them, and they were tossed about all night; the heroic
girl, anxious only for the safety of her charge, encouraged the oarsmen to exert their utmost strength, while
the Prince sang songs he had learned round the Highland watchfires, and recited wild legends of the olden
time. At dawn they approached the island. The
sight of a band of soldiers drawn up on the shore,
turned them back; the soldiers fired after them, and
while the balls were whistling past, they pursued their
course eastwardly, landing about noon, near the residence of Sir Alexander M'Donald, the Laird of Sleite

Concealing the Prince in a hollow rock on the beach, Flora repaired to the chieftain's house, the hall of which was full of officers in search of the royal fugitive. The Laird himself, at that time absent, was known to be hostile to his pretensions; but Flora appealed not in vain to the generous enthusiasm of woman. Lady M'Donald's compassionate heart responded to her confidence; she sent refreshments to the weary wanderer by the Laird of Kingsburg, her husband's Baillie, and as it was deemed safest to depart immediately, he accompanied them to Kingsburg. The country people whom they met returning from church looked with much curiosity at the coarse, clumsy, long-legged female-figure with the Laird and the maiden; but they reached unsuspected the place of their destination, and Kingsburg conducted the Prince to his house, where he was to pass the night. His wife came to receive him and his guests, and it is said, was terrified on saluting the supposed Betty, at the rough beard which encountered her cheek. The next morning Flora accompanied the Prince to Portaree, and bade him adieu, as he was to embark for the Isle of Raarsay. At parting, he kissed her, and said, " Gentle, faithful maiden, I hope we shall yet meet in the Palace Royal." But the youthful heroine never again met the Prince who owed so much to woman's tenderness, and the loyal feelings of Scottish hearts.

After the escape of Charles Edward to France, the indignation of the officers of the crown fell upon those who had aided his flight. Flora was . arrested with others, and imprisoned in the Tower of London, to be tried for her life.   The nobility of England became deeply interested in the beautiful and high-spirited girl, who, without any political or religious bias, had exhibited such romantic devotion to the cause of royalty. Prince Frederick, the heir apparent, visited her in prison, and by his exertions at length succeeded in obtaining her release.   After being set at liberty, she was introduced into the court society by Lady Primrose, a partisan of Charles Edward, and a person of wealth and distinction.   It is said that Flora's dwelling in London was surrounded by the carriages of the aristocracy, who came to pay their respects and congratulate her on her release; and that presents were showered upon her, more than sufficient to meet the expenses of her detention and return.   The tradition in Carolina is, that " she received gold ornaments and coin enough to fill a half bushel."   She was presented to George the Second ; and when he asked how she dared render assistance to the enemy of his crown, she answered with modest simplicity, " It was no more than I would have done for your Majesty, had you been in a like situation."   For her escort back to Scotland, she chose a fellow-prisoner, Malcolm M'Leod, who used afterwards to boast, " that he came to London to be hanged, but rode back in a chaise-and-four with Flora M'Donald."

Four years after her return she married Allen M'Donald, son of the Laird of Kingsburg, and thus became eventually mistress of the mansion in which the Prince had passed his first night in the Isle of Skye.   Here

Doctor Johnson and Mr. Boswell were hospitably entertained in 1773; at which time Flora, though a matron
and a mother, was still blooming and graceful, and full
of the enthusiasm of her youth.　She put her distinguished guest to sleep in the same bed which the unfortunate
Charles Edward had occupied.　It is mentioned in the
tour to the Hebrides, that M'Donald then contemplated
a removal to America, on account of pecuniary em-
barassments.

In 1775, with his family and some friends, he landed
in North Carolina, so long a place of refuge for the
distressed Scottish families, and settled first at Cross
Creek—so called from the intersection of two streams
—the seat of the present town of Fayetteville.　It was
a stormy period, and those who came to seek peace
and security found disturbance and civil war.　The
Colonial governor summoned the Highland emigrants
to support the royal cause ; General Donald M'Donald,
a kinsman of Flora's, who was the most influential
among them, erected his standard at Cross Creek, and
on the first of February, 1776, sent forth his proclama-
tion, calling on all his true and loyal countrymen to
join him.　Flora herself espoused the cause of the
English monarch with the same spirit and enthusiasm
she had shown thirty years before in the cause of the
Prince she saved.　She accompanied her husband when
he went to join the army, and tradition even says she
was seen among the soldiers, animating their courage
when on the eve of their march.　Though this may be
an exaggeration, there is no doubt that her influence

went far to inspire her assembled clansmen and neighbors with a zeal kindred to her own.

The celebrated battle of Moore's Creek proved another
Culloden to the brave but unfortunate Highlanders.
The unhappy General M'Donald, who had been prevented by illness from commanding his troops in the
encounter, was found, when the engagement was over,
sitting alone on a stump near his tent ; and as the victorious American officers advanced towards him, he
waved in the air the parchment scroll of his commission,
and surrendered it into their hands.   Captain M'Donald,
the husband of Flora, was among the prisoners of that
day, and was sent to Halifax : while Flora found herself once more in the condition of a fugitive and an
outlaw.

The M'Donalds, with other Highlanders, suffered
much from the plunderings and confiscations to which
the royalists were exposed.   It is said that Flora's house
was pillaged and her plantation ravaged.   Allen, after his
release, finding his prospects thus unpropitious, determined to return with his family to his native land—and they
embarked in a sloop of war.   On their voyage home, an
incident occurred, illustrative of the character of this
remarkable woman.   The sloop encountered a French
vessel of war, and an action ensued.   The courage of
the sailors appearing to fail, capture seemed inevitable,
when Flora ascended the quarter-deck in the fiercest of
the battle, and, nothing daunted by a wound received,
or according to one account, an arm broken in the
tumult, encouraged the men to a more desperate con-

flict. The enemy was beaten off, and the heroine safely landed on her native soil. She was accustomed
afterwards to say pleasantly, that she had hazarded her
life for both the house of Stuart and the house of Hanover; but that she did not perceive she had· greatly
profited by her exertions.

Notwithstanding her masculine courage, her character was thoroughly feminine, and blended modesty and
dignity with sensibility and benevolence. Her eventful life closed March 5th, 1790. An immense concourse
assembled at her funeral, and not less than three thousand persons followed her remains to the cemetery of
Kilmuir, in the Isle of Skye. According to a wish long
previously expressed, her shroud was made of the sheets
in which the Prince had slept the night he lodged at
Kingsburg. It is said she had carried them with her
through all her migrations.

The town of Fayetteville covers the former metropolis of the Highland clans. It was surrounded by a
sandy, barren country, sprinkled with lofty pines, and
the American home of Flora M'Donald stood in the
midst of this waste. The place of her residence has
been destroyed by fire; but her memory is still cherished in that locality, and the story of her romantic enthusiasm, intrepidity, and disinterested self-devotion, has
extended into lands where in life she was unknown.

XXXVI.

RACHEL CALDWELL.

The history of the Rev. David Caldwell is in many ways identified with that of North Carolina. He was for almost sixty years the pastor of the two oldest and largest Presbyterian congregations in the county of Guilford, and kept a celebrated classical school, for a long time the only one of note in the State, in which for forty years nearly all its professional men, and many from adjoining States, were educated. Not only was he thus the father of education in North Carolina, but before and during the Revolutionary struggle, he exerted a strong influence in favor of the promotion of national independence, and bore an active part in the prominent events of that period. The influence of Mrs. Caldwell in his school was great and beneficial, increasing the respect of the students towards him, and disposing their minds to religious impressions. They bore uniform testimony to her intelligence and zeal, and to the value of her counsels, while her kindness won their regard and confidence. The success with which she labored to inculcate the lessons of practical piety, gave currency to the saying throughout the country—" Dr. Caldwell makes

the scholars, and Mrs. Caldwell makes the preachers."
She was the third daughter of Rev. Alexander Craighead, the pastor of the Sugar Creek congregation, and a
man of eminent piety and usefulness. In early life she
had a share in many of the perils and hardships of the
Indian war—the inroads of the savages being frequent
and murderous, and her home in an exposed situation.
She often said, describing these incursions, that as the
family would escape out of one door, the Indians would
come in at another. When Braddock's defeat left the
Virginia frontier at the mercy of the savages, Mr.
Craighead fled, with some of his people, and crossing
the Blue Ridge, passed to the more quiet regions of
Carolina, where he remained till the close of his life.
Rachel married Dr. Caldwell in 1766.

For some days before the battle at Guilford Court-
house, the army of Cornwallis was encamped within
the bounds of Dr. Caldwell's congregations; and most
of the men being with General Greene, the distress fell
on the defenceless women and children. In the detail
of spoliation and outrage, their pastor suffered his
share. He had been repeatedly harassed by the British
and tories, who bore him special enmity; a price had
been set upon his head, and a reward of two hundred
pounds offered for his apprehension.* On the 11th of
March, while he was in Greene's camp, the army was
marched to his plantation and encamped there, the
officers taking possession of his house. Mrs. Caldwell

---

* The reader is referred to the Life and Character of Rev. David
Caldwell, D. D., by Rev. E. W. Caruthers, Greensboro', N. C.

was at home with her children when they arrived. They at first announced themselves as Americans, and asked to see the landlady; but a female domestic who had ascertained by standing on the fence and seeing red coats at a distance, that they belonged to the army of Cornwallis, quickly communicated her discovery to her mistress. Excusing herself by saying that she must attend to her child, Mrs. Caldwell retired within the house, and immediately gave warning to two of her neighbors who happened to be there, that they might escape through the other door and conceal themselves. She then returned to the gate. The party in front when charged with being British soldiers, avowed themselves such, and said they must have the use of the dwelling for a day or two. They immediately established themselves in their quarters, turning out Mrs. Caldwell, who with her children retired to the smoke house, and there passed a day with no other food than a few dried peaches and apples, till a physician interposed, and procured for her a bed, some provisions, and a few cooking utensils. The family remained in the smoke house two days and nights—their distress being frequently insulted by profane and brutal language. To a young officer who came to the door for the purpose of taunting the helpless mother, by ridiculing her countrymen, whom he termed rebels and cowards, Mrs. Caldwell replied, "Wait and see what the Lord will do for us." "If he intends to do anything," pertly rejoined the military fop, "'tis time he had begun." In reply to Mrs. Caldwell's application to one of the soldiers for protection, she was told she could expect no favors, for that the women were as great rebels as the men.

After remaining two days, the army took their departure from the ravaged plantation, on which they had destroyed every thing; but before leaving Dr. Caldwell's house, the officer in command gave orders that his library and papers should be burned. A fire was kindled in the large oven in the yard, and books which could not at that time be replaced, and valuable manuscripts which had cost the study and labor of years, were carried out by the soldiers, armful after armful, and ruthlessly committed to the flames. Not even the family Bible was spared, and the house, as well as plantation, was left pillaged and desolate.

On the fifteenth was heard the roar of that battle which was to compel the retreat of the invaders, and achieve the deliverance of Carolina. The women of Dr. Caldwell's congregation met, as has been mentioned, and while the conflict was raging fiercely between man and man, wrestled in earnest prayer for their defenders. After the cold, wet night which succeeded the action, the women wandered over the field of battle to search for their friends, administer the last sad rites to the dead, and bear away the wounded and expiring. One officer who had lain thirty hours undiscovered, was found in the woods by an old lady, and carried to his house, where he survived long enough to relate how a loyalist of his acquaintance had passed him the day after the battle, had recognized him, and bestowed a blow and an

6*

execration, instead of the water he craved to quench his consuming thirst. Conscience, however, sometimes avenged the insulted rights of nature ;—the man who had refused the dying request of a fellow creature, was found after the officer's death, suspended on a tree before his own door.*

The persecution of Dr. Caldwell continued while the British occupied that portion of the State. His property was destroyed, and he was hunted as a felon ; snares were laid for him, and pretences used to draw him from his hiding-place ; he was compelled to pass nights in the woods, and ventured only at the most imminent peril to see his family. Often he escaped captivity or death, as it were, by a miracle. At one time when he had ventured home on a stolen visit, the house was suddenly surrounded by armed men, who seized him before he could escape, designing to carry him to the British camp. One or two were set to guard him, while the others went to gather such articles of provisions and clothing as could be found worth taking away. When they were nearly ready to depart, the plunder collected being piled in the middle of the floor, and the prisoner standing beside it with his guard, Mrs. Dunlap, who with Mrs. Caldwell had remained in an adjoining apartment, came forward. With the promptitude and presence of mind for which women are often remarkable in sudden emergencies, she stepped behind Dr. Caldwell, leaned over his shoulder, and whispered to him, as if intending the question for his ear alone, asking if it

* Sketches of North Carolina

was not time for Gillespie and his men to be there.
One of the soldiers who stood nearest caught the
words, and with evident alarm demanded what men
were meant. The lady replied that she was merely
speaking to her brother. In a moment all was confusion ; the whole party was panic-struck ; exclamations
and hurried questions followed ; and in the consterna-
tion produced by this ingenious though simple ma-
nœuvre, the tories fled precipitately, leaving their
prisoner and their plunder. The name of Gillespie was
a scourge and terror to the loyalists, and this party
knew themselves to be within the limits of one of the
strongest whig neighborhoods in the State.

Sometime in the fall of 1780, a stranger stopped at
the house of Dr. Caldwell, faint and worn with fatigue,
to ask supper and lodging for the night. He announced
himself an express bearing despatches from Washington to General Greene, then on the Pedee river. He
had imagined that he would be free from danger under
the roof of a minister of the gospel; but Mrs. Caldwell
soon undeceived him on this point. She was alone ;
her husband was an object of peculiar hatred to the
tories, and she could not tell the day or hour when an
attack might be expected. Should they chance to hear
of the traveller, and learn that he had important papers
in his possession, he would certainly be robbed before
morning. She said he should have something to eat
immediately—but advised him to seek some safer place
of shelter for the night. This intelligence so much
alarmed the stranger that his agitation would not permit

him to eat, even when the repast was prepared and placed before him. But a short time had passed before voices were heard without, with cries of "Surround the house!" and the dwelling was presently assailed by a body of tories. With admirable calmness, Mrs. Caldwell bade the stranger follow her, and led him out at the opposite door. A large locust tree stood close by, and the night was so dark that no object could be discerned amid its clustering foliage. She bade him climb the tree, thorny as it was, and conceal himself till the men should be engaged in plundering the house. He could then descend on the other side, and trust to flight for his safety. The house was pillaged as she had expected; but the express made his escape, to remember with gratitude the woman whose prudence had saved him with the loss of her property.

One little incident is characteristic. Among such articles as the housewife especially prizes, Mrs. Caldwell had an elegant table cloth, which she valued as the gift of her mother. While the tories on one occasion were in her house collecting plunder, one of them broke open the chest or drawer which contained it, and drew out the tablecloth. Mrs. Caldwell seized and held it fast, determined not to give up her treasure. When she found that her rapacious enemy would soon succeed in wresting it from her, unless she could make use of some other than muscular force to prevent him, she turned to the other men of the party, whose attention had been attracted by the struggle, so that they had gathered around her. Still keeping her hold on the tablecloth, she appealed to them with all a woman's eloquence, asking if some of them had not wives or daughters for whose sake they would interfere to cause her to be treated with more civility. A small man who stood at the distance of a few feet presently stepped up, with tears in his eyes, and said that he had a wife—a fine little woman she was, too! and that he would not allow any rudeness to be practised towards Mrs. Caldwell. His interference compelled the depredator to restore the valued article.

It was not unfrequently that female prudence or intrepidity was successful in disappointing the marauders. The plantations of Dr. Caldwell and his brother Alexander were near each other. One evening, during Alexander's absence from home, two soldiers entered his house, and began rudely to seize upon every thing they saw worth carrying off, having ordered his wife to prepare supper for them. They were supposed to belong to the army of Cornwallis, at that time foraging in the neighborhood. Not knowing what to do, Mrs. Caldwell sent to her brother-in-law for advice. He sent word in answer that she must treat the men civilly, and have supper ready as soon as practicable; but that she must observe where they placed their guns, and set the table at the other end of the house. He promised to come over in the meantime and conceal himself in a haystack close by; and she was to inform him as soon as the men had sat down to supper. These directions were implicitly followed. The house was a double cabin, containing two rooms on the same floor. While the men were leisurely discussing their repast, Dr. Caldwell quietly entered the other apartment, took up one of the guns, and stepping to the door of the room where they were so comfortably occupied, presented the weapon, and informed them they were his prisoners, and their lives would be the forfeit, should they make the least attempt to escape. They surrendered immediately, and Dr. Caldwell marched them to his own house, where he kept them till morning, and then suffered them to depart, after putting them on their parole by causing them to take a solemn oath upon the family Bible, that they would no longer bear arms against the United States, but would return to him upon a day named. This pledge was faithfully kept.

After the war, Dr. Caldwell resumed his labors as a teacher and preacher—his pastoral services being continued till within about four years of his death. He died in the summer of 1824, in the hundredth year of his age. His wife, who had accompanied him in the vicissitudes of his long pilgrimage, aiding him in his useful work, followed him to the grave in 1825, at the age of eighty-six. All who knew, regarded her as a woman of remarkable character and influence, and she is remembered throughout the State with high respect.

THE influence of Colonel Hamilton, of the British army, contributed greatly—at the time Lord Cornwallis, on his last ill-fated expedition, was in the neighborhood of Halifax—to mitigate the evils usually attendant upon the march of a hostile force. Hamilton had resided there before the Revolution, and showed a regard for his old acquaintances by inducing the Commander to forbid the molestation of the persons or property of non-combatants.

It is not improbable that female influence had something to do with this magnanimity. The tone of public opnion in Halifax and its neighborhood was affected in no slight degree by three women, who were rendered prominent by the position of their husbands, and by their own talents and example. These women were Mrs. Willie Jones, Mrs. Allen Jones, and Mrs. Nicholas Long. Their husbands were men of cultivated minds, of wealth and high consideration, having great influence in public councils, and being zealously devoted to the achievement of independence. The importance of the principles for which they contended, was vindicated not less impressively by the conversation and patriotic zeal of their wives, than by their own efforts in more striking appeals.

Colonel Nicholas Long was Commissary general for the forces raised in North Carolina, and superintended the preparation, in workshops erected on his premises, of warlike implements, military equipments, and clothing for the soldiers. His wife was a most efficient co-operator in this business. She possessed great energy and firmness, with mental powers of no common order. Her praises were the theme of conversation among the old officers of the army as long as any were left who had known her. Her maiden name was M'Kinney. She died when about eighty years of age, leaving a numerous offspring.

Mrs. Allen Jones was a Miss Edwards, the sister of Isaac Edwards, the English secretary of Governor Tryon. She had the reputation of being the most accomplished woman of her day, and was remarkable for the elegance and taste shown in all her domestic arrangements. She died shortly after the Revolution, leaving an only daughter, who married the son of Mrs. Long.

Mrs. Willie Jones was the daughter of Colonel Montfort, and was married at a very early age. She is regarded as the most conspicuous among the Revolutionary heroines in the region where she lived, and is said to have been eminent in every quality that constitutes excellence in female character. She possessed a remarkable faculty of gaining influence by the affections. One of her acquaintances says: "She is the only person with whom it has been my fortune to be acquainted, who was loved—devotedly, enthusiastically loved—by every human being who knew her." Born to an ample fortune, she dispensed it with a munificent and elegant hospitality rarely seen in a new country, while her charities were extended to all proper objects of her beneficence. A native nobility of soul rendered her superior to the influence of any selfish feeling, or of accidental circumstances, which often mould the character of ordinary minds. The enjoyments of life were partaken by her with sobriety, while the troubles and

privations that fell to her lot were borne with calmness
and cheerful fortitude. She died about 1828, leaving
five children, of whom two are living in North Carolina.

The celebrated retort to Tarleton's sneering remark
concerning Colonel William Washington, a witticism
variously repeated, has been generally attributed to
Mrs. Jones; but I have been assured by her daughter
that it was incorrectly ascribed to her. Mrs. Jones
often related the occurrence to this lady, and disclaimed
the merit of the retort, which belonged to her sister
Mrs. Ashe. The circumstances were as follows:
During the stay of General Leslie and the British
troops in Halifax, several of his officers were quartered
at the house of Colonel Ashe, and Mrs. Ashe was in
the habit of playing backgammon with them. Among
these was Tarleton, who often conversed with her,
and was especially fond of indulging his sarcastic wit in
her presence at the expense of her favorite hero Colonel
Washington. On one occasion he observed, jestingly,
that he should like to have an opportunity of seeing
that man, who he had understood was very small. Mrs.
Ashe replied quickly: "If you had looked behind you,
Colonel Tarleton, at the battle of the Cowpens, you
would have had that pleasure." The taunt was keenly
felt, and the British Colonel so moved, that his hand in-
voluntarily sought the hilt of his sword. At this moment
General Leslie entered the room, and observing that
Mrs. Ashe was much agitated, inquired the cause of her
emotion. She explained what had passed, to which
General Leslie answered with a smile; "Say what you

please, Mrs. Ashe ; Colonel Tarleton knows better than
to insult a lady in my presence."

~~~~~~~~~

THE following illustrative incident was communicated
to the Rev. J. H. Saye, by two Revolutionary officers,
one of whom lived in the vicinity where it occurred—
the other being of the party concerned in the adventure.

Early in the war, the inhabitants on the frontier of
Burke County, North Carolina, being apprehensive of
an attack by the Indians, it was determined to seek
protection in a fort in a more densely populated neighborhood in an interior settlement. A party of soldiers
was sent to protect them on their retreat. The families
assembled, the line of march was taken towards their
place of destination, and they proceeded some miles
unmolested—the soldiers marching in a hollow square,
with the refugee families in the centre. The Indians,
who had watched these movements, had laid a plan for
their destruction. The road to be travelled lay through
a dense forest in the fork of a river, where the Indians
concealed themselves, and waited till the travellers were
in the desired spot. Suddenly the war-whoop sounded
in front, and on either side ; a large body of painted
warriors rushed in, filling the gap by which the whites
had entered, and an appalling crash of fire-arms followed.
The soldiers, however, were prepared ; such as chanced
to be near the trees darted behind them, and began to
ply the deadly rifle ; the others prostrated themselves
upon the earth, among the tall grass, and crawled to

trees. The families screened themselves as best they could. The onset was long and fiercely urged ; ever and anon amid the din and smoke, the warriors would rush, tomahawk in hand, towards the centre ; but they were repulsed by the cool intrepidity of the back-woods riflemen. Still they fought on, determined on the destruction of the victims who offered such desperate resistance. All at once, an appalling sound greeted the ears of the women and children in the centre ; it was a cry from their defenders—a cry for powder! "Our powder is giving out," they exclaimed. "Have you any? Bring us some, or we can fight no longer!" A woman of the party had a good supply. She spread her apron on the ground, poured her powder into it, and going round from soldier to soldier as they stood behind the trees, bade each who needed powder put down his hat, and poured a quantity upon it. Thus she went round the line of defence, till her whole stock, and all she could obtain from others, was distributed. At last the savages gave way, and pressed by their foes, were driven off the ground. The victorious whites returned to those for whose safety they had ventured into the wilderness. Inquiries were made as to who had been killed, and one running up, cried, "Where is the woman that gave us the powder! I want to see her!" "Yes!—yes!—let us see her!" responded another and another ; "without her we should have been all lost!" The soldiers ran about among the women and children, looking for her and making inquiries. Directly came in others from the pursuit, one of whom observing the commotion, asked the cause, and was told. "You are looking in the wrong place," he replied "Is she killed? Ah, we were afraid of that!" exclaimed many voices. "Not when I saw her," answered the soldier. "When the Indians ran off, she was *on her knees in prayer* at the root of yonder tree, and there I left her." There was a simultaneous rush to the tree—and there, to their great joy, they found the woman safe, and still on her knees in prayer. Thinking not of herself, she received their applause without manifesting any other feeling than gratitude to Heaven for their great deliverance.

XXXVII.

~~~~~~~~~

THE WOMEN OF WYOMING.

THE name of Wyoming is celebrated from its association with events of thrilling interest. Its history from its first settlement is well known to the American reader, nor is there needed another recital of the catastrophe of July, 1778, which converted the fertile and thriving settlement into a field of slaughter, and recorded in characters of blood one of the darkest pages in the annals of our race. The pen of the historian—the eloquence of the orator—the imagination of the poet and novelist—have by turns illustrated the scene—the realities of which transcend the wildest creations of fiction, and over which hovers the solemn glory that enshrines the resting place of heroes. The very ground speaks of the past

> " And on the margin of yon orchard hill
> Are marks where time-worn battlements have been,
> And in the tall grass traces linger still
> Of ' arrowy frieze and wedged ravelin ;'
> Five hundred of her brave that valley green
> Trod on the morn, in soldier spirit gay ;
> But twenty lived to tell the noonday scene."*

<p align="center">* Halleck.</p>

Vain was the bravery of that little band—the population of the valley having been drained of its strength to supply the continental army—to stem the fury of the tories and savages, gathering strength with success, till it swept in a tempest of blood and fire over their devoted homes. Their gallant deeds—their fate—have been told in song and story.

The wives and daughters of Wyoming deserve to share in the tribute due to their unfortunate defenders. While the men were engaged in public service, they had cheerfully assumed such a portion of the labor as they could perform; had tilled the ground to plant and make hay, husked and garnered the corn, and assisted in manufacturing ammunition.* They, too, were marked out for the enemy's vengeance, and were victims in the scene of carnage and horror. Dreadful was the suspense in which they awaited, with their children, the event of the battle; and when the news was brought in the night—warned that instant flight would be their only means of escape, they fled in terrified confusion, without clothes or food—looking back only to behold "the light of burning plains," repressing their groans for fear of Indians in ambush, and fortunate if they escaped butchery—to implore the aid of strangers in a distant land. Many an aged matron, after the lapse of half a century, "could tell you where the foot of battle stepped, upon the day of massacre;" for the spot was marked by the blood of her nearest and dearest.

* Miner's History of Wyoming, page 212, &c. See this work for notices of the women.

A nearer view may be given by the mention of one
or two instances among the sufferers. Two sons of
Esther Skinner, in the flower of early manhood, went
forth to the desperate conflict of that day, and were
seen no more by their widowed mother. A young man
who afterwards married her daughter—one of the twenty
who was saved—related an incident of his escape.
" Driven to the brink of the river, he plunged into the
water for safety, and swam to a small island. Here,
immersed in water, protected by the bushes at the
water's edge, and screened by the darkness of night, he
happily eluded the search of the pursuing foe, thirsting
for blood ; while about twenty of his companions, who
had retreated to the same spot, were all massacred
within a few yards of him. He heard the dismal
strokes of the tomahawk, and the groans of the dying,
expecting every moment himself to become the next
victim. One savage foot trod upon the very bush to
which he clung. A solitary individual besides himself
was left, at the departure of the savages, to weep with
him over the mangled bodies of their friends."*

Mrs. Skinner was in the company of women who
fled amid the horrors of the conflagration. With her
six surviving children, the youngest but five years of
age, she hastened to the water-side, where boats were
prepared for their conveyance down the river. The
little ones, half destitute of clothing, "were ready to
cry with the anguish of their bruised and lacerated

* Extract from a sermon preached at the funeral of Esther Skinner,
1831.

feet; but the chidings of the wary mother, and the dread of being heard by the lurking savage, repressed their weeping, and made them tread in breathless silence their painful way."

The widow's little property plundered, her home in ashes, her husband buried, and her eldest son lying mangled on the field of battle, her thoughts were turned towards the land of her birth, formidable as the journey was on foot, with six helpless children, and without money, clothes, or provisions. Her way lay in part through Dutch settlements, where she could only by signs tell the story of her sufferings, or make known her wants. The tale of woe, however, swifter in its flight, had spread far and wide, and she received many kindnesses from the people of a strange language. Sometimes, indeed, she was refused admission into their houses; "but," she would add in her narration, "they had nice barns, with clean straw, where my children lodged very comfortably." After travelling one hundred miles by water, and nearly three hundred by land, she arrived in safety at the place of her former residence in Connecticut; where, having survived all her children but one, she died in 1831, in the hundreth year of her age.

~~~~~~~~~~

MRS. MYERS was one of the crowd who resorted to Forty Fort, and was about sixteen years old at the time of the massacre. Her maiden name was Bennett, and her father's family stood conspicuous among the patriots of that day. A relative, Mrs. Bennett, was liv-

ing in 1845, at the age of eighty-three, and though
blind, was one of the clearest chroniclers of the scenes
witnessed in her eventful youth.   Whether she was the
" woman, withered, gray, and old," with whom the poet
conversed, sitting and smoking—as he says, in her
chimney-corner—is uncertain ; for she was not the only
one who had a lively recollection of those times.   Mrs.
Myers had even preserved the table on which had been
signed the terms of capitulation, and repeated the conversation between Colonel Denison and Colonel Butler,
overheard by herself and another girl on a seat within
the Fort ; with Butler's acknowledgment of his inability
to check the savages in their plunder and slaughter
of the inhabitants.   At one time the Indians, to show
their power, came into the fort.   One took the hat from
Colonel Denison's head, and another demanded his
frock.   The savage raised his tomahawk menacingly,
and the Colonel was obliged to yield ; but seeming to
find difficulty in taking off the garment, he stepped back
to where the young women were sitting.   The girl who
sat by Miss Bennett was an inmate of his family—understanding the movement, she took from the pocket of
the frock a purse, which she hid under her apron.   The
frock was then delivered to the Indian, and the town
money thus saved ; for the purse, containing a few dollars, was the whole military chest of Wyoming.

Another patriotic sufferer, MRS. LUCY IVES, was a
child of ten years old at Forty Fort.   She had two
brothers and a brother-in-law in the battle, and both
her brothers were killed.   Her father and family escaped

8

through the swamp; but on his return to secure a part of his harvest, he was killed by the Indians. The mother and children, having lost all their property, sought refuge in Canterbury, Connecticut, their native place, whence they did not return till peace was established. With broken fortunes and blighted hopes, left to grapple with a hard world—while a compensating degree of prosperity awaited many of the ancient sufferers—the night of bloodshed and woe was not succeeded to them as to others, by a bright and cheering morning of sunshine.

MRS. BIDLACK was the daughter of Obadiah Gore, and about twenty years old at the time of the battle. Her family were devoted to the cause of liberty. The aged father was left in Forty Fort to aid in its defence, while five sons with two brothers-in-law marched to the conflict! At sunset five of the seven lay mangled corpses on the field. Mrs. Murfee, another sister, begged her way, among the rest of the fugitives, across the wilderness, and sought a home in the State from which she had emigrated. The mother of the Gore family lived to see prosperity return to her remaining children.

The death of MRS. YOUNG was particularly noticed in the newspapers at the time of its occurrence, on account of the many vicissitudes that had marked her life. Her father, Mr. Poyner, was a Huguenot, who had been driven by religious persecution from France, and had been a commissary in the old French war. Mrs. Young was the last survivor of those who occupied the fort at

Mill Creek. She made her escape with six others, in a canoe, on hearing of the issue of the battle, and the enemy's approach—and pushed off into the river, without provisions, to seek safety from the murderous tomahawk. Meeting a boat coming up with stores for Captain Spalding's company, the sufferings of hunger were relieved; and the distressed fugitives, not knowing the fate of their friends, after a dangerous navigation of one hundred and twenty miles—landed near Harrisburg, where, being hospitably received and kindly treated, they remained till Sullivan's army came to Wyoming and rendered it safe to return. She died at the age of eighty-nine.

MRS. DANA took with her in her flight a pillow-case of valuable papers—her husband being engaged in public business; and the preservation of these has thrown light on the path of research. The names of a hundred others, who shared that memorable flight, might be mentioned; but these are sufficient.

In the enemy's ranks, some of the women were foremost in the work of carnage. Esther, the queen of the Seneca tribe of Indians—a fury in female form—it is said, took upon herself the office of executioner, passing with her tomahawk round the circle of prisoners, counting with a cadence, and sinking the weapon into the heads of the victims. In the journal of one of Sullivan's officers, her plantation is described—an extensive plain near the Susquehanna, where she dwelt in sullen retirement.

The story of the captivity of Frances Slocum has

some romantic interest. Her father was a member of
the Friends' Society, and having always been kind to
the Indians, was at first left unmolested; but when they
learned that one of his sons had been in the battle, the
family was marked out for sure vengeance. A shot,
and cry of distress, one day summoning Mrs. Slocum
to the door, she saw an Indian scalping a lad to whom,
with his brother, her husband had given a home, their
father being taken prisoner. The savages soon after
entered the house, seized her little boy, Ebenezer, and
when the mother interposed to save the child, caught
up her daughter Frances, about five years old, and fled
swiftly to the mountains. This was within a hundred
rods of Wilkesbarre fort; but, though the alarm was
instantly given, the Indians eluded pursuit, and no trace
of their retreat could be discovered.

The cup of vengeance was not yet full—the father
being afterwards murdered. The widowed mother
heard nothing of her lost child, though peace came
in time, and prisoners returned. When intercourse
with Canada was opened, two of her sons, then among
the most intelligent and enterprising young men in the
valley, determined, if living, to find their sister, and
connecting business with their search, traversed the
Indian settlements, and went as far as Niagara. But
vain were their inquiries and offered rewards; and the
conclusion seemed probable that she had been killed by
her merciless captors. Still the fond mother saw the
lost one in her dreams, and her soul clung to the hope
of recovering her daughter, as the great and engrossing

object of her life. At length a girl was found, who had been carried away captive from Susquehanna River, and could not remember her parents. She was brought to Mrs. Slocum's home; but the mysterious sympathy which exists between a mother and her offspring did not draw them together. Mrs. Slocum could not believe the orphan to be her own child, and the girl, feeling a persuasion that she had no claim of relationship, at length returned to her Indian friends. Time extinguished the last ray of hope, and the bereaved parent, at an advanced age, descended to the grave.

In August, 1837, fifty-nine years after the capture, a letter appeared in the Lancaster Intelligencer, written by Mr. Ewing of Logansport, Indiana, and dated a year and a half previous. It stated that an aged white woman was living in that vicinity, among the Miami tribe of Indians, who had recently informed the writer that she had been brought, when very young, from the Susquehanna, and that her father's name was Slocum; that he was a Quaker, and that his house was near a village where there was a fort. Her attachment to Indian life, and fear of being claimed by her kindred, had prevented her, in past years, from disclosing her name and history—which she did then from a conviction that her life was drawing to an end. She was a widow, with two daughters—wealthy, respected and bearing an excellent character.

The sensation produced throughout Wyoming by this letter, can scarcely be imagined. Joseph Slocum, the brother of Frances, moved by affection, duty, and the known wishes of his deceased parent, made immediate preparations for the journey, though a thousand miles intervened; and with his younger brother, Isaac, who lived in Ohio, hastened to Logansport. The lost sister, whose residence was about twelve miles distant, was informed of their arrival, and came to the village to meet them, riding a high-spirited horse, and accompanied by her two daughters, tastefully dressed in the Indian costume. Her bearing was grave and reserved; she listened, through an interpreter, to what they had to say—but doubt, amounting to jealous suspicion, possessed her mind. She returned home, and came again the next day, desiring further explanation, ere she would recognize those who claimed such near kindred. At length Joseph Slocum mentioned that his sister, at play in their father's smithshop with the children, had once received a blow from a hammer on the middle finger of the hand, which crushed the bone; and that his mother had always said the injury would leave a mark that could not be mistaken. This was conviction to the long separated sister; her countenance was instantly lighted up with smiles, while tears ran down her cheeks, as she held out the scarred hand; the welcome recognition, the tender embrace, the earnest inquiries for her parents—showed the awakening of the long slumbering affections, and filled every heart present to overflowing.

The events of her life, as detailed by herself, were truly remarkable. On her capture, she had been carried to a rocky cave on the mountain, where a bed of

blankets and dried leaves had been prepared for the
accommodation of the Indians. Thence taken to the
Indian country, she was treated with kindness, and
brought up as an adopted daughter of their people.
When her Indian parents died, she married a young
chief of the nation, and removed to the waters of the
Ohio. Changed completely by time and education—
exempted from the tasks usually imposed on women in
the savage state, the most flattering deference being
paid to her superior understanding—invested with the
dignity of a queen among them—and happy in her family and connections—she had been led to regard the
whites with a degree of fear and aversion, and to deem
return to her kindred a calamity rather than a blessing;
so that when prisoners were inquired for, she always
earnestly entreated that she might not be betrayed.

When her narration was finished, Frances, or Macona-
quah, as she was called, appealed with solemnity to the
Great Spirit, to bear witness to its truth. The next
day, her brothers, with the interpreter, rode out to visit
her. Every thing bore the appearance, not only of
plenty, but of rude abundance; the cattle and horses
were numerous; the house, though roughly constructed, was better than the Indian wigwams; and
the repast, of venison, honey, and cakes of flour, was
excellent. Frances caused her brothers to enter into a
formal covenant of recognition and affection, by lifting
a snow-white cloth from a piece of venison she had
placed beneath it. The visit was prolonged for several
days; and was afterwards repeated by another member

of the family—Mrs. Bennett, the daughter of Joseph Slocum, and wife of the Hon. Ziba Bennett, who accompanied her father on his second visit to Indiana.

~~~~~~~~~~~~~~~~

The sufferings of families during the depredations of the Indians on the frontier, in Wawasink and its vicinity, were not exceeded even by those of Wyoming. The women bore their share not only in these, but in the efforts made for defence—loading guns for their defenders, and carrying water to extinguish the flames of their dwellings. In an attack upon the house of the widow Bevier, when, after it was fired, the two women sought refuge in the cellar, the daughter, Magdalen, took with her the Dutch family Bible. When the flames approached them, they decided to deliver themselves up to the savages, and made their way through the cellar window—the mother in advance. The daughter threw her apron over her head, fearing to see her parent killed. As she feared, the widow fell a prey to the cruel tomahawk, while the Bible was wrested from Magdalen's hands and stamped in the mud—she herself being retained a prisoner. When afterwards released, she was fortunate enough to recover the treasure she had saved from the flames—some of the leaves only being soiled by the mud—and it is still preserved as a precious relic in the family.

The house of Jesse Bevier at the Fantinekill, was assailed afterwards, and defended successfully by the spirit and resolution of its inmates. Their powder was

laid in basins on the table, and the women helped to
load the pieces, till at length the old log house was fired
at a point where the little band of heroes could not bring
their guns to bear.   Their situation now became most
alarming, and the women applied every drop of liquid
in the house to check the progress of the flames; taking
milk, and even swill, in their mouths, and spirting it
through the cracks of the logs, in hopes thus to protract
existence till relief might come from Naponoch.   At
this awful crisis, when death appeared inevitable, the
pious mother, knowing that "with God all things are
possible," proposed that they should suspend their exertions, and unite in petitions to the throne of grace for
mercy.   Her son replied that she must pray, and they
would continue to fight.   And fervent were the prayers
of that mother—till it seemed as if they were answered
by direct interposition from heaven.   The brother of
Bevier, warned of danger by the mute appeal of the
dog belonging to the house, came with another to his
assistance, and the Indians and tories, not knowing,
when they heard the firing of their sentry, how large a
force was coming, withdrew from the house just as the
flames had extended to the curtains of the bed.

A solemn and affecting scene in this tragedy was that
at the bedside of Jacob Bevier, who lay ill, and unable
to move, when all the family had fled across the mountain, except an insane brother, who was sitting on the
fence, unconscious of danger, and a daughter, who in
spite of entreaties and expostulations, would not leave
her suffering parent.

7*

The old stone fort at Wawasink was also the scene of active operations. It was the courage and presence of mind of Catharine Vernooy, that saved the fort when first assailed by the enemy. She was going to milk when she heard them coming; but returned quickly to the fort, closed the door, and called to the sentry to assist her in getting the brace against it. At the house of Peter Vernooy, too, the females were active in rendering assistance. They loaded the pieces, of which there was a double set, and stood with axes, determined to plunge them into their foes, if they should attempt to break through the windows. The wife of Vernooy had a family of small children, but kept them quiet by her authority, while all was going on.

XXXVIII.

JANE CAMPBELL.

MRS. CAMPBELL was a distinguished representative of the female actors in the Revolutionary drama in the section of country where she lived. Prominent in position and character, her influence was decided; and in the extraordinary trials through which she was called to pass, her firmness and fortitude, her intrepid bearing under sufferings that would have crushed an inferior nature, her energy, constancy, and disinterested patriotism—render her example a bright and useful one, and entitle her to a conspicuous place among those to whom her country pays the willing tribute of honor and gratitude.

Jane Cannon was born on the first day of January, 1773, in the county of Antrim, Ireland, almost within hearing of the ocean as it beat around the Giant's Causeway. Her early years were spent upon this coast; and it was perhaps her familiarity with nature in the wild and sublime scenery of this romantic region, that nourished the spirit of independence, and the strength of character, so strikingly displayed by her in after life, amid far distant scenes. The permanency of the impressions received in childhood is shown by her frequent recurrence, towards the close of a protracted life, to these juvenile associations, to her school and her youthful companions, and the customs and manners of that day. At the age of ten she left Ireland with her family, her father—Captain Matthew Cannon, who was a sea-faring man, having determined to emigrate to the North American Colonies. His first settlement was at New Castle in the present State of Delaware, where he remained for ten or eleven years engaged in agricultural pursuits. He then, with his family, penetrated the wilderness to the central part of the State of New York, and fixed his home in the extreme frontier settlement, within the limits of the present county of Otsego, and about seven miles from the village of Cherry Valley. A year after the removal of the family to this new abode, Jane Cannon was married to Samuel Campbell, a son of one of the first settlers of Cherry Valley, a young man twenty-five years of age, and already distinguished for his energy of character and bold spirit of enterprise. At the very commencement of the Revolutionary war, the father and the husband of Mrs. Campbell embraced the quarrel of the Colonies with great ardor. They were both on the committee of safety; both at an early period, pledged themselves to the achievement of national independence, and in the long and bloody warfare on the frontier, both were actively engaged. Both also lost every thing, save life and honor—in the contest. Mr. Campbell was early chosen to the command of the militia in that

region; and at the general request converted his own
house into a garrison, where for two years—and until a
fort was erected in the settlement, the inhabitants of
that exposed frontier were gathered for protection. In
all his patriotic efforts, he not only had the sympathy of
his wife, but found her a zealous and efficient co-operator. Her feelings were ardently enlisted in behalf of
her adopted country, and she was ready to give her
own exertions to the cause, as well as to urge forward
those who had risen against the oppressor.

In August, 1777, Colonel Campbell, with his regiment,
was engaged in the disastrous battle of Oriskany, the
bloodiest, in proportion to the number engaged, of any of
the battles of the Revolution. His brother was killed
by his side; and he himself narrowly escaped. In the
July following, occurred the massacre at Wyoming;
and in November, 1778, a part of the same force,
composed principally of Indians and tories, invaded and
utterly destroyed the settlement at Cherry Valley. The
dreadful tragedy here enacted, says Dunlap, "next
to the destruction of Wyoming, stands out in history as
conspicuous for atrocity." The horrors of the massacre,
and the flight, indeed likened the scene to that

"Whose baptism was the weight of blood that flows
From kindred hearts."

Some extraordinary instances of individual suffering
are recorded.* One young girl, Jane Wells, was
barbarously murdered by an Indian near a pile of wood,

* See Annals of Tryon County, by William W. Campbell.

behind which she had endeavored to screen herself.
The wife of Colonel Clyde fled with her children into
the woods, where she lay concealed under a large log
during a cold rainy day and night, hearing the yells of
the savages as they triumphed in their work of death,
and seeing them pass so near that one of them trailed
his gun upon the log that covered her. Colonel Campbell was absent from home at the time; but the father
of Mrs. Campbell, who was in her house, attempted
almost single-handed to oppose the advance of the
enemy—and notwithstanding that resistance was mad-
ness, the brave old man refused to yield till he was
wounded and overpowered. Imagination alone can
depict the terror and anguish of the mother trembling for
her children in the midst of this scene of strife and
carnage, the shrieks of slaughtered victims, and the
yells of their savage foes. They were dragged away
as prisoners by the triumphant Indians, and the house
was presently in flames. The husband and father—
who had hastened homeward on the alarm of a cannon
fired at the fort, arrived only in time to witness the
destruction of his property, and was unable to learn
what had become of his wife and children.

Leaving the settlement a scene of desolation, the
enemy took their departure the same night, with their
prisoners, of whom there were between thirty and forty.
That night of wretchedness was passed in a valley
about two miles south of the fort. " A large fire was
kindled, around which they were collected, with no
shelter, not even in most cases an outer garment, to

protect them from the storm.   There might be seen the
old and infirm, and the middle-aged of both sexes, and
'shivering childhood, houseless but for a mother's arms,
couchless but for a mother's breast.'   Around them at
a short distance on every side, gleamed the watchfires
of the savages, who were engaged in examining and
distributing their plunder.   Along up the valley they
caught occasional glimpses of the ruins of their dwellings, as some sudden gust of wind, or falling timber,
awoke into new life the decaying flame."

The prominent position and services of Colonel
Campbell had rendered him peculiarly obnoxious to the
enemy.   It was well known that his wife had constantly aided his and her father's movements, and that
her determined character and excellent judgment had
not only been of service to them, but to the friends of
liberty in that region.   Hence both the husband and
wife were marked objects of vengeance.   Mrs. Campbell and her children were considered important captives, and while most of the other women and little
ones were released, after the detention of a day or two,
and permitted to return to their homes, to them no such
mercy was extended.   Mrs. Campbell was informed
that she and her children must accompany their captors
to the land of the Senecas. · On the second day after
the captivity her mother was killed by her side.   The
aged and infirm lady was unable to keep pace with
the rest; and her daughter was aiding her faltering
steps, and encouraging her to exert her utmost strength,
when the savage struck her down with his toma-

hawk. Not a moment was Mrs. Campbell suffered
to linger, to close the dying eyes, or receive the last
sigh, of her murdered parent; the same Indian drove
her on with his uplifted and bloody weapon, threatening
her with a similar fate, should her speed slacken. She
carried in her arms an infant eighteen months old;
and for the sake of her helpless little ones, dragged
on her weary steps in spite of failing strength, at the
bidding of her inhuman tormentors.

This arduous, long, and melancholy journey was
commenced on the 11th of November. Mrs. Campbell
was taken down the valley of the Susquehanna to its
junction with the Tioga, and thence into the western
part of New York, to the Indian Castle, the capital of
the Seneca nation, near the site of the present beautiful village of Geneva. The whole region was then
an unbroken wilderness, with here and there an Indian
settlement, and the journey was performed by Mrs.
Campbell partly on foot, with her babe in her arms.
Her other children were separated from her on the way,
being given to Indians of different tribes; and on her
arrival at the village, her infant also—the last link
which visibly bound her to home and family and civili-
zation—was taken from her. This, to the mother's
heart, was the severest trial; and she often spoke of it
in after years as the most cruel of all her sufferings.
The helpless babe clung to her when torn away by
savage hands, and she could hear its piercing cries till
they were lost in the distance. Long and dreary was
the winter that followed. In one respect Mrs. Camp-

bell was fortunate. She was placed in an Indian family, composed of females, with the exception of one aged man, and with the tact which always distinguished her she began at once to make herself useful; thus early securing the confidence and even the admiration of these daughters of the forest. She taught them some of the arts of civilized life, and made garments not only for the family to which she belonged, but for those in the neighborhood, who sent corn and venison in return. In acknowledgment of these services, care and protection were extended to her; she was allowed the command of her own time, and freedom from restraint, and was permitted to abstain from her usual avocations on the sacred day of rest.

One day an Indian who came to the house, observing her cap, promised to give her one; and inviting her to his cabin, pulled from behind a beam a cap of a smoky color, and handed it to her, saying he had taken it from the head of a woman at Cherry Valley. Mrs. Campbell recognised it as having belonged to the unfortunate Jane Wells.- It had a cut in the crown made by the tomahawk, and was spotted with blood. She shrank with horror from the murderer of her friend. Returning to her cabin, she tore off the lace border, from which, however, she could not wash the stains of blood, and laid it away, to give to the friends of the murdered girl, should any have escaped the massacre. In the midst of her own sorrows she lost not her sympathy with the woes of others.

The proposed exchange of Mrs. Campbell and her

children for the wife and sons of Colonel John Butler—
the noted partisan leader—being agreed upon by Governor Clinton and General Schuyler, early in the spring
Colonel Campbell despatched an Indian messenger to
Colonel Butler at Fort Niagara. Butler came soon after
to the village of Canadaseago, to confer with the Indian
council on the subject of giving up their prisoners.
The families who adopted captives in the place of deceased relatives were always unwilling to part with
them ; and Butler had some difficulty in obtaining their
assent.   It was necessary also to procure the consent of
a family in the Genesee village, with whom Mrs. Campbell was to have been placed in the spring.   They were
kinsfolk of the king of the Senecas ; and it is no small
evidence of the esteem Mrs. Campbell had won from
the Indians, that he volunteered to go himself, and persuade them to yield their claim.   Though aged, the
kind-hearted savage performed the journey on foot ; and
returning, informed Mrs. Campbell that she was free,
bade her farewell, and promised to come and visit her
when the war was over.   In June, 1799, she was sent
to Fort Niagara, where many persons took refuge—preparation being made for an expected attack by General
Sullivan.   Among them came Katrine Montour, a fury
who had figured in the horrors of Wyoming.   One of
her sons having taken prisoner in Cherry Valley the
father of Mrs. Campbell, and brought him to the Indian
country, it may be conceived what were the feelings of
the captive on hearing her reproach the savage for not

having killed him at once, to avoid the incumbrance of
an old and feeble man!

Mrs. Campbell was detained a year as a prisoner in
the fort; but had the solace of her children, all except
one of whom Butler obtained from the Indians and
restored to her. She associated freely, too, with the
wives of the officers of the garrison. In the summer
of 1780 she received the first letter from her husband,
sent by a friendly Oneida Indian. In June, she was
sent to Montreal, where she recovered her missing
child—a boy seven years old, whom she had not seen
since the day after the massacre at Cherry Valley.
He had been with a branch of the Mohawk tribe, and
had forgotten his native tongue, though he remembered
his mother, whom, in the joy of seeing her, he addressed
in the Indian language.

At Montreal the exchange of prisoners was effected.
In the fall, Mrs. Campbell and her children reached
Albany, escorted into that city by a detachment of
troops under the command of Colonel Ethan Allen.
Here Colonel Campbell awaited their arrival, and
the trials of a two years' captivity were almost forgotten in the joy of restoration. They remained there
till the close of the war, and in 1783, returned to
Cherry Valley, and literally began the world anew.
Their lands had gone to waste, and were overgrown
with underbrush; all besides was destroyed; and with
no shelter save a small log-cabin hastily put up—they
felt for a time that their lot had been a hard one. But

the consciousness of having performed the duty of patriots, sustained them under misfortune. By the close of the following summer a more comfortable log-house was erected on the ruins of their former residence, and the farm began to assume the aspect of cultivation. Here General Washington was received and entertained on his visit to Cherry Valley, accompanied by Governor George Clinton and other distinguished officers. It was on this occasion that Mrs. Campbell presented her sons to Washington, and told him she would train them up to the service of their country, should that country ever need their services.

From this time Mrs. Campbell was eminently blessed in all things temporal; being permitted in old age to see around her a large and prosperous family. Her oldest son was the Hon. William Campbell, late Surveyor general of the State of New York. Her second son, James S. Campbell, though educated as a farmer—inheriting the "old homestead"—was for many years a magistrate, and one of the judges of the Court of Common Pleas in Otsego; while the youngest son, the late Robert Campbell, of Cooperstown, an able and eminent lawyer, enjoyed in a high degree the confidence of the people of that county. Colonel Campbell, after an active life, died in 1824, at the age of eighty-six. His wife lived, in the enjoyment of almost uninterrupted health, to the age of ninety-three, and died in 1836—the last survivor of the Revolutionary women in the region of the head waters of the Susquehanna. All her children but two have followed her to the grave.

Mrs. Campbell's latter days—to the close of a life marked with so much of action, enterprise and stirring incident—were days of industry. Like the Roman matron, she bore the distaff in her hand, and sat with her maidens around her; and her characteristic energy was infused into every thing she did. Yet she was in every sense of the term a lady: scrupulously neat in her apparel, combining dignity with affable and pleasing manners—the expression of real kindness of heart; and with a mind naturally vigorous and clear improved by reading, and still more by observation and society—and conversation enriched by the stores she had gathered in her experience, she was well fitted to shine in any sphere of life. For many years before her death she was designated throughout the country, as "old Lady Campbell." Her memory unimpaired, she was a living chronicler of days gone by; the peculiar circumstances in which she was placed during the war having brought her into personal acquaintance with almost all the prominent men engaged on both sides.

The feminine and domestic virtues that adorned her character, rendering her beloved in every relation—especially by those towards whom she so faithfully discharged her duties—were brightened by her unaffected piety. It was the power of Christian principle that sustained her through all her wanderings and trials, and in her lonely captivity among a barbarous people. It was this which cheered her closing days of existence, and supported her when, almost on the verge of a century—having survived the companions who had commenced life with her, surrounded by her children, and her descendants to the fourth generation—she passed calmly to her rest.

CORNELIA BEEKMAN.

C Beekman

XXXIX.

～～～～

CORNELIA BEEKMAN.

A MEMOIR of the long and eventful life of Mrs. Beekman, describing scenes in which those connected with her were prominent actors, would form a valuable contribution to American history. But it is not possible, at this distant day, without the materials afforded by letters or contemporaneous details, to give an adequate idea of the influence she exercised. There are many who retain a deep impression of her talents and noble qualities; but no record has preserved the memory of what she did for America, and her character can be but imperfectly illustrated by the anecdotes remembered by those who knew her most intimately. The active part she sustained in the contest, her trials and the spirit exhibited under them, her claims for substantial service to the gratitude of her country, and a name in its annals, cannot now be appreciated as they deserve. But it may be seen that hers was no ordinary character, that she was a true patriot, and that her part must have been a very important one in directing the judgment and movements of others.

Her family was one of distinction, from which nu-

merous branches have proceeded.   The ancestor, Oloff
Stevenson Van Cortlandt, died in this country about
1683, leaving seven children ; and in 1685, his eldest
son obtained from Governor Dongan a patent for large
tracts of land purchased from the Indians, in Westchester, Putnam, and Dutchess Counties.   For many
years preceding the Revolution, the family resided in
the Cortlandt manor house, an old-fashioned stone
mansion situated upon the banks of the Croton River.
It was here that Cornelia, the second daughter of Pierre
Van Cortlandt and Joanna Livingston, was born, in
1752.   Her father, who was Lieutenant Governor of
the State of New York, under George Clinton, from
1777 to 1795, was distinguished for his zealous main-
tenance of American rights.   From him she imbibed
the principles to which, in after life, she was so ardently
devoted.

The childhood and youth of Cornelia passed in peace
and happiness in her pleasant home.   On her marriage,
about the age of seventeen, with Gerard G. Beekman,
she removed to the city of New York, where her
residence was in the street which bears her name.   Her
husband was in mind, education, and character, worthy
of her choice.   Not many years of her married life had
passed, when the storm of war burst upon the land,
and, taught to share in aspirations for freedom, she
entered into the feelings of the people with all the
warmth of her generous nature.   She often spoke with
enthusiasm of an imposing ceremonial procession she
witnessed, of the mechanics of the city, who brought

their tools and deposited them in a large coffin made for the purpose—marched to the solemn music of a funeral dirge, and buried the coffin in Potter's Field; returning to present themselves, each with musket in hand, in readiness for military service.

Finding a residence in New York not agreeable in the state of popular excitement, she returned with her husband and family to the home of her childhood at Croton, till the Peekshill Manor House could be completed. This was a large brick building situated on a flat about two miles north of Peekskill, at the foot of Regular Hill, the place of encampment for the American army. The top of Anthony's Nose can be seen from its rear. Here she resided during the war, marked out as an object of aggression and insult by the royalists, on account of the part taken by her relatives and friends, and her own ardent attachment to the American cause. At intervals of the struggle, when portions of the British army were ranging through Westchester, she was particularly exposed to their injuries. But her high spirit and strong will contributed to her safety, and supported her through many scenes of trial. Only once was she prevailed upon to leave her residence, being persuaded by her brother, Colonel Philip Van Cortlandt, to retire with her family some miles back in the country for safety from a scouting party on their way from Verplanck's Point. She yielded to the counsel, contrary to her own judgment and wishes; and after being absent a day and night, not hearing of any depredations committed, returned to the manor house.

9

She found it a scene of desolation! Not an article of furniture was left, except a bedstead; a single glass bottle was the only drinking utensil; and one ham was all that remained of the provisions, having, by good fortune, been hung in an obscure part of the cellar. This disaster, and the inconveniences to which she was obliged to submit in consequence, were borne with fortitude, and even formed subject of merriment. Soon after, she was called upon by two of the American officers—Putnam and Webb—who asked how she had fared, not supposing she had been visited with annoyance, and were much surprised at her description of the state of the house on her return. The General promised, if she would be satisfied with army conveniences, to send her the next day a complete outfit to recommence housekeeping. On the morrow a horseman arrived, carrying a bag on either side, filled with all kinds of woodenware—a welcome and useful present —for such things were not at that time easy to be obtained. Some of these articles were still in the house at the time of Mrs. Beekman's decease.

The leading officers of the American army were often received and entertained at her hospitable mansion. General Patterson was at one time quartered there; and the room is still called "Washington's," in which that beloved Chief was accustomed to repose. He visited her frequently, their acquaintance being of long standing, and while his troops were stationed in the neighborhood, made her house his quarters. The chairs used by his aids as beds are still in the possession of her

descendants. Her hospitality was not limited to persons
of distinction ; she was at all times ready to aid the
distressed, and administer to the necessities of those
who needed attention.   Nor were her acts of humanity
and benevolence confined to such as were friendly to
the cause in which her warmest feelings were enlisted,
many in the enemy's ranks experiencing her kindness,
and that in return for grievance and outrage.   Of this
she had more than her share—and sometimes the most
daring robberies were committed before her eyes.   On
one occasion the favorite saddle-horse which she always
rode, was driven off with the others by marauders.   The
next day Colonel Bayard, mounted upon the prize,
stopping at the gate, Mr. Beekman claimed the animal
as belonging to his wife, and demanded that it should be
restored.   The insolent reply was, that he must here-
after look upon his property as British artillery horses ;
and the officer added, as he rode away, "I am going
now to burn down your rebel father's paper mill !"

At another time, in broad day, and in sight of the
family, a horse was brought up with baskets fastened
on either side, and a deliberate ransacking of the poultry
yard commenced.   The baskets were presently filled
with the fowls, and the turkey-gobbler, a noisy patriarch,
was placed astride the horse, the bridle being thrown over
his head.   His uneasiness when the whip was used,
testified by clamorous complaints, made the whole scene
so amusing that the depredators were allowed to
depart without a word of remonstrance.   One day
when the British were in the neighborhood, a soldier

entered the house, and walked unceremoniously towards the closet. Mrs. Beekman asked what he wanted; "Some brandy;" was his reply. When she reproved him for the intrusion, he presented his bayonet at her breast, and calling her a rebel, with many harsh epithets, swore he would kill her on the spot. Though alone in the house, except an old black servant, she felt no alarm at the threats of the cowardly assailant; but told him she would call her husband, and send information to his officer of his conduct. Her resolution triumphed over his audacity; for seeing that she showed no fear, he was not long in obeying her command to leave the house. Upon another occasion she was writing a letter to her father, when, looking out, she saw the enemy approaching. There was only time to secrete the paper behind the frame-work of the mantle-piece; where it was discovered when the house was repaired after the war.

The story of Mrs. Beekman's contemptuous repulse of the enemy under Bayard and Fanning is related by herself, in a letter written in 1777. A party of royalists, commanded by those two colonels, paid a visit to her house, demeaning themselves with the arrogance and insolence she was accustomed to witness. One of them insultingly said to her: "Are you not the daughter of that old rebel, Pierre Van Cortlandt?" She replied with dignity: "I am the daughter of Pierre Van Cortlandt—but it becomes not such as you to call my father a rebel!" The tory raised his musket, when she, with perfect calmness, reproved him for his insolence and bade him begone, He finally turned away abashed.

The persecutors of Mrs. Beekman were sometimes disappointed in their plundering expeditions. One day the miller came to her with the news that the enemy had been taking a dozen barrels of flour from the mill. "But when they arrive at the Point," he added, "they will find their cakes not quite so good as they expect; as they have taken the lime provided for finishing the walls, and left us the flour." Often, however, the depredators left nothing for those who came after them.

One morning a captain serving in the British army rode up to the house, and asked for Mrs. Beekman. When she appeared, he told her he was much in want of something to eat. She left the room, and soon returning, brought a loaf of bread and a knife. This, she assured him, was all she had in the house, the soldiers of his army having taken away every thing else. "But I will divide this," she said: "you shall have one-half, and I will keep the other for my family." This magnanimity so struck the officer, that he thanked her cordially, and requested her to let him know if in future any of his men ventured to annoy her, promising that the offence should not be repeated. It is not known that this promise was of any avail.

In one instance the firmness and prudence displayed by Mrs. Beekman were of essential service. John Webb, familiarly known as "Lieutenant Jack," who occasionally served as an acting aid in the staff of the Commander-in-chief, was much at her house, as well as the other officers, during the operations of the army on the banks of the Hudson. On one occasion, passing through

Peekskill, he rode up and requested her to oblige him by taking charge of his valise, which contained his new suit of uniform and a quantity of gold. He added, "I will send for it whenever I want it; but do not deliver it without a written order from me or brother Sam." He threw in the valise at the door, from his horse, and rode on to the tavern at Peekskill, where he stopped to dine. A fortnight or so after his departure, Mrs. Beekman saw an acquaintance—Smith—whose fidelity to the whig cause had been suspected, ride rapidly up to the house. She heard him ask her husband for "Lieutenant Jack's" valise, which he directed a servant to bring and hand to Smith. Mrs. Beekman called out to ask if the messenger had a written order from either of the brothers. Smith replied that he had no written order, the officer having had no time to write one; but added—"You know me very well, Mrs. Beekman; and when I assure you that Lieutenant Jack sent me for the valise, you will not refuse to deliver it to me, as he is greatly in want of his uniform." Mrs. Beekman often said she had an instinctive antipathy to Smith, and, by an intuition for which it is difficult to account, felt convinced that he had not been authorized to call for the article she had in trust. She answered—"I do know you very well—*too well* to give you up the valise without a written order from the owner or the colonel." Smith was angry at her doubts, and appealed to her husband, urging that the fact of his knowing the valise was there, and that it contained Lieutenant Jack's uniform, should be sufficient evidence that he came by authority ; but his representations had no effect upon her resolution. Although even her husband was displeased at this treatment of the messenger, she remained firm in her denial, and the disappointed horseman rode away as rapidly as he came. The result proved that he had no authority to make the application ; and it was subsequently ascertained that at the very time of this attempt Major Andrè was in Smith's house. How he knew that the uniform had been left at Mrs. Beekman's was a matter of uncertainty ; but another account of the incident—given by the accomplished lady who furnished these anecdotes of Mrs. Beekman— states that Lieutenant Webb, dining at the tavern the same day, had mentioned that she had taken charge of his valise, and what were its contents. He thanked Mrs. Beekman, on his return, for the prudence that had saved his property, and had also prevented an occurrence which might have caused a train of disasters. He and Major Andrè were of the same stature and form ; "and beyond all doubt," says one who heard the particulars from the parties interested, "had Smith obtained possession of the uniform, Andrè would have made his escape through the American lines." The experience that teaches in every page of the world's history what vast results depend on things apparently trivial, favors the supposition, in dwelling on this simple incident, that under the Providence that disposes all human events, the fate of a nation may here have been suspended upon a woman's judgment.

Many of Mrs. Beekman's letters written during the

war, breathe the most ardent spirit of patriotism. The wrongs she was compelled to suffer in person, and the aggressions she witnessed on every side, roused her just indignation ; and her feelings were expressed in severe reproaches against the enemy, and in frequent prayers for the success of the American arms. But although surrounded by peril and disaster, she would not consent to leave her home ; her zeal for the honor of her family and her country inspiring her with a courage that never faltered, and causing her to disregard the evils she had so continually to bear.

Years rolled on, and peace came at last to smile upon those who had shed their blood, or sacrificed their possessions for the achievement of national independence. The lands in the manor of Philipsburgh having become vested in the State of New York by the attainder of Frederick Philipse, were parcelled out and sold ; and Mr. Beekman purchased the tract in the vicinity of Tarrytown, on which the old manor-house is situated. To this he removed with his family in 1785. Historical recollections, and the classic creations of genius, combine to shed a romance and a glory around this spot. The manor-house—Castle Philipse—the ancient residence of the lords of Philipsburgh—was strongly fortified in the early days of the colony, being built for defence against the Indians. The embrasures or portholes now form the cellar windows. Rodolphus Philipse made additions to this fort, to render it suitable for a place of residence. It faces the east, and looks upon the old Dutch church, which stands at a little distance, with

its time-honored walls and antique belfry—a fit memorial
of the past. This church was built about 1699 by
Frederick Philipse and Catharina Van Cortlandt his
wife, who, according to tradition, was in the habit of
riding up from the city of New York on horseback—
upon moonlight nights—mounted on a pillion behind
her brother, Jacobus Van Cortlandt, for the purpose of
superintending its erection.* It was struck by lightning
some years since, and was in part rebuilt, with modern
improvements. Many readers will remember the description of this church in the " Legend of Sleepy Hollow," with the wide woody dell beside it, and the bridge
over the stream shaded by overhanging trees; for it
was there that the Yankee pedagogue Ichabod Crane
met with the adventure so renowned in story. The
ravine on the *other side* of the hill forms the dreamy
region of "Sleepy Hollow." This locality bore a reputation more than equivocal—less, however, on account
of its haunting goblins, than its human inhabitants; and
often did our heroine express her regret and indignation
that Mr. Irving's description had given the name to a
spot so near her own residence. The Pocanteco—
or Mill river—wanders hereabouts in a region of
romantic beauty; winding through dark woodlands, or
grassy meadows, or stealing along beneath rugged
heights, replenished by a thousand crystal rills that glide
murmuring down to mingle with the stream. The
venerable manor-house is seen to advantage from the
bridge, the trees intercepting the view in other direc-

* See History of Westchester County.

9*

tions.   The stately trees that surrounded a silver sheet
of water before the door, have been felled ; and the old
mill with its moss-covered roof, where in its palmy days
so many bushels of grain were ground free of toll for
the neighboring poor, exhibits tokens of decay.   All is,
however, in mellow keeping with the surrounding
scenery.   A picturesque view is presented from the
windows of the manor-house, of the stream flowing in
its serpentine windings to lose itself in the bosom of the
majestic Hudson.

It was here that Mrs. Beekman resided to the day of
her death, enjoying life among the friends she loved, and
contributing to the improvement and happiness of those
who had the advantage of her society.   She was one
of the company who welcomed the arrival of La Fayette,
and conversed with the veteran general of times gone
by.   Mr. Beekman died in 1822, at the age of seventy-
six; and on the 14th of March, 1847, in her ninety-fifth
year, did she too "like tired breezes fall asleep."   The
day on which her remains were borne to the family
burial-ground, is described by one who was present as
not soon to be forgotten.   At an early hour the inhabitants for miles around began to assemble, until the
crowd became so great, that as far as the view extended,
the space seemed alive with carriages, and persons on
foot and on horseback.   After the funeral services, "the
coffin was placed in the hall, and not a dry eye beheld
the loved relics.   Domestics who had grown gray in
her service, sobbed to part with their kind mistress; and
when the hoary-headed pall-bearers had placed the

coffin in the sable hearse, before which were two milk white horses with black trappings, the solemn silence was broken by the tolling of the old church bell," and one sentiment of grief seemed to pervade the assemblage.

Mrs. Beekman is described as an accomplished lady of the old school. She was remarkable for force of will, resolution, and a lofty sense of honor. Steadfast in her principles, she had a mind of uncommon vigor, and a heart alive to all kindly and noble feelings. In the prime of life she possessed a great share of personal beauty, while her manners were courteous, dignified and refined. Her conversation, brilliant and interesting, was enlivened by stores of anecdote supplied by a memory unusually retentive, and many were the thrilling tales of the olden time heard from her lips. Her sight failed during the last three or four years; but her mental faculties continued clear and unimpaired in strength to the close of her almost century of existence. She could dwell with minuteness of detail on the scenes her childhood had witnessed, while the realities she described were fading traditions to those who listened. Thus was she a faithful type of a past generation, on few of which any can look again.

The energy of mind which had characterized her through life, was evinced on her death-bed. With her usual disinterestedness, she refused to summon those among her nearest relatives whose age and infirmities rendered their separation inevitable, to behold the progress of disease they could not alleviate. Calmly and quietly, bearing much suffering, but disturbed by no apprehension, she awaited with her accustomed fortitude, the coming of that last enemy, whose nearer and yet nearer approach she announced unshrinkingly to those about her.   When it was necessary to affix her signature to an important paper, and being supposed too weak to write, she was told that her mark would be sufficient, she immediately asked to be raised, called for a pen, and placing her left hand on the pulse of her right, wrote her name as distinctly as ever.   It was the last act of her life.   Literally counting, it is said, the failing beats of her pulse, she "looked death in the face with the same high resolve and strong will with which she had been wont, in her lifetime, to encounter less powerful enemies."   It was the strength of Christian faith, which thus gave her victory over the king of terrors.

Of her brothers and sisters, only Mrs. Van Rensselaer and General Pierre Van Cortlandt survived her.   The latter died recently at Peekskill.   Her daughter, Mrs. De Peyster, resides in New York; and her son, Dr. S. D. Beekman, at Tarrytown, on a part of the old place.

XL.

~~~~~

FRANCES ALLEN.*

OF the men of strong energy of thought or action, who arrested public attention during the momentous period of the Revolution, there is scarcely one who assimilates at all to the zealous and erratic, yet firm and indomitable Ethan Allen. He had been schooled in the fierce conflicts in which New Hampshire on the one side, and New York on the other, contended for legal jurisdiction and sovereignty over the present area of Vermont; and his bold character had fitted him, when the people refused to submit to either, to be the functionary of popular will, in administering justice without law, and maintaining independence without a government. He possessed traits in common with William Tell, Wat Tyler, and Brennus, the conqueror of Rome; but was in himself unique and original, act-ing and thinking on the spur of occasion, as few other men have ever done. His views of theology were as curious as those of politics; yet he had *fixed points* for both; and when the contest of 1775 drew on, he boldly

* The reader is indebted for this sketch to the pen of Mr. H. R. Schoolcraft.

grasped his sword, and by a sudden movement summoned Ticonderoga to surrender, " in the name of God
and the Continental Congress." Here, then, were the
two points of his faith, which led him forward in a
series of bold and masterly movements and adventures;
in which he was indeed but the exponent of the feelings
and views of a bold, hardy, Tyrolese-like yeomanry, who
had settled on the sides of the Green Mountains, and
glowed with an unquenchable love of civil liberty.   The
result was, that they cast off effectually both the authority
of New Hampshire and New York, and coming patrioti-
cally to the rescue of the United Colonies, at a time of
" bitter need," secured their own independence, and
gave the name of VERMONT to the pages of future history.   In all this Ethan Allen was the leader ; and it is
upon him, more than any other individual, that we are
to look as the founder of that patriotic State.

Whom such a man married—who became the counsellor and companion of his secret and private hours, it
may be interesting to inquire ! The results of such an
inquiry are indeed as unique and original as the rest of
the traits of his life, and show a curious correspondence,
acting by reverse affinities, in the mysterious chain of
the marriage tie.

The wild and adventurous character of Allen's early
life prevented him from forming a youthful attachment ;
and he had enacted his most daring scenes before he appears to have thought of it.   It was owing to the curiosity and interest arising from the domestic recital of
one of these daring adventures of the Green Mountain

hero, that an acquaintance was brought about, which resulted in an attachment between two individuals from the antipodes of American society—the one a bold, rough, free-spoken democrat, and stickler for the utmost degree of power in the people ; the other a well-educated and refined young lady of high aristocratic feelings, the daughter of a British field-officer who had served with distinction in the ante-revolutionary French wars, and the grand-daughter of a proud veteran British artillerist, who had also served with reputation under the Duke of Marlborough, and came to America after the treaty of Utrecht, with the most extravagantly exalted notions, not only of the part he had borne in the field, but of the glorious reign of Queen Anne, under whose banners he had served. Miss Fanny Brush, who was destined to be the wife of the bold Vermonter, was the daughter of Colonel Brush of the British army, whose military acts at Boston just before the Revolution, gave notoriety to his name. This officer had served under General Bradstreet, commanding at Albany, at whose mansion he became acquainted with, and married Miss Elizabeth Calcraft, the daughter of James Calcraft,* a retired veteran of the army of Queen Anne, who enjoyed in a high degree the friendship and confidence of the British general. After the death of Colonel Brush, Mrs.

* This name is changed to SCHOOLCRAFT in that county, in a rather too graphic allusion to the last employment of the declining days of a soldier of fortune—a pilgrim of the sword from England, and withal a man of letters.

Brush, by whom he had but a single child, married Mr. Edward Wall, and removed with him to the township of Westminster, in Vermont. The position chosen by him for his residence, was one of the most beautiful and picturesque in that section of the fertile valley of the Connecticut. The settlement in that town, is one of the oldest and best cultivated in the State ; and the society of that portion of the new district, which had originally been settled as part of the " New Hampshire grants," excelled, as it preceded others, in comforts and refinement. Such was at least the wealth and position of Mr. Wall, that he spared no expense in the education of his daughter, Miss Brush, who was sent to the capital of New England to complete her accomplishments. She was in her eighteenth year when Ethan Allen, liberated from the Tower of London, returned to his native State, with the fame of his daring deeds not a little exalted by reports of his sayings and doings beyond the water. Among other reports which probably had very little foundation, it was said that he had bit off a tenpenny nail while in the Tower of London. " I should like," said Miss Brush, one evening, in a mixed company in her father's parlor, " above all things to see this Mr. Allen, of whom we hear such incredible things." This saying reached the ears of Allen, who soon after paid a visit to the house of Mr. Wall, and was introduced to Miss Brush. There was mutually an agreeable surprise. Both were manifestly pleased with the tone of thought and conversation, which ran on with a natural flow, and developed traits of kindred sympathies of intellect and feeling. It was late in the evening before Mr. Allen rose. He had not failed to observe the interest his conversation had excited in Miss Brush. "And now," said he, as he stood erect before her, and was about to depart—" and now, Miss Brush, allow me to ask, *how do you like' this Mr. Allen?'*"

This was the initiative to an offer which resulted in the marriage of the parties. Mrs. Allen was a woman of more than the ordinary intellectual endowment; bold, striking, and original in her conceptions, and of singular facility and clearness in her expression. She was educated from early life to disbelieve in the capacity or general intelligence of the masses for efficient self-government. All her prejudices were nurtured in favor of the British Constitution as developed by Magna Charta, and administered by a king and ministers responsible to the nation; which form of government she believed to be above all comparison the best in the world. Yet, in spite of all these deeply-rooted prejudices, with a grasp of thought that could look at and examine questions of inherent right, on their original basis—with the abiding principles of the Christian faith to serve as a guide in judging of human duty in governments, and with the daily recurring practical examples of the conflicts of opinion between the Colonies and the mother country, which the American Revolution presented, she saw and acknowledged the wrongs inflicted on the Colonies—the justice of that cause in which they had, at length, banded for a higher measure of liberty, and the growing capacity of the people to maintain those rights, both by the sword and the pen. She was thus made an intellectual convert to the doctrines of the Revolution, and became a most useful and capable counsellor to Allen, in the subsequent critical periods of his life. Her mind was, indeed, a counterpart, in its boldness and originality, to that of her husband, whose intuitive mode of reaching conclusions enabled him to put into the shape of *acts*, what it might have sorely puzzled him sometimes to reason out; and what, indeed, if he could have reasoned ever so well, his bold and fiery zeal, and crushing rapidity of action, put him out of all temper to submit to the slow process of ratiocination. He also felt the happy influences of manners, opinions, and sentiments at once dignified and frank, yet mild and persuasive.

We have no means of access to Mrs. Allen's correspondence, which it is hoped some member of the family will give to the public. It is known that Allen did not confine his notions of human freedom and right, to questions of government only, in which he devoted himself so effectually during the struggle for independence; but that, mistaking the great theory of a SUBSTITUTE for the LOST TYPE OF RIGHTEOUSNESS IN MAN, he as boldly attacked the doctrines of revelation, as he had done the divine right of kings, in the person of George III., and the Guelph family. We have no copy of his writings on this head to refer to, and only allude to them for the purpose of denoting the meliorating effects of Mrs. Allen's opinions, superior reading, and influence on his mind. For he is believed to have relinquished these dangerous anti-Christian views prior to his death. One of his daughters, who inherited a disquisitive and metaphysical mind, and intellectual vigor, from her parents, joined a convent of nuns at the city of Montreal, in which she became an eminent example of charity in her order, and devoted her life to the most inflexible obedience to her vows.

Ethan Allen was many years his wife's senior. After his death, she married Dr. Penniman, of Colchester, Vermont, where she resided during the latter years of her life. By this marriage she had several children, and her descendants of the names of Allen and Penniman are numerous in that State. It was during her residence here, in the year 1814, that the writer of this sketch became personally acquainted with her. She visited his residence at Lake Dunmore, during that winter. She was then, perhaps, a lady past fifty years of age, of an erect figure, middle size, with an energetic step, and a marked intellectual physiognomy. Her animated eyes assumed their full expression, in speaking of her grand-father Calcraft, whose true name she said had been changed among the Palatine Germans of Queen Anne; whom she pronounced "a loyal Briton;" and whose military services under the Duke of Marlborough, she appeared to hold in lively remembrance.

In writing this sketch, the author has neither time to refer to Mrs. Allen's relatives in Vermont, for details to fill out the picture which is here attempted, nor even to refer to his own notes, made many years ago, when his memory of events, and of conversations with her,

was fresh.   This tribute may, at least, excite some other
hand to do full justice to her character and memory.

> " Man is not born *alone* to act, or be
>   The sole asserter of man's liberty ;
>   But so God shares the gifts of head and heart,
>   And crowns blest woman with a hero's part."

XLI.

~~~~~~

MARGARET ARNOLD.

THE wife of Benedict Arnold was Margaret Shippen, of Philadelphia. One of her ancestors—Edward Shippen, who was Mayor of the city in the beginning of the eighteenth century, suffered severe persecution from the zealots in authority at Boston for his Quakerism; but, successful in business, amassed a large fortune, and according to tradition, was distinguished for "being the biggest man, having the biggest house, and the biggest carriage in Philadelphia."* His mansion, called 'the governor's house'—'Shippen's great house'—and 'the famous house and orchard outside the town,'—was built on an eminence, the orchard overlooking the city; yellow pines shaded the rear, a green lawn extended in front, and the view was unobstructed to the Delaware and Jersey shores;—a princely place, indeed, for that day—with its summer-house, and gardens abounding with tulips, roses and lilies! It is said to have been the

* See Watson's Annals of Philadelphia. It is singular that this "zealous chronicler" should have been led into the mistake of stating that Mrs. Arnold's name was Sarah, and that she died in Massachusetts in 1836, at the age of eighty-three !

residence, for a few weeks, of William Penn and his family. An account of the distinguished persons who were guests there at different times, would be curious and interesting.

Edward Shippen, afterwards Chief Justice of Pennsylvania, was the father of Margaret. His family, distinguished among the aristocracy of the day, was prominent after the commencement of the contest, among those known to cherish loyalist principles—his daughters being educated in these, and having their constant associations and sympathies with those who were opposed to American independence. The youngest of them—only eighteen years of age—beautiful, brilliant and fascinating, full of spirit and gaiety—the toast of the British officers while their army occupied Philadelphia—became the object of Arnold's admiration. She had been " one of the brightest of the belles of the Mischianza ;" and it is somewhat curious that the knight who appeared in her honor on that occasion, chose for his device a bay-leaf—with the motto—"Unchangeable." This gay and volatile young creature, accustomed to the display connected with 'the pride of life'—and the homage paid to beauty in high station, was not one to resist the lure of ambition, and was captivated, it is probable, through her girlish fancy, by the splendor of Arnold's equipments, and his military ostentation. These appear to have had their effect upon her relatives; one of whom, in a manuscript letter still extant, says : " We understand that General Arnold, a fine gentleman, lays close siege to Peggy ;"—thus noticing his brilliant and imposing exterior, without a word of information or inquiry as to his character or principles.

A letter from Arnold to Miss Shippen, which has been published—written from the camp at Raritan—February 8th, 1779—not long before their marriage, shows the discontent and rancor of his heart, in the allusions to the President and Council of Pennsylvania. These feelings were probably expressed freely to her, as it was his pleasure to complain of injury and persecution; while the darker designs, of which no one suspected him till the whole community was startled by the news of his treason, were doubtless buried in his own bosom.

Some writers have taken delight in representing Mrs. Arnold as another Lady Macbeth—an unscrupulous and artful seductress, whose inordinate vanity and ambition were the cause of her husband's crime; but there seems no foundation even for the supposition that she was acquainted with his purpose of betraying his trust. She was not the being he would have chosen as the sharer of a secret so perilous, nor was the dissimulation attributed to her consistent with her character. Arnold's marriage, it is true, brought him more continually into familiar association with the enemies of American liberty, and strengthened distrust of him in the minds of those who had seen enough to condemn in his previous conduct; and it is likely that his propensity to extravagance was encouraged by his wife's taste for luxury and display, while she exerted over him no saving influence.

In the words of one of his best biographer: "He had no domestic security for doing right—no fireside guardianship to protect him from the tempter. Rejecting, as we do utterly, the theory that his wife was the instigator of his crime—all common principles of human action being opposed to it—we still believe that there was nothing in her influence or associations to countervail the persuasions to which he ultimately yielded. She was young, gay and frivolous; fond of display and admiration, and used to luxury; she was utterly unfitted for the duties and privations of a poor man's wife. A loyalist's daughter, she had been taught to mourn over even the poor pageantry of colonial rank and authority, and to recollect with pleasure the pomp of those brief days of enjoyment, when military men of noble station were her admirers. Arnold had no counsellor on his pillow to urge him to the imitation of homely republican virtue, to stimulate him to follow the rugged path of a Revolutionary patriot. He fell, and though his wife did not tempt or counsel him to ruin, there is no reason to think she ever uttered a word or made a sign to deter him."

Her instrumentality in the intercourse carried on while the iniquitous plan was maturing, according to all probability, was an unconscious one. Major André, who had been intimate in her father's family while General Howe was in possession of Philadelphia, wrote to her from New York, in August, 1779, to solicit her remembrance, and offer his services in procuring supplies, should she require any, in the millinery department, in which, he says playfully, the Mischianza had given him skill and experience.* The period at which this missive was sent—more than a year after Andrè had parted with the "fair circle" for which he professes such lively regard, and the singularity of the letter itself, justified the suspicion which became general after its seizure by the Council of Pennsylvania—that its offer of service in the detail of capwire, needles, and gauze, covered a meaning deep and dangerous. This view was taken by many writers of the day; but, admitting that the letter was intended to convey a mysterious meaning, still, it is not conclusive evidence of Mrs. Arnold's participation in the design or knowledge of the treason, the consummation of which was yet distant more than a year. The suggestion of Mr. Reed seems more probable—that the guilty correspondence between the two officers under feigned names having been commenced in March or April, the letter to Mrs. Arnold may have been intended by Andrè to inform her husband of the name and rank of his New York correspondent, and thus encourage a fuller measure of confidence and regard. The judgment of Mr. Reed, Mr. Sparks, and others who have closely investigated the subject, is in favor of Mrs. Arnold's innocence in the matter.

It was after the plot was far advanced towards its denouement, and only two days before General Washington commenced his tour to Hartford, in the course of which he made his visit at West Point—that Mrs.

---

* This letter is published in the Life and Correspondence of President Reed, which see—Vol. II., pp. 272—275.

10

Arnold came thither, with her infant, to join her husband
travelling by short stages, in her own carriage.* She
passed the last night at Smith's house, where she was
met by the General, and proceeded up the river in his
barge to head-quarters. When Washington and his
officers arrived at West Point, having sent from Fish-
kill to announce their coming, La Fayette reminded the
Chief, who was turning his horse into a road leading to
the river—that Mrs. Arnold would be waiting breakfast ;
to which Washington sportively answered—" Ah, you
young men are all in love with Mrs. Arnold, and wish
to get where she is as soon as possible. Go, breakfast
with her—and do not wait for me."

Mrs. Arnold was at breakfast with her husband and
the aids-de-camp—Washington and the other officers
having not yet come—when the letter arrived which
bore to the traitor the first intelligence of Andrè's
capture. He left the room immediately, went to his
wife's chamber, sent for her, and briefly informed her
of the necessity of his instant flight to the enemy.
This was, probably, the first intelligence she received
of what had been so long going on ; the news overwhelmed her, and when Arnold quitted the apartment,
he left her lying in a swoon on the floor.

Her almost frantic condition—plunged into the depths
of distress—is described with sympathy by Colonel
Hamilton, in a letter written the next day : " The
General," he says, " went to see her ; she upbraided him
with being in a plot to murder her child, raved, shed

* See Sparks' Life of Arnold.

tears, and lamented the fate of the infant. * * All the sweetness of beauty—all the loveliness of innocence— all the tenderness of a wife, and all the fondness of a mother, showed themselves in her appearance and conduct." He, too, expresses his conviction that she had no knowledge of Arnold's plan, till his announcement to her that he must banish himself from his country for ever. The opinion of other persons qualified to judge without prejudice, acquitted her of the charge of having participated in the treason. John Jay, writing from Madrid to Catharine Livingston, says—"All the world here are cursing Arnold, and pitying his wife."* And Robert Morris writes—"Poor Mrs. Arnold! was there ever such an infernal villain!"†

Mrs. Arnold went from West Point to her father's house; but was not long permitted to remain in Philadelphia. The traitor's papers having been seized, by direction of the Executive Authorities, the correspondence with Andrè was brought to light; suspicion rested on her; and by an order of the Council dated October 27th, she was required to leave the State, to return no more during the continuance of the war. She accordingly departed to join her husband in New York. The respect and forbearance shown towards her on her journey through the country, notwithstanding her banishment, testified the popular belief in her innocence. M. de. Marbois relates that when she stopped at a village where the people were about to burn Arnold in effigy, they put it off till the next night. And when

---

* MS. letter, 17th Dec. 1780.   † MS. letter.

she entered the carriage on her way to join her husband, all exhibition of popular indignation was suspended, as if respectful pity for the grief and shame she suffered for the time overcame every other feeling.

Mrs. Arnold resided with her husband for a time in the city of St. Johns, New Brunswick, and was long remembered by persons who knew her there, and who spoke much of her beauty and fascination. She afterwards lived in England. Mr. Sabine says that she and Arnold were seen by an American loyalist in Westminster Abbey, standing before the cenotaph erected by command of the king, in memory of the unfortunate Andrè. With what feelings the traitor viewed the monument of the man his crime had sacrificed, is not known; but he who saw him standing there turned away with horror.

Mrs. Arnold survived her husband three years, and died in London in 1804, at the age of forty-three. Little is known of her after the blasting of the bright promise of her youth by her husband's crime, and a dreary obscurity hangs over the close of her career; but her relatives in Philadelphia cherish her memory with respect and affection.

Hannah, the sister of Arnold, whose affection followed him through his guilty career, possessed great excellence of character; but no particulars have been obtained, by which full justice could be done to her. Mr. Sabine says: "That she was a true woman in the highest possible sense, I do not entertain a doubt;" and the same opinion of her is expressed by Mr. Sparks.

XLII.

~~~~~~

JANE M'CREA.

So many wild tales have been told of the tragical fate of Jane M'Crea, that the reader of different accounts, inconsistent with each other, knows not which to receive as truth. That given in the Life of Arnold, by Mr. Sparks, has the authority of an eye witness; the particulars having been related to him by Samuel Standish, who was present at the murder, and confirmed by General Morgan Lewis, one of the party that found Miss M'Crea's body, and superintended her funeral. It is therefore given with entire confidence in its correctness.

The headquarters of the division of the American army commanded by Arnold were at the time between Moses Creek and Fort Edward. Jane M'Crea was residing with her brother, one of the pioneer settlers, about four miles from Fort Edward, on the western bank of the Hudson. Her father was James M'Crea, an Episcopal clergyman of New Jersey, who died before the Revolution.

In the solitude of those wilds she had formed an intimacy with a young man named David Jones, to whom she was betrothed, and who had taken part with the British. He had gone to Canada after the commencement of the war, had there been made captain of a company, and was now serving among the provincials in Burgoyne's army. The lovers had kept up a correspondence, and Jones was informed that his affianced bride was on a visit to Mrs. M'Niel, a widow lady whose house stood near the foot of the hill, about one-third of a mile northward from the fort. Fort Edward, then in possession of a guard of one hundred Americans, was situated on the eastern margin of the river, very near the water, and surrounded by a cleared and cultivated plain of considerable extent.

It is evident that Miss M'Crea felt no assurance of her own safety, notwithstanding her friendly relations with the English; having been alarmed by the rumors that had reached her of the approach of the Indians, and reminded of her danger by the people at the fort. It is not known why she remained unprotected in so exposed a situation ; but it is conjectured that she had been counselled by her lover not to leave her friend's house, till the advance of the British troops should enable her to join him, in company with Mrs. M'Niel. The woods being filled with American scouting parties, it would be dangerous for him to attempt a visit to her, as the tory captain, if taken prisoner, could expect no mercy at the hands of his countrymen.

The anxiety may be conceived with which the timid but confiding girl expected, from hour to hour, intelligence from her betrothed, and awaited the long desired moment when they should meet to part no more. She was young—some authorities say nineteen, some twenty-three—but all agree that she was beautiful, with auburn hair, blue eyes, and a fresh complexion ; and endowed with accomplishments and virtues not less attractive than her personal charms. With the trustfulness of youth she yielded her own fears and scruples implicitly to the judgment of him she loved, resolving to be guided by his directions.

The catastrophe took place about the latter part of July or first of August, 1777. It should be borne in mind that the side of the hill, near the foot of which stood Mrs. M'Niel's house, was covered with bushes, while a quarter of a mile above, on the summit of the hill, a huge pine tree shadowed a clear spring. On the hill—a little beyond, within the cover of the woods, was stationed at the time a picket-guard under the command of Lieutenant Van Vechten.

Jane and her friend were at first alarmed by seeing a party of Indians advancing towards the house. The savages had been a terror to all that part of the country; and the tales told of their unsparing cruelty were fresh in the remembrance of the women. Their first impulse was to endeavor to escape; but the Indians made signs of a pacific intent, and one of them held up a letter, intimating that it would explain their business. This removed all apprehensions, and the letter was taken from the messenger. It proved to be from Captain Jones. He entreated Jane and her friend to put themselves under the protection of the Indians, whom he had sent for the purpose of taking charge of them, and who would escort them in safety to the British camp. The story that he sent his horse for the use of Miss M'Crea appears to be unfounded.

The two women, notwithstanding some misgivings, lost no time in preparation, and set off under the guidance of the savages. It happened that two separate parties of Indians, commanded by two independent chiefs, had come forth on this enterprise. They had another object in view—an attack upon the picket stationed in the woods on the hill. This arrangement, it is probable, was not known to Jones, or he would hardly have trusted the safety of Miss M'Crea to the contingencies of such an expedition.

The party attacking the guard rushed upon it through the woods from different points, making the forest resound with their horrible yelling; killing the lieutenant and five others, and wounding four more. One of the guard was Samuel Standish, whose post was near the pine-tree. He discharged his musket at an Indian, and ran down the hill towards the fort; but being intercepted on the plain by three Indians, who rushed from the thicket, fired at and wounded him slightly, and then secured him, he was forced to re-ascend the hill, where he saw several Indians at the spring beneath the pine-tree.

Here he was left alone, bound, and expecting death every moment, to witness, at a short distance, the appalling scene that ensued. Another party of Indians came in a few minutes up the hill, bringing with them Miss M'Crea and her companion. The two parties of savages here met ; and it was presently apparent that a violent altercation had arisen between them. The dispute was about the division of the reward they were to receive for the service rendered. The savages to whom the mission had been entrusted, it appears, were not aware of the relation in which the girl stood to their employer, and looked upon her rather as a prisoner, decoyed by a stratagem into their power. This supposition accounts for their conduct, consistently with the usages of the Indians in the case of captives whom they feared to lose. The quarrel became furious ; violent words and blows ensued, and in the midst of the fray, one of the chiefs fired at Miss M'Crea. The shot entered her breast; she sank to the ground, and instantly expired. The Indian grasped her long flowing locks, drew his knife, and took off the scalp ; then leaping from the ground with a yell of savage exultation, he brandished it in the air, and tossed it in the face of a young warrior who stood near him.

This murder terminated the quarrel, and the Indians, fearful of being pursued by men from the fort, where the alarm had already been given, hurried away with their two prisoners, Standish and Mrs. M'Niel, towards General Frazer's encampment on the road to Fort Anne.

The body of the murdered girl was left under the tree, gashed in several places by a tomahawk or scalping knife, and was found, with the others who had been slain, by the party in pursuit. A messenger was immediately despatched with the dreadful tidings to her brother, who soon after arrived and took charge of his

10*

sister's corpse. It was buried on the east side of the river, about three miles below the fort.

Imagination may depict the state of mind of the unfortunate Captain Jones, when the bloody trophy was presented to him, which revealed the horrible truth. To the anguish of his bereavement was added the reflection that the innocent girl had fallen a victim to her confidence in him. Time could not give him strength to bear the burden of his grief; he lived but a few years, and went down heart-broken to the grave.

General Gates reproached Burgoyne for this murder; and the frightful story spread rapidly over the country, the glowing description given of it by Burke in one of his celebrated speeches rendering it familiar throughout Europe. The remembrance of the tragedy, Mr. Sparks says, is yet cherished with sympathy by the people in the village of Fort Edward, who not many years since removed the remains of the hapless girl from their obscure resting place to the public burial-ground. "The little fountain still pours out its clear waters near the brow of the hill; and the venerable pine is yet standing in its ancient majesty—broken at the top, and shorn of its branches by the winds and storms of half a century, but revered as marking the spot where youth and innocence were sacrificed."

XLIII.

~~~~~~~~~~

NANCY HART.

At the commencement of the Revolutionary war, a large district in the State of Georgia, extending in one direction from Newson's Ponds to Cherokee Corner near Athens, and in the other, from the Savannah River to Ogeechee River and Shoulderbone, had been already organized into a county which received the name of Wilkes, in honor of the distinguished English politician. At the commencement of hostilities, so great a majority of the people of this county espoused the whig cause, that it received from the tories the name of the "Hornet's Nest." In a portion of this district, near Dye's and Webb's ferries on Broad River, now in Elbert County, was a stream known as "War-woman's Creek"—a name derived from the character of an individual who lived near the entrance of the stream into the river.

This person was NANCY HART, a woman entirely uneducated, and ignorant of all the conventional civilities of life, but a zealous lover of liberty and of the "liberty boys," as she called the whigs. She had a husband whom she denominated a "poor stick," because he did not take a decided and active part with the defenders of his country; although she could not conscientiously charge him with the least partiality to the tories. This vulgar and illiterate, but hospitable and valorous female patriot could boast no share of beauty; a fact she would herself have readily acknowledged, had she ever enjoyed an opportunity of looking in a mirror. She was cross-eyed, with a broad, angular mouth—ungainly in figure, rude in speech, and awkward in manners—but having a woman's heart for her friends, though that of a tigress or a Katrine Montour for the enemies of her country. She was well known to the tories, who stood somewhat in fear of her vengeance for any grievance or aggressive act; though they let pass no opportunity of teasing and annoying her, when they could do so with impunity.

On the occasion of an excursion from the British camp at Augusta, a party of loyalists penetrated into the interior; and having savagely massacred Colonel Dooly in bed in his own house, proceeded up the country with the design of perpetrating further atrocities. On their way, a detachment of five from the party diverged to the east, and crossed Broad River to examine the neighborhood and pay a visit to their old acquaintance Nancy Hart. When they arrived at her cabin, they unceremoniously entered it, although receiving from her no welcome but a scowl, and informed her they had come to learn the truth of a story in circulation, that she had secreted a noted rebel from a company of "king's men" who were pursuing him, and who, but for her interference, would have caught and

hung him. Nancy undauntedly avowed her agency in
the fugitive's escape. She had, she said, at first heard
the tramp of a horse, and then saw a man on horseback approaching her cabin at his utmost speed. As
soon as she recognized him to be a whig flying from
pursuit, she let down the bars in front of her cabin,
and motioned him to pass through both doors, front
and rear, of her single-roomed house—to take to the
swamp, and secure himself as well as he could. This
he did without loss of time; and she then put up the
bars, entered the cabin, closed the doors, and went
about her usual employments. Presently, some tories
rode up to the bars, calling vociferously for her. She
muffled up her head and face, and opening the door,
inquired why they disturbed a sick, lone woman.
They said they had traced a man they wanted to catch
near to her house, and asked if any one on horseback
had passed that way. She answered, no—but she saw
some one on a sorrel horse turn out of the path into the
woods, some two or three hundred yards back. " That
must be the fellow!" said the tories; and asking her
direction as to the way he took, they turned about and
went off, " *well fooled*," concluded Nancy, " in an opposite course to that of my whig boy; when, if they
had not been so lofty minded—but had looked on the
ground inside the bars, they would have seen his horse's
tracks up to that door, as plain as you can see the
tracks on this here floor, and out of t'other door down
the path to the swamp."

This bold story did not much please the tory party,

but they would not wreak their revenge upon the woman who so unscrupulously avowed the cheat she had put upon the pursuers of a rebel. They contented themselves with ordering her to prepare them something to eat. She replied that she never fed traitors and king's men if she could help it—the villains having put it out of her power to feed even her own family and friends, by stealing and killing all her poultry and pigs, " except that one old gobbler you see in the yard." " Well, and *that* you shall cook for us," said one who appeared to be a leader of the party; and raising his musket he shot down the turkey, which another of them brought into the house and handed to Mrs. Hart to be cleaned and cooked without delay. She stormed and swore awhile—for Nancy occasionally swore—but seeming at last disposed to make a merit of necessity, began with alacrity the arrangements for cooking, assisted by her daughter, a little girl ten or twelve years old, and sometimes by one of the party, with whom she seemed in a tolerably good humor—now and then ex- changing rude jests with him. The tories, pleased with her freedom, invited her to partake of the liquor they had brought with them—an invitation which was ac- cepted with jocose thanks.

The spring—of which every settlement has one near by—was just at the edge of the swamp; and a short distance within the swamp was hid among the trees a high snag-topped stump, on which was placed a conch- shell. This rude trumpet was used by the family to convey information, by variations in its notes, to Mr.

Hart or his neighbors, who might be at work in a field, or "clearing," just beyond the swamp; to let them know that the "Britishers" or tories were about—that the master was wanted at the cabin—or that he was to keep close, or "make tracks" for another swamp. Pending the operation of cooking the turkey, Nancy had sent her daughter Sukey to the spring for water, with directions to blow the conch for her father in such a way as should inform him there were tories in the cabin; and that he was to "keep close" with his three neighbors who were with him, until he should again hear the conch.

The party had become merry over their jug, and sat down to feast upon the slaughtered gobbler. They had cautiously stacked their arms where they were in view and within reach; and Mrs. Hart, assiduous in her attentions upon the table and to her guests, occasionally passed between the men and their muskets. Water was called for; and our heroine having contrived that there should be none in the cabin, Sukey was a second time despatched to the spring, with instructions to blow such a signal on the conch as should call up Mr. Hart and his neighbors immediately. Meanwhile Nancy had managed, by slipping out one of the pieces of pine which form a "chinking" between the logs of a cabin, to open a space through which she was able to pass to the outside two of the five guns. She was detected in the act of putting out the third. The whole party sprang to their feet; when quick as thought Nancy brought the piece she held, to her shoulder, declaring she would kill the first man who approached her. All were terror-struck; for Nancy's obliquity of sight caused each to imagine himself her destined victim. At length one of them made a movement to advance upon her; and true to her threat, she fired and shot him dead! Seizing another musket, she levelled it inštantly, keeping the others at bay. By this time Sukey had returned from the spring; and taking up the remaining gun, she carried it out of the house, saying to her mother—"Daddy and them will soon be here." This information much increased the alarm of the tories, who perceived the importance of recovering their arms immediately; but each one hesitated, in the confident belief that Mrs. Hart had one eye at least on him for a mark. They proposed a general rush. No time was to be lost by the bold woman;—she fired again, and brought down another of the enemy. Sukey had another musket in readiness, which her mother took, and posting herself in the doorway, called upon the party to surrender "their d—— tory carcasses to a whig woman." They agreed to surrender, and proposed to "shake hands upon the strength of it." But the victor, unwilling to trust their word, kept them in their places for a few minutes, till her husband and his neighbors came up to the door. They were about to shoot down the tories, but Mrs. Hart stopped them, saying they had surrendered to *her;* and her spirit being up to boiling heat, she swore that "shooting was too good for them." This hint was enough; the dead man was dragged out of the house; and the wounded tory and the others were bound, taken out beyond the bars and hung! The tree upon which they were suspended was shown in 1828 by one who lived in those bloody times, and who also pointed out the spot once occupied by Mrs. Hart's cabin; accompanying the mention of her name with the emphatic remark—"Poor Nancy! she was a honey of a patriot—but the devil of a wife!"

XLIV.

~~~~~~~~

REBECCA BIDDLE.

THE husband of this lady, Colonel Clement Biddle, was among the first of those who took an active part on the breaking out of the war, resolved to sacrifice everything in the cause. Both he and his wife were members of the Society of Friends, and as a consequence of his taking up arms he was "read out of meeting" by that peace-loving community; while Mrs. Biddle, as ardent a patriot—expressing her approval of the war, and encouraging her husband in his course—was subjected to similar discipline.

Mrs. Biddle gave up the comforts of home to join the army with her husband, and was with the camp during the greater part of the war. With Mrs. Greene and Mrs. Knox, who were also with the army, she formed a lasting friendship, and was intimate with Mrs. Washington—being moreover on terms of personal friendship with the Commander-in-chief, for whom she entertained the highest respect and admiration. His letters to her husband, with whom a correspondence was kept up during his life, are still in the possession of her children. This intimacy, with the unusual facilities she enjoyed

for observing the events of the war, and the characters
of the distinguished men engaged in it, render it a matter of regret that the spirited anecdotes and graphic details, so well worthy of being embodied in history, with
which her conversation abounded in after life, should
not have been recorded as they fell from her lips. One
or two of these, however, received from a member of
her family, may illustrate her character.

When the American army was encamped near the
Brandywine, Mrs. Biddle was informed by an aid of
Washington, that a large British foraging party was
within the distance of a few miles; that orders had been
issued for a party to start before day for the purpose of cutting off their retreat, and that, as an engagement might be expected, the women were directed
to leave the camp. Mrs. Biddle, not willing to consider
herself included in the order, told General Washington,
when an opportunity of addressing him occurred, that as
the officers would return hungry and fatigued from the
expedition, she would, if allowed to stay, make provision
for their refreshment. He assured her she might remain
in safety, but recommended that she should hold herself
in readiness to remove at a moment's warning, promising, in the event of any disaster, to send her timely
information. She immediately despatched her servant
through the neighborhood to collect provisions; and all
the food cooked that day in the camp was thus procured
by her. The enemy, informed by spies of the movement against them, made a hasty retreat, and at a late
hour the American troops returned after a fatiguing

march.   Mrs. Biddle had the pleasure of giving the dinner she had provided to at least a hundred officers; each
remarking, as he entered, "Madam, we hear that you
feed the army to-day," which she really did till not a
crust remained.

Among her guests on that occasion was the gallant
La Fayette, who on his last visit paid his respects to
her in Philadelphia.   One of the Revolutionary reminiscences which they talked over in the presence of
her deeply interested children and friends, was that entertainment, to which the General alluded with marked
satisfaction.   He also recalled to Mrs. Biddle's memory
the suffering condition of the army at Valley Forge,
where the want of provisions was at one time provi-
dentially supplied by a flight of wild pigeons in such
vast numbers, and so near the ground, that they were
killed with clubs and poles.   Even the officers were at
that time so destitute of decent clothing, that it was
jocosely remarked, that a single suit of dress uniform
served them all for dining in, when invited by turns to
headquarters, where the repast consisted of pigeons
prepared in as many ways as the cook could devise.

In no instance did the enthusiasm and patriotic spirit
which animated the heroines of that day, shine more
brightly than in this high-minded woman.   The purest
and most disinterested love of country induced a cheerful submission, on her part, to all the inconveniences,
hardships, and losses rendered inevitable by a protracted
war; and often, in subsequent years, did her detail of
those difficulties serve for the amusement of her family

circle. Her attachment to General Washington and
his family continued through life ; and during their residence in Philadelphia, she and Colonel Biddle were
always honored guests at their table. She survived her
husband many years, living till upwards of seventy, and
to the last retaining in all their strength and freshness,
the faculties and feelings of her prime. She ever loved
to dwell on the signal display of the hand of Providence
in the contest with the mother country, and whenever
allusion was made to the Revolutionary war, it was a
source of new delight to her children to hear her "fight
her battles o'er again."

Mrs. GRAYDON has been made known to us in her
son's "Memoirs" of his own life and times. She was
the eldest of four daughters ; was born in the island of
Barbadoes, and when but seven years old came with her
family to Philadelphia. Her father was a German who
had been engaged in trade in Barbadoes—her mother a
native of Glasgow ; but notwithstanding the want of
national affinity, and the still greater differences of
dialect and religion, there was no lack of harmony in
their judgment with respect to the training of their
children, who were brought up in strict principles, and
after good example in both parents. The mother died
before the commencement of hostilities, and it is not
ascertained at what time the subject of this notice married Mr. Graydon. She was pronounced by one of her
acquaintances (Dr. Baird), who has transmitted the

record to posterity, to be "the finest girl in Philadelphia, having the manners of a lady bred at court." Her house was the seat of hospitality, and the resort of numerous guests of distinction, including officers of the British army. The Baron de Kalb was often there; and among persons of rank from the mother country, were Lady Moore, the wife of Sir Henry Moore, and her daughter; Lady Susan O'Brien and her husband; Major George Etherington, and others. Sir William Draper, who attained the rank of general in the British army, and, in 1779, was appointed Lieutenant Governor of Minorca, was also a frequent guest.

The account of Mrs. Graydon's visit to her son Alexander, who had been taken prisoner at the battle of Fort Washington, has interest as exhibiting the strength of her maternal affection, with a fortitude and patriotic spirit worthy of an American matron. After having addressed a letter to General Washington, who could do nothing to accomplish the release of her son, she resolved on going herself to New York, notwithstanding the opposition of her friends on account of the difficulties of travelling, for the purpose of soliciting his freedom on parole, from the British commander. She accordingly purchased a horse and chair, and set out for Philadelphia, her residence being then at Reading. On her arrival in the city, one Fisher, a distant relative, was officious in tendering his service to drive her to New York, and the offer was accepted; but when they had nearly reached Princeton, they were overtaken, to their great astonishment, by a detachment of American

cavalry—Fisher, it seems, being a loyalist. The lady
found in such evil company was taken also into custody,
and after some delay, was obliged to retrace her road to
Philadelphia, under an escort of horse. When they
reached Bristol on their return, means were found for
the prisoner to go on without the chair, and Mrs. Graydon was accompanied by Colonel M'Ilvaine, an old
friend, to the head quarters of the American army,
where proper measures could be taken for her proceed-
ing within the British lines. After being conducted
to the lines, she was committed to the courtesy of some
Hessian officers. It happened, during the ceremony
of the flag, that a gun was somewhere discharged
on the American side. This infringement of military
etiquette was furiously resented by the German officers; and their vehement gestures, and expressions
of indignation, but imperfectly understood by the lady,
alarmed her not a little. She supported herself as
well as she could, under this inauspicious introduction into the hostile territory, and had her horse led
to the quarters of the general who commanded in
Brunswick, where she alighted, and was shown into
a parlor. Weary and faint from fatigue and agitation,
she partook of some refreshment offered her, and then
went to deliver a letter of introduction she had received
from Mr. Vanhorne of Boundbrook to a gentleman in
Brunswick. Five of the Misses Vanhorne, his nieces,
were staying at the house, and with them Mrs. Graydon
became well acquainted, as they avowed whig principles.
Their uncle had been compelled to leave Flatbush on

account of his attachment to the American cause; but was permitted not long afterwards to return to his house there, accompanied by Mrs. Vanhorne and her daughters.

After a detention of a week or more at Brunswick, Mrs. Graydon embarked in a sloop or shallop for New York. The vessel was fired upon from the shore, but no one was injured, and she reached in safety the destined port. Mr. Bache allowed Mrs. Graydon to occupy his part of Mr. Suydam's house during her stay at Flatbush. Here, in the society of her son, her accustomed flow of good spirits returned: she even gave one or two tea drinkings to the "rebel clan," and "learned from Major Williams the art of making Johnny cakes in the true Maryland fashion." These recreations did not interfere with the object of her expedition, nor could her son dissuade her from her purpose of proving the result of an application. When she called in New York on Mr. Galloway, who was supposed to have much influence at headquarters, he advised her to apply to Sir William Howe by memorial, and offered to draw up one for her. In a few minutes he produced what accorded with his ideas on the subject, and read to her what he had written, commencing with— "Whereas Mrs. Graydon has always been a true and faithful subject of His Majesty George the Third; and whereas her son, an inexperienced youth, has been deluded by the arts of designing men—"

"Oh, sir,"—cried the mother—"that will never do! my son cannot obtain his release on those terms."

"Then, madam"—replied the officer, somewhat peevishly, "I can do nothing for you!"

Though depressed by her first disappointment, Mrs. Graydon would not relinquish her object; but continued to advise with every one she thought able or willing to assist her. In accordance with the counsel received from a friend, she at length resolved upon a direct application to General Howe.

After several weeks of delay, anxiety and disappointment, through which her perseverance was unwearied, the design was put in execution. Without having informed her son of what she meant to do, lest he might prevent her, through his fear of improper concessions on her part, she went one morning to New York, and boldly waited upon Sir William Howe. She was shown into a parlor, and had a few moments to consider how she should address him who possessed the power to grant her request, or to destroy her hopes. He entered the room, and was near her, before she perceived him.

" Sir William Howe—I presume?" said Mrs. Graydon, rising. He bowed; she made known her business —a mother's feelings doubtless giving eloquence to her speech—and entreated permission for her son to go home with her on parole.

" And then immediately to take up arms against us, I suppose!" said the General.

" By no means, sir; I solicit his release upon parole; that will restrain him until exchanged; but on my own part I will go further, and say that if I have any influence over him, he shall never take up arms again."

11

" Here," says Graydon, " the feelings of the patriot were wholly lost in those of the ' war-detesting' mother." The General seemed to hesitate; but on the earnest renewal of her suit, gave the desired permission.

The mother's joy at her success was the prelude to a welcome summons to the prisoners, to repair to New York for the purpose of being transported in a flag-vessel to Elizabethtown.   The captives having been kept in the dark on subjects concerning which they most desired information—the state of the army and public affairs—one of those left behind furnished Graydon with a kind of cypher, by which intelligence could be conveyed to him.   The disguise consisted in the substitution of one piece of information for another; for instance—a lady named, was to signify the army; if that was prosperous, the fact was to be indicated by announcing the health and charming looks of the belle in question; there being a scale in the key, by which intelligence might be graduated.

After some adventures, the travellers reached Philadelphia, where they dined at President Hancock's.   He had opposed Mrs. Graydon's scheme of going to New York; and though apparently pleased with her success, could not be supposed cordially gratified by an event which might give to the adverse cause any reputation for clemency.   Such is the policy of war, and so stern a thing is patriotism!

XLV.

ANN ELIZA BLEECKER.

Ann Eliza Bleecker, whose name is prominent on the list of the female poets of our country, was the youngest child of Brandt Schuyler, of New York, where she was born, in 1752. In her early years she was passionately fond of books, and wrote verses, which, however, were shown to none but her most intimate acquaintances. After her marriage, at the age of seventeen, to John J. Bleecker, of New Rochelle, she removed to Poughkeepsie, and thence to Tomhanick, a pretty and secluded village about eighteen miles from Albany, where her residence was well suited to her romantic tastes. The house commanded a beautiful view ; on one side was a fine garden, filled with flowers and fruit trees, and beyond it the Tomhanick River dashed foaming over a bed of broken rocks. On the other lay wide cultivated fields ; a wood, through the openings of which cottages might be descried, bounded the orchard in the rear, and in front a meadow, through which wandered a clear stream, stretched itself to join a ridge of tall pines, on the shelving side of a mountain. To the imagination of Mrs. Bleecker, the dark forest, the green valley and the rushing river had more charms than the gay city she had quitted ; but her tranquil enjoyment of these lovely scenes, in the cultivation of her flowers and grounds, and the indulgence of her poetical tastes, was destined to be short-lived.

The approach of Burgoyne's army, in 1777, drove the family from their rural retreat. While Mr. Bleecker was gone to Albany to seek a place of refuge for them, his wife was terrified by news that the enemy were close to the village, burning and murdering all before them. With her children and one servant, she fled to a place called Stony Arabia. The roads were crowded with carriages loaded with women and children ; distress and weeping were every where ; no one spoke to another, and the tramping of horses and the dismal creaking of burdened wheels, alone interrupted the mournful silence. Mrs. Bleecker obtained a place for her children in one of the wagons, and herself performed the journey on foot. But when she reached the place where she hoped to find friends, no door was open to her. She wandered from house to house, and at length obtained an asylum in the garret of a rich acquaintance, where a couple of blankets, spread on boards, were given her as a bed. The night was passed in tears ; but the next day Mr. Bleecker came and brought them to Albany, whence they set off with several other families by water. A more severe distress here overtook the mother—her little daughter being taken so ill that they were obliged to go on shore, where she died, and was buried on the banks of the river. This bereavement was followed in rapid succession by the death of her mother and sister.

In August of the year 1781, while Mr. Bleecker was assisting in the harvest, he was taken prisoner by one of the scouting parties from Canada. His wife abandoned herself to hopeless grief. She says, "My hour of darkness and astonishment was very great; I lifted my broken heart in despair." But after the agonizing suspense of a few days, her husband returned, having been rescued by a party of Americans.

Amid the scenes of distress, in many of which Mrs. Bleecker was a principal sufferer, she was sustained by the hope of yet seeing the footsteps of desolation effaced from the soil. She was not destined, however, to behold the recovery of her native land from the ravages of war. After a rapid decline, the struggles of this calm and lovely spirit were ended in death, in November, 1783.

The benevolence of Mrs. Bleecker's heart overflowed on all with whom she associated. "To the aged and infirm," says her daughter, "she was a physician and a friend; to the orphan a mother, and a soother of the widow's woes." She is said to have possessed a considerable share of beauty, her figure being tall and graceful; and her easy, unaffected deportment and engaging manners prepossessed strangers in her favor. Her letters describing the scenes around her, show her ardent and poetical temperament. An intense love of nature appears in her poems, and a warmth of heart, with a delicacy and taste, that cannot fail to please;

though they lack the high finish a greater severity of critical judgment would have bestowed.

~~~~~~~~~~~~~~~

MRS. BLEECKER's daughter, Margaretta Faugeres, was also a poet, and has sung in sweet strains "the hoar genius of old Hudson's stream," including a description of the scenery of Fort Edward and West Point. In the latter portion is introduced a highly poetical "Vision of Arnold," where Treason is personified, plotting her dark schemes while bending over the bright waters, and stealing softly to the traitor's couch. Margaretta became distinguished after the war, in New York fashionable society, as a gifted and accomplished woman, although her married life was rendered unhappy by a profligate husband. After his death in 1798, she assisted in a female academy in New Brunswick ; but her sufferings had broken her heart. She died, a hopeful Christian, at the early age of twenty-nine.

~~~~~~~~~~~~~~~

THE correspondence of Ralph Izard was published a few years since by his daughter, Anne Izard Deas, at the desire of her mother, whose anxiety to do justice to the memory of her husband proves her worthy of sharing in his fame. Moving in her youth in the gayest circles of New York society, her amiable qualities, and the discretion and modesty joined to her singular personal attractions, won the admiration and regard of all her acquaintances, and gave promise of those virtues which shone amid the trials of after life.

She was the daughter of Peter De Lancey, of West-chester, and niece to James De Lancey, Lieutenant Governor of the province of New York. It is remarkable how many women of this distinguished family have married eminent men. Susan, the daughter of Colonel Stephen De Lancey, whose first husband was Lieutenant Colonel William Johnson, became the wife of Lieutenant General Sir Hudson Lowe, and was the beautiful Lady Lowe praised by Bonaparte. Charlotte De Lancey, who married Sir David Dundas, did not escape her share of trials during the war. When their house at Bloomingdale was burned, her mother hid herself in a kennel, and not being able on account of her deafness to discover when the enemy departed, narrowly escaped death. On a visit afterwards from a party of soldiers, the young girl was put into a bin for concealment by the servants, and covered with oats, into which the soldiers, who were in search of a prisoner they might hold as a hostage, plunged their bayonets repeatedly, but luckily did not touch her. A Miss De Lancey was the wife of Sir William Draper. In later years one of this family married a distinguished American, whose genius is the pride of his country.*

Alice was married in 1767, to Ralph Izard; and after some years accompanied him to Europe. After the breaking out of the war, her anxious desire was to return with him to this country; but not being able to do so, she remained in France during his absence, devoting herself to the care and improvement of her children.

* J. Fenimore Cooper.

On their arrival at home, after the establishment of peace, their estate was found in a state of lamentable dilapidation; but the energy and good management of Mrs. Izard soon restored a degree of order, and rendered "the Elms"—the old family residence—the seat of domestic comfort and liberal hospitality. During her husband's illness, which lasted seven years, she was his devoted nurse, while the management of his large estate, embarrassed by losses sustained during the war, devolved upon her. She wrote all his letters of business, besides attending to the affairs of her family, then augmented by the addition of two orphan grandchildren; yet found time to read to him several hours of every day. The charge of two other families of grandchildren was afterwards undertaken by her. Notwithstanding these multiplied cares, each day was marked by some deed of unostentatious charity. Her piety, though deep and sincere, was cheerful, for a humble faith directed her steps, and taught resignation in trials the most severe— the loss of many children. In the faithful performance, from day to day, of the duties before her, and the promotion of the good of others, her useful life was closed in 1832, in the eighty-seventh year of her age.

AN INTERESTING anecdote is related of another Mrs. Ralph Izard, a relative of the patriot, who resided near Dorchester, within the range of excursions made by the British, at that time in the neighborhood of Charleston. When the enemy ventured beyond their lines, the inhabitants of the country were frequently subjected to depredations. The plantation of Mr. Izard, who at that time acted as aid-de-camp to the commanding officer of the Light Troops, was often visited, but had been preserved from destruction by the prudent deportment of his wife. She invariably received the officers with polite attention, and by the suavity and gentle dignity of her manners, disarmed their hostility, and induced them to retire without disturbance. On one occasion her courage was put to a severe trial. Her husband was at home, when the alarm was suddenly given by the appearance of a party of British soldiers, from whom there was no way of escape, the house being surrounded. Mr. Izard hastily concealed himself in a clothes-press, while his wife awaited the entrance of his enemies, who had been informed of the visit of the master of the house, and were determined on his capture. A search was instituted, which proving unsuccessful, the soldiers threatened to fire the house, unless he surrendered himself. In their rage and disappointment, they proceeded to outrages they had never before ventured upon; Mr. Izard's wardrobe was robbed, and several of the marauders arrayed themselves in his best coats; valuable articles were seized in the presence of the mistress of the mansion and an attempt was even made to force her rings from her fingers. Through all this trying scene, Mrs. Izard preserved, in a wonderful manner, her firmness and composure; her bearing, on which she knew her husband's safety depended, was marked with her accustomed courtesy and urbanity, and she betrayed no

11*

apprehension, notwithstanding the indignities offered. So calm, so dignified was her deportment, that the plunderers, doubting the correctness of the information they had received, and perhaps ashamed of their insolence, withdrew. No sooner were they gone, than Mr. Izard made his escape, and quickly crossing the Ashley, gave notice to the Americans on the other side of the river of the proximity of the enemy. Meanwhile, the British soldiers, returning to the house, again entered Mrs. Izard's apartment, and burst open the press, which they had before forgotten to examine. Finding no one there, they retired; but were speedily intercepted by a body of cavalry that had pushed across Bacon's bridge, and so completely routed, that but a few of their number returned within their lines to relate the disaster. The property taken from Mr. Izard's house was recovered, and restored by the conquerors to the owner, with a compliment to the matron whose strength of spirit had proved the means of their obtaining the victory.

XLVI.

~~~~~

ANNA BAILEY.

A⊤ the time of the burning of New London, in Connecticut, a detachment of the army of the traitor Arnold was directed to attack Fort Griswold, at Groton, on the opposite side of the river. This fort was little more than a rude embankment of earth, thrown up as a breast-work for the handful of troops it surrounded, with a strong loghouse in the centre. The garrison defending it, under the command of the brave Colonel Ledyard, was far inferior to the force of the assailants; but the gallant spirits of the commander and his men could not brook the thought of retreat before a marauding enemy, without an effort at resistance. They refused to yield, and stood their ground, till, overwhelmed by numbers, after a fierce and bloody encounter, hand to hand, with the foe, it was found to be impossible to maintain the post. No mercy was shown by the conquerors—the noble Ledyard was slain in the act of surrender, with the sword he had placed in the hand of the commander of the assailants—and after an indiscriminate butchery, such of the prisoners as showed signs of life, were thrown into a cart, which heaped with mangled bodies, was started down a steep and rugged hill towards the river.

The course of the cart being interrupted by stones and logs, the victims were not precipitated into the water ; and, after the enemy had been driven off by the roused inhabitants of the country, friends came to the aid of the wounded, and several lives were preserved. Their sufferings before relief could be obtained, were indescribable. Thirty-five men, covered with wounds and blood, trembling with cold, and parched with thirst, lay all night upon the bare floor, almost hopeless of succor, and looking to death as a deliverance from intolerable anguish. With the first ray of morning came a ministering angel to their aid—one who bore a name imperishably connected with the event—Miss Fanny Ledyard—a near relative of the commander who had been so barbarously murdered. She brought warm chocolate, wine, and other refreshments ; and while Dr. Downer of Preston was dressing their wounds, she went from one to another, administering her cordials, and breathing into their ears gentle words of sympathy and encouragement. In these labors of kindness she was assisted by another relative of the lamented Colonel Ledyard—Mrs. John Ledyard—who had also brought her household stores to refresh the sufferers, and lavished on them the most soothing personal attentions. The soldiers who recovered from their wounds were accustomed, to the day of their death, to speak of these ladies in terms of fervent gratitude and praise.

The morning after the massacre at Fort Griswold, a

young woman, now Mrs. Anna Bailey, left her home, three miles distant, and came in search of her uncle, who had joined the volunteers on the first alarm of invasion, and was known to have been engaged in the disastrous conflict. He was among those wounded unto death. His niece found him in a house near the scene of slaughter, where he had shared the attention bestowed on the rest. His wounds had been dressed, but it was evident that he could bear no further removal, and that life was fast departing. Still perfect consciousness remained, and with dying energy he entreated that he might once more behold his wife and child.

Such a request was sacred to the affectionate and sympathizing girl. She lost no time in hastening home, where she caught and saddled the horse used by the family, placed upon the animal the delicate wife, whose strength could not have accomplished so long a walk; and taking the child herself, bore it in her arms the whole distance, and presented it to receive the blessing of its expiring father.

With pictures of cruelty like the scene at Groton fresh in her recollection, it is not surprising that Mrs. Bailey, during the subsequent years of her life, has been noted for bitterness of feeling towards the ancient enemies of her country. She was emphatically a daughter of the Revolution, and in those times of trial was nourished the ardent love of her native land for which she has ever been distinguished, and the energy and resolution which in later days prompted the patriotic act that has made her name so celebrated as "the heroine of Groton." This act was performed in the last war with Great Britain. On the 13th July, 1813, a British squadron appearing off New London harbor, an attack, evidently the enemy's object, was momentarily expected. The most intense excitement prevailed among the crowds assembled on both sides of the river, and the ancient fort was again manned for a desperate defence. In the midst of the preparations for resistance, it was discovered that there was a want of flannel to make the cartridges. There being no time to cross the ferry to New London, Mrs. Bailey proposed appealing to the people living in the neighborhood—went herself from house to house to make the collections, and took even a garment from her own person to contribute to the stock.* This characteristic instance of enthusiasm in the cause of her country, with the impression her remarkable character has produced, has acquired for her a degree of popularity, which brings many curious visitors, from time to time, to see and converse with the heroine of whom they have heard so much, and to look at her museum of Revolutionary relics.

Her maiden name was Anna Warner, and she

* A graphic account of this incident, and of "Mother Bailey," appeared in the Democratic Review for January, 1847. But as a piece of historical justice, it is due to this heroine to state that she *denies* having used the coarse and profane expression there attributed to her. The highly intelligent lady residing in New London, who received the particulars I have mentioned from Mrs. Bailey's own lips, also says that she has never claimed the credit of being among those who ministered to the wants of the wounded, after the massacre at Fort Griswold.

married Captain Elijah Bailey, of Groton. She is
still living, in her eighty-ninth year, in the possession
of her mental faculties, able to describe the scenes of
hardship and peril in which she shared in the nation's
infancy, and still glowing with the ardent feelings of
love to America and hatred to America's foes, which
have given a coloring to her life.

The following extract from Butler's " History of
Groton," may show that the women of Massachusetts
were not behind their sisters of other States in patriotic
daring.

"The patriotism of the women in those times 'which
tried men's souls,' must not be passed over in silence.
After the departure of Colonel Prescott's regiment of
'minute-men,' Mrs. David Wright of Pepperell, Mrs.
Job Shattuck of Groton, and the neighboring women,
collected at what is now Jewett's Bridge, over the
Nashua, between Pepperell and Groton, clothed in their
absent husbands' apparel, and armed with muskets,
pitchforks, and such other weapons as they could find;
and having elected Mrs. Wright their commander,
resolutely determined that no foe to freedom, foreign or
domestic, should pass that bridge. For rumors were
rife, that the regulars were approaching, and frightful
stories of slaughter flew rapidly from place to place,
and from house to house.

" Soon there appeared one* on horseback, supposed

* "Captain Leonard Whiting, of Hollis, N. H., a noted tory. He

to be treasonably engaged in conveying intelligence to the enemy. By the implicit command of Sergeant Wright, he is immediately arrested, unhorsed, searched, and the treasonable correspondence found concealed in his boots. He was detained prisoner, and sent to Oliver Prescott, Esq., of Groton, and his despatches were sent to the Committee of Safety."

The worthy author of the History of Groton has omitted, in his account of this transaction, one of the most important and characteristic particulars, which I cannot, as a faithful chronicler, neglect to notice, having received it on the authority of America's most distinguished historian. The officer thus taken prisoner, being a politic gentleman, and probably somewhat experienced in the tactics of gallantry, endeavored, when thus arrested and disarmed, to win his way by kissing his fair captors. But they were proof against his arts as well as his arms.

~~~~~~~~~~~~~~~

IT is not generally known that Joel Barlow—the poet, philosopher and politician, the author of the Columbiad and other works—owed much of the formation of his mind and character to the wife of his elder brother Aaron. Much of his time in early life was spent in the society of his sister-in-law, who was a woman

was in reality the bearer of despatches from Canada to the British in Boston. An article was some time after inserted in a warrant for town meeting: 'To see what the town will vote or order to be paid to Mr. Solomon Rogers, for entertaining Leonard Whiting and his guard.' Not acted upon."

of strong mind, and united the qualities of gentleness
and resolute firmness.   Her residence was at Redding,
Connecticut, in the south part of the town, called by the
Indian name of "Umpawag," which it still retains.   The
country is much broken, and the ground almost entirely
covered with stones; yet the soil was rich enough to
reward the labor of the husbandman, and for some years
after their marriage the young couple lived there in
comfort.   When the stirring scenes of the Revolution
commenced, both were called to act their part.   The
husband entered the army in the service of his country,
and in a short time was promoted to the rank of colonel.
His military duties required long absences from home,
and the young wife was left to take the entire charge of
her helpless little ones.   The courage and resolution
she displayed, in the midst of many trials, moved the
admiration of those who knew her, and presented an
example which ought to be recorded for the benefit of
her countrymen.   No feminine fears were strong enough
to prevent the calm discharge of her duty to her family.
At one time a rumor came that the British army was
approaching and would probably reach Umpawag that
very night.   The terrified inhabitants resolved on
instant flight, and each family, gathering together such
of their effects as they could take with them, quitted the
village, and were travelling nearly the whole night to
reach a place of refuge from the enemy.   Mrs. Barlow
could not carry away her children, and to leave them
was out of the question ; she therefore remained to protect them, or share their fate, being deserted by all her

neighbors.   No enemy, however, was near ; the ground-less alarm having been caused by the firing of some guns below.

At one time during the war, a brigade of the Ameri-can troops under the command of General Putnam, was quartered during the winter months at Redding.   The head-quarters of the General were in an old-fashioned house, standing at some distance from the road, with a green lawn in front.   A lane led from this to the public highway.   Nearly a quarter of a mile distant, and parallel with this ancient mansion, stood the residence of Colonel Barlow.

The story of Mrs. Barlow's heroism, in remaining alone in the village when the attack from the British was apprehended, was of course told to the bluff General, and gained his admiration for the intrepid young mother.   He also heard much of her fortitude amidst the privations to which she was obliged to submit, of her gentle and courteous, though retiring deportment, and her cheerful endurance of evils common to all, which she hoped might result in the accomplishment of great good to her country.   It is said that, feeling a curi-osity to make the acquaintance of one whose character met with his strong approbation, he took a stroll over the fields towards her house, on a frosty morning in February—wearing the simple dress of a countryman—and made her a visit; his ostensible errand being a neighborly request that Mrs. Barlow would be kind enough to give or lend him a little yeast for a baking.*

* This incident is related by a descendant of Mrs. Barlow.

He entered the kitchen without ceremony, where the matron was busily engaged in preparing breakfast, and stopping a moment to look at her, asked for the yeast. But she had none to give, and told him so, each time his request was repeated, without suspending her employment to look at her visitor. It was not till after his departure, that she was informed by her old black servant who it was, who had asked the favor with such importunity.

" I suppose"—was her remark—"had I known him, I should have treated him with rather more civility ; but it is no matter now." And Putnam, who had observed her cheerful countenance, and attention to her domestic affairs, saw that she was of the proper material for the matrons of the infant nation.

The house in which General Putnam had his headquarters at this time, was long celebrated on that account. It was taken down a few years since, and a new and elegant mansion erected on the spot where it stood. The inhabitants of Umpawag saw with regret what they could not but deem the sacrilegious destruction of a dwelling so hallowed by association, and rich with reminiscences of the early and glorious struggle of our country for freedom—that a more costly edifice might be built on the ground it occupied.

Rebecca Barlow was the daughter of Elnathan Sanford, of Redding, and was born in the village where she resided after her marriage. A few years after the war ended, Colonel Barlow, with his family, removed to Norfolk in Virginia, where he subsequently fell a victim to the yellow fever. The whole family suffered with the disease; and after the burial of her husband and daughter, and the recovery of the others, the widow returned to her former home at Umpawag. She died at an advanced age. Some of her sons have rendered important services to their country as statesmen. The youngest, Thomas, accompanied his uncle Joel, the Minister Plenipotentiary at the Court of France, as his Secretary; and after the death of Joel at Zarnovica, in the winter of 1812, escorted his wife, who had been left in Paris, to America. The remains of the minister were brought with them, and placed in the family vault at Washington.

XLVII.

~~~~~~

THE WOMEN OF KENTUCKY.

MANY were the brilliant exploits of the pioneers of Kentucky, and among them many a tale of woman's fortitude, intrepidity, and heroism, lived long in the recollection of those who witnessed or mingled in the stirring scenes. No materials can be gathered for extended memoirs of those dwellers in the forest, whose history, were it recorded, would throw so strong a light upon early western life; but a few detached anecdotes —illustrative of their trials in the times of civil war— may be found interesting.*

The wife of the distinguished pioneer Daniel Boone —after whom Boone County was named—and her daughters, were the first white women who stood upon the banks of the Kentucky River. They removed to the new fort, afterwards known as Boonesborough, in the summer of 1775. This place soon became the central object of Indian hostilities. A cabin, not far distant, erected to found a new fort some years afterwards, was attacked by the savages, one man and his wife killed, and the other, Mr. Duree, mortally wounded.

* See Collins's Historical Sketches of Kentucky.

His wife, who had barred the door, grasped a rifle, and told her husband she would help him to fight, but received the answer that he was dying. Having presented the gun through several port-holes in quick succession, she sat down beside her husband with the calmness of despair, and closed his eyes in death. Some hours passed, in which nothing more was heard of the Indians, and taking her infant in her arms—her son, three or four years older, following her, she sallied forth in desperation to make her way to the fort at White Oak Spring. Wandering in the woods, and running till she was nearly exhausted, she came at length to the trail, and pursuing it, met her father-in-law, with his wife and son, on their way to the new station. The melancholy tidings changed their course; they led their horses into an adjoining cane brake, unloaded them of the baggage, and regained the White Oak Spring before daylight.

The wife of Whitley, another of the enterprising hunters whose adventurous exploits have shed a coloring of romance over the early history of Kentucky, manifested a spirit of adventure and a love of independence equal to his own. To his observation that he had heard a fine report of Kentucky, and thought they could obtain a living there with less hard work—her answer was—"Then, Billy, I would go and see;" and in two days he was on his way with axe and plough, and gun and kettle. She afterwards collected his warriors to pursue the Indians. This was on an occasion when the emergency called for prompt action—the camp of an emigrant named M'Clure having been assaulted in the night and six whites killed. His wife fled into the woods with her four children; but the cries of the infant she bore in her arms betrayed her place of retreat. She heard the savages coming towards the spot, eager to imbrue their hands in innocent blood; she could have escaped with three of the children by abandoning the youngest; the night, the grass, and the bushes, offered concealment—but how could the mother leave her helpless babe to certain destruction? She resolved to die with it. The other affrighted little ones clung to her for protection; she dared not bid them fly and hide themselves, lest the savages should discover them; she *hoped* her arms might shield them, should the inhuman enemy find them at her side. The Indians came, and quickly extinguished both hopes and fears in the blood of three of the children. The hapless mother and infant were taken to their camp, where she was compelled to cook the meal on which the murderers feasted. In the morning they pursued their way, forcing her to accompany them, riding an unbroken horse.

Whitley was not at home when the news of this outrage was brought to his station. His wife immediately despatched a messenger for him, and sent, in the meantime, to warn and assemble his company. When he returned, he found twenty-one men awaiting his orders. Directing his course to the war-path, he gained it in advance of the savages, who had stopped to divide their plunder; concealed his men, and opening a deadly fire upon them as they approached, soon dispersed them, and rescued the captives.

The siege of Bryant's station, near Lexington, which took place in August, 1782, gave occasion for a brilliant display of female intrepidity. The garrison was supplied with water from a spring at some distance from the fort, near which a considerable body of the Indians had been placed in ambush. Another party in full view was ordered to open a fire at a given time, with the hope of enticing the besieged to an engagement without the walls, when the remaining force could seize the opportunity of storming one of the gates. The more experienced of the garrison felt satisfied that Indians were concealed near the spring, but conjectured that they would not unmask themselves, until the firing on the opposite side of the fort should induce them to believe that the men had come out and were engaged with the other party. The need of water was urgent, and yielding to the necessity of the case, they summoned all the women. "Explaining to them the circumstances in which they were placed, and the improbability that any injury would be offered them, until the firing had been returned from the opposite side of the fort, they urged them to go in a body to the spring, and bring up each a bucket full of water. Some, as was natural, had no relish for the undertaking, and asked why the men could not bring water as well as themselves, observing that they were not bullet-proof, and the Indians made no distinction between male and female scalps. To this it was answered, that the women were in the habit of bringing water every morning to the fort; and that if the Indians saw them engaged as usual, it would induce them to think their ambuscade was undiscovered; and that they would not unmask themselves for the sake of firing at a few women, when they hoped, by remaining concealed a few moments longer, to obtain complete possession of the fort. That if men should go down to the spring, the Indians would immediately suspect something was wrong, would despair of succeeding by ambuscade, and would instantly rush upon them, follow them into the fort, or shoot them down at the spring.

"The decision was soon made. A few of the boldest declared their readiness to brave the danger, and the younger and more timid rallying in the rear of these veterans, they all marched down in a body to the spring, within point blank shot of more than five hundred Indian warriors! Some of the girls could not help betraying symptoms of terror; but the married women, in general, moved with a steadiness and composure that completely deceived the Indians. Not a shot was fired. The party were permitted to fill their buckets, one after another, without interruption; and although their steps became quicker and quicker, on their return, and when near the fort, degenerated into a rather unmilitary celerity, with some little crowding in passing the gate, yet not more than one-fifth of the water was spilled, and the eyes of the youngest had not dilated to more than double their ordinary size."*

M'Clung's Sketches of Western Adventure.

12

At the siege of Logan's fort, while the men composing the small garrison were constantly at their posts, engaged in a vigorous defence, the women were actively employed in moulding bullets. In 1779, General Simon Kenton owed his liberty to female compassion. He was one of the most celebrated pioneers of the west, and was honored by having his name given to one of the counties of Kentucky. In an expedition for taking horses from the Indians, he was captured, and for eight months suffered incredible cruelties at their hands, till at length, being transferred to a Canadian trader, he was delivered to the British commander at Detroit. Here, while he worked for the garrison, his hard lot excited the commiseration of Mrs. Harvey, the wife of an Indian trader. His exterior was calculated to interest in his fate the gentle and enthusiastic sex; he was but twenty-four years of age, and according to one who served with him, "was fine looking, with a dignified and manly deportment, and a soft, pleasing voice, being wherever he went a favorite among the ladies." He appealed to Mrs. Harvey for assistance, and she promised at his solicitation to aid him and two other Kentuckian prisoners in their escape, and to procure them rifles and ammunition, which were indispensable on a journey through the wilderness. It was not long before she found opportunity to execute her benevolent design. A large concourse of Indians was assembled at Detroit, in western parlance, " to take a spree ;" and before indulging in their potations, several stacked their guns near Mrs. Harvey's house. As soon as it was

dark, she stole noiselessly out, selected three of the best
looking, hid them quickly in her garden in a patch of peas,
and, careful to avoid observation, hastened to Kenton's
lodgings, to inform him of her success.   Her directions
were, that he should come at midnight to the back of
the garden, where he would find a ladder, by means of
which he could climb the fence and get the guns.   She
had previously collected such articles of ammunition,
food and clothing, as would be necessary in their journey,
and with Kenton's knowledge had hid them in a hollow
tree some distance from the town.   No time was lost
by the prisoners in their secret preparations for flight.
At the hour appointed, they came to the end of the
garden; the ladder was there, and Kenton climbing over,
saw Mrs. Harvey already waiting for him, seated by
the place where she had concealed the guns.   No
woman ever appeared half so beautiful in the eyes of
the grateful young hunter.   His thanks were expressed
with the eloquence of true feeling; but she would not
suffer the fugitives to waste a moment; the night was
far advanced, the shoutings of the Indians, in their
drunken revelry, could be heard all around them; a few
hours would reveal their escape and the loss of the guns,
and instant pursuit would be made.   She bade him
make haste to be gone; and with a brief farewell Kenton
joined his companions, with whom, hastening from the
city, he travelled towards the prairies of the Wabash.
He never ceased to remember and acknowledge, in
language glowing with gratitude and admiration, the
kindness of the trader's wife; but when the lapse of

half a century had changed the aspect of the whole country, still delighted to dwell on this adventure, saying that he had seen her a thousand times in his reveries as he had last beheld her—"sitting by the guns in the garden."

The presence of mind, and cool deliberate courage of Mrs. Daviess, of Lincoln County, brought about the deliverance of herself and family from the savages. Early one morning, her husband having left the house for a few moments, four Indians rushed into the room where she was still in bed with her children. They ordered her, by signs, to rise immediately ; and one of them inquired how far it was to the next house. She instantly comprehended that it was important to make the distance appear as great as possible, for the purpose of detaining them at the house till her husband, who had evidently taken the alarm, should have time to bring assistance. Counting on her fingers, she made them understand that it was eight miles. She then rose and dressed herself ; after which she showed the savages various articles of clothing one after another—their pleased examination delaying them nearly two hours. Another Indian, who had been in pursuit of her husband, now entered the house, and holding up in her sight his hands stained with pokeberry juice, at the same time using violent gestures and brandishing his tomahawk, endeavored to persuade her that the fugitive had been slain. Her quick eye, however, at once discovered the deception, and she rejoiced in the evidence that her husband had escaped uninjured.

The house was now plundered of every thing that could be carried away, and the savages set out, taking with them Mrs. Daviess and all her children as prisoners. The mother's care was in requisition to provide for their safety, and she was obliged to make the two oldest carry the younger ones, for well she knew that death would be the penalty of any failure of strength or speed. The Indians watched them closely, that no twigs nor weeds were broken off, as they passed along, which might serve to mark the course they had taken. Even the length of Mrs. Daviess' dress interfering, as they thought, with their movements, one of them drew his knife and cut off some inches of it.

Meanwhile this courageous woman was revolving projects for accomplishing a deliverance. She determined at length, if not rescued in the course of the day, to make a desperate attempt at night, when the Indians should be asleep, by possessing herself of their arms, killing as many as she could, and inducing the belief of a night attack to frighten the others. To such extremity was female resolution driven in those times. Those who knew Mrs. Daviess entertained little doubt that her enterprise would have succeeded; but she was prevented from the perilous attempt—being overtaken and rescued by nine o'clock, by her husband and a party of friends.

Another act of courage displayed by Mrs. Daviess, strikingly illustrates her character. A marauder who had committed extensive depredations on the property of Mr. Daviess and his neighbors, was pursued by them with the purpose of bringing him to justice. During the pursuit, not aware that they were on his track, he came to the house, armed with gun and tomahawk, to obtain refreshment, and found Mrs. Daviess alone with her children. She placed a bottle of whiskey on the table, and requested him to help himself. While he was drinking, she went to the door, took his gun, which he had set there on his entrance, and placing herself in the doorway, cocked the weapon and levelled it at him. He started up, but she ordered him, on pain of instant death, to sit down, and remain quiet. The terrified intruder asked what he had done; she replied that he had stolen her husband's property, that he was her prisoner, and she meant to stand guard over him. She kept him thus, not daring to make the slightest movement towards escape, till her husband and his party returned and took him into custody.

The wife of Joseph Russell, who, with her children, was taken captive, had the presence of mind, when on their march, to leave signs which might show the direction they had taken, by occasionally breaking off a twig and scattering along their route pieces of a white handkerchief which she had torn in fragments; so that General Logan's party found no difficulty in the pursuit. At the house of Mr. Woods, near the Crab orchard in Lincoln County, a singular adventure occurred. He had gone one morning to the station, not expecting to return till night, and leaving his family, which consisted only of his wife, a young daughter, and a lame negro man. Mrs. Woods was at a short distance from her

cabin, when she saw several Indians approaching it.
Screaming loudly to give the alarm, she ran to reach
the house before them, and succeeded; but before she
could close the door, one of the savages had pushed his
way into the house. He was instantly grappled with
by the negro, a scuffle ensued, and both fell on the
floor, the black man underneath. Mrs. Woods could
render no assistance, having to exert all her strength in
keeping the door closed against the party without; but
the lame domestic, holding the Indian tightly in his
arms, called to the young girl to take the axe from
under the bed and despatch him by a blow on the head.
Self-preservation demanded instant obedience, and after
an ineffectual blow, the Indian was killed. The negro
then proposed to his mistress to let in another of those
still trying to force open the door, and dispose of him
in the same manner; but the experiment was thought
too dangerous. Shortly after, some men from the
station discovered the situation of the family, and soon
scattered the besiegers.

It was at the Blue Lick Springs, the most noted
watering place in the west, that the bloody battle was
fought with the Indians which shrouded Kentucky in
mourning, and is only less famous than Braddock's defeat, in the annals of savage warfare. A romantic incident is related as having occurred after that fatal
action.* Among the unfortunate captives who had
survived the ordeal of the gauntlet, and had been paint-

* Judge Robertson's Address on the Fourth of July, at Camp Madi-
son, in 1843.

ed black by the savages, as devoted to torture and death,
was an excellent husband and father. By some unac-
countable freak of clemency, his life was spared when
all his fellow prisoners were butchered. For about a
year his friends believed him numbered with the slain of
that disastrous day. His wife was wooed by another;
but continued to hope against hope that he yet lived
and would return to her. Persuaded, at length, through
the expostulations of others, that her affectionate instinct
was a delusion, she reluctantly yielded a consent to the
second nuptials, which, however, she postponed several
times, declaring that she found it impossible to divest
herself of the belief that her husband lived. Again she
submitted to the judgment of friends, and the day of her
marriage was appointed. Just before the dawn of that
day, when we may suppose her wakeful from reflection,
the crack of a rifle was heard near her lonely cabin.
Startled by the familiar sound, she leaped out "like a
liberated fawn," exclaiming as she sprang towards the
door, "That's John's gun!" and in an instant was
clasped in the arms of her lost husband. In poetical
justice to the disappointed suitor, it should perhaps be
mentioned, that nine years afterwards the same husband
was killed at "St. Clair's defeat"—and that in proper
time he obtained the hand of the fair widow. The
scene of this occurrence was in Garrard County,
Kentucky.

An incident that occurred at a fort on Green River,
shows the magnanimity which the dangers besetting the
emigrants of that period often gave opportunity to exer-

cise. Several young persons belonging to the fort were
pulling flax in one of the distant fields. They were
joined by two of their mothers, the younger carrying
an infant. The whole party was attacked by some Indians, who rushed from the woods, and pursued them
towards the fort, yelling and firing upon them. The
elder of the two mothers, recollecting in her flight that
the younger, a small and feeble woman, was encumbered with her child, turned back in the face of the enemy,
who were still firing, and rending the air with hideous
yells, snatched the babe from its almost exhausted
mother, and ran with it to the fort. She was twice shot
at when the foe was near, and one arrow passed through
her sleeve; but she escaped without injury.

The attack on the house of John Merrill, in Nelson
County, Kentucky, is related differently in some particulars by different authorities; but they agree in citing it
as a remarkable instance of female heroism.* Merrill
was alarmed at midnight by the barking of the dog, and
on opening the door, was fired upon by several Indians.
He fell back wounded, and the door was instantly closed
by his wife, who, an Amazon in strength and courage,
stood on guard with an axe, and killed or wounded
four as they attempted to enter through a breach.
They then climbed to the roof to come down the chimney. She hastily ripped a feather-bed, and threw it on
the fire. The blaze and smoke brought down two Indians, whom she despatched, while she wounded the cheek

* Drake's Book of the Indians. McClung's Sketches of Western
Adventure, etc.

12*

of another who meanwhile assailed the door.   He fled
with a loud yell; and afterwards at Chillicothe gave an
exaggerated account of the strength and fierceness of
the "long knife squaw."

XLVIII.

~~~~~~~

ELIZABETH ZANE.

THE name of Elizabeth Zane is inseparably associated with the history of one of the most memorable incidents in the annals of border warfare. The most reliable account of it is that prepared by Mr. Kiernan for the "American Pioneer," a Cincinnati journal devoted to sketches relative to the early settlement of the country. In this a full history is given of the establishment of Fort Fincastle—afterwards called Fort Henry, in honor of Patrick Henry—under the superintendence of Ebenezer Zane and John Caldwell.

This fort stood on the left bank of the Ohio, a little above the mouth of Wheeling Creek, and near the foot of a hill that rose abruptly from the inner margin of the bottom land. Of this land, the portion next the river was cleared, fenced, and planted with corn. Between the fort and the base of the hill, the forest had also been cleared away, and there stood some twenty or thirty log houses; a rude village, which, though of little importance then, was the germ of one of the fairest cities that now grace the domain of Virginia. The fort covered about three quarters of an acre of ground,

and had a block house at each corner, with lines of
stout pickets about eight feet high, extending from one
to the other.   Within the enclosure were a number of
cabins for the use of families, and the principal entrance
was through a gateway on the side next to the straggling
village.

In May and June, 1777, a number of savage forays
upon the settlements took place, and as the season
advanced, these depredations became more bold and
frequent. So imminent was the danger, that the people
threw aside their private pursuits; the troops were
constantly in service, and civil jurisdiction gave place
for months to martial law throughout the country. In
September it was ascertained that a large Indian force
was concentrating on the Sandusky River, under the
direction of the notorious white renegade and tory,
Simeon Girty. This savage host, numbering, according
to various estimates, from three hundred and eighty to
five hundred warriors, having completed the preparations
for their campaign, took up their line of march in the
direction of Limestone, Kentucky; and were brought
by their leader before the walls of Fort Henry, before
the scouts employed by Colonel Shepherd were able to
discover his real design.

They were made aware of this in the night by seeing
the smoke caused by the burning of a block-house
twelve miles below; and the inhabitants of the village
and several families in the neighborhood betook themselves to the fort for safety. At break of day, a man
despatched to bring in some horses having been killed,

a party of fourteen was sent to dislodge the savages from a corn-field near the fort. They found themselves unexpectedly and furiously assailed by the whole of Girty's army, and but two survived the skirmish. Others who had pressed to their relief, fell into an ambuscade, and two thirds of their number perished. The Indians then advanced with loud whoops to take their position before the fort. The garrison, which had at first numbered forty-two fighting men, was now reduced to twelve, including boys. Girty, having posted his forces, appeared with a white flag, and demanded their surrender in the name of His Britannic Majesty; but Colonel Shepherd promptly replied that he should only obtain possession of the fort when there remained no longer an American soldier to defend it. The little band had a sacred charge to protect; their mothers, sisters, wives and children were assembled around them, and they resolved to fight to the last extremity, trusting in Heaven for a successful issue.

For many hours, after the opening of the siege, the firing of the Indians, eager for butchery, was met by a sure and well-directed fire from the garrison, which was composed of excellent marksmen. But the stock of gunpowder in the fort was nearly exhausted! A favorable opportunity was offered by the temporary suspension of hostilities, to procure a keg of powder known to be in the house of Ebenezer Zane, about sixty yards from the gate. The commandant explained the matter to his men, and, unwilling to order any one upon an enterprise so desperate, asked who would volunteer for the perilous service. The person going and coming would necessarily be exposed to the danger of being shot down by the Indians; yet three or four young men promptly offered to undertake it. The Colonel answered that only one man could be spared, and left it to them to decide who it should be. While they disputed—every moment of time being precious, from the danger of a renewal of the attack before the powder could be procured—the interposition of a young girl put an end to their generous contention. Elizabeth, the sister of Ebenezer and Silas Zane, came forward, and requested that she might be permitted to go for the powder. Her proposition at first met with a peremptory refusal; but she renewed her petition with steadfast earnestness; nor would she be dissuaded from her heroic purpose by the remonstrances of the commandant and her anxious relatives. Either of the young men, it was represented, would be more likely than herself to perform the task successfully, by reason of greater familiarity with danger, and swiftness in running. Her answer was—that her knowledge of the danger attending the undertaking was her reason for offering to perform the service; *her* loss would not be felt, while not a single soldier could be spared from the already weakened garrison. This argument prevailed; her request was granted; and when she had divested herself of such portions of clothing as might impede her speed, the gate was opened for her to pass out.

The opening of the gate arrested the attention of several Indians straggling through the village, and it could be seen from the fort that the eyes of the savages were upon Elizabeth as she crossed the open space— walking as rapidly as possible, to reach her brother's house. But probably deeming a woman's life not worth the trouble of taking, or influenced by some sudden freak of clemency, they permitted her to pass without molestation.

In a few moments she re-appeared, carrying the powder in her arms, and walked at her utmost speed towards the gate. One account says the powder was tied in a table-cloth, and fastened round her waist. The Indians doubtless suspected, this time, the nature of her burden; they raised their firelocks, and discharged a leaden storm at her as she went on; but the balls whistled past her harmless—and the intrepid girl reached the fort in safety with her prize.

The story of this siege has been preserved in the collections of Virginia as the most important event in the history of Wheeling, and is enumerated among the battles of the Revolution. The brothers Silas and Ebenezer Zane received honor for having contributed to its final success; nor did the courageous conduct of the women pass unacknowledged. The wife of Ebenezer, and others, undismayed by the bloody strife going on, employed themselves in running bullets and preparing patches for the use of the garrison, and by their presence at every point where they could perform useful service, and their cheering encouragement of their defenders, inspired the soldiers with new energy for desperate resistance. The noble act of Elizabeth, in particular, caused an enthusiasm which contributed to sustain their courage when fate seemed against them—till the arrival of relief.

Elizabeth had but recently returned from school in Philadelphia, and was totally unused to such scenes as were daily exhibited on the frontier. She married twice, and afterwards lived in Ohio with Mr. Clarke, her last husband.* An Ohio newspaper states that she has raised a family of children, and was living, a short time since, near St. Clairsville.

Withers.

XLIX.

MARGARET MORRIS.

A JOURNAL—which has never been published, but of which a few copies were printed for private circulation many years since—kept during the Revolutionary war for the amusement of a sister, by Margaret Morris, of Burlington, New Jersey, presents a picture of the daily alarms to which a private family was liable, and of the persecution to which obnoxious individuals were subjected. The writer was a patriot in principle and feeling, but sympathized with the distresses she witnessed on both sides. She had, however, no liking for war—being a member of the Society of Friends. Her maiden name was Hill. Her father, Richard Hill, had been engaged in the wine trade, and lived long with his family on the island of Madeira; her brother, Henry, accumulated a large fortune in the same business, and died of the yellow fever in Philadelphia. Margaret was eminently pious, and cheerful through many years of illness and suffering. In this character she is best remembered by her grandchildren and connections, among whom she was greatly beloved and venerated for her example of Christian benevolence and humble

reliance on Providence in every trial. She was left a
widow early in life, and died at the age of seventy-nine,
at Burlington, in 1816. The sister for whom the
journal was written was Milcah Martha Moore, the
wife of Dr. Charles Moore, of Philadelphia.

The following extracts are from the "Journal."
DECEMBER 16th, 1776 :

"About noon this day, a very terrible account of
thousands coming into town, and now actually to be seen
off Gallows Hill—my incautious son caught up the spy-
glass, and was running towards the mill to look at them.
I told him it would be liable to misconstruction, but he
prevailed on me to allow him to gratify his curiosity.
He went, but returned much dissatisfied, for no troops
could he see. As he came back, poor Dick took the
glass, and resting it against a tree, took a view of the
fleet. Both were observed by the people on board, who
snspected it was an enemy who was watching their
motions. They manned a boat and sent her on shore.

"A loud knocking at my door brought me to it. I was
a little fluttered, and kept locking and unlocking that I
might get my ruffled face a little composed. At last I
opened it, and half a dozen men, all armed, demanded
the key of the empty house. I asked what they wanted
there; they replied—' To search for a d—d tory who
had been spying at them from the mill.''

"The name of a *tory*, so near my own door, seriously
alarmed me; for a poor refugee, dignified by that name,
had claimed the shelter of my roof, and was at that
very time concealed, like a thief in an augerhole. I

rang the bell violently—the signal agreed upon if they came to search ; and when I thought he had crept into the hole, I put on a very simple look and exclaimed— 'Bless me ! I hope you are not Hessians !'

"'Do we look like Hessians?' asked one rudely.

"'Indeed, I don't know.'

"'Did you never see a Hessian?'

"'No—never in my life ; but they are *men ;* and you are men ; and may be Hessians for aught I know ! But I'll go with you into Colonel Cox's house ; though indeed it was my son at the mill ; he is but a boy, and meant no harm ; he wanted to see the troops.'

"So I marched at the head of them, opened the door, and searched every place ; but we could not find the tory. Strange where he could be ! We returned— they greatly disappointed ; I pleased to think my house was not suspected. The Captain, a smart little fellow named Shippen, said he wished they could see the spyglass. So Dick produced it, and very civilly desired his acceptance of it ; which I was sorry for, as I often amused myself looking through it.

" They left us and searched James Verree's and the two next houses ; but no tory could they find. This transaction reached the town, and Colonel Cox was very angry and ordered the men on board. In the evening I went to town with my refugee, and placed him in other lodgings. I was told to-day of a design to seize upon a young man in town, as he was esteemed a tory. I thought a hint would be kindly received ; and as I came back, called upon a friend of his, and told him. Next day he was out of reach of the gondolas."

"DEC. 17th. More news! great news! very great news! (J. V.'s). The British troops actually at Mount Holly! guards of militia placed at London and York bridges—gondola-men in arms patrolling the street, and diligent search making for fire-arms, ammunition, and tories—another attempt last night to enter into R. Smith's house. Early this morning, J. V. sent in, to beg I would let my son go a few miles out of town on some business for him. I consented, not knowing of the formidable doings up town; when I heard of it I felt a mother's pangs for her son all the day; but when night came, and he did not appear, I made no doubt of his being taken by the Hessians. A friend made my mind easy, by telling me he had passed through the town where the dreadful Hessians were said to be 'playing the very mischief,' (J. V. again); it is certain there were numbers of them at Mount Holly, but they behaved very civilly to the people, excepting only a few persons who were actually in rebellion, as they termed it, whose goods, etc., they injured.

"This evening every gondola-man sent on board with strict orders not to set a foot on the Jersey shore again —so far, so good."

"DEC. 27th. This evening about three thousand of the Pennsylvania militia and other troops landed in the Neck, and marched into town with artillery, baggage, etc., and are quartered on the inhabitants.

" An officer spent the evening with us, and appeared to be in high spirits, and talked of engaging the English as a very trifling affair—nothing so easy as to drive them over the North River, etc.; not considering that there is a God of battle as well as a God of peace, who may have given them the late advantage, in order to draw them out to meet the chastisement that is reserved for them."

" DEC. 29th. This morning the soldiers at the next house prepared to depart; and as they passed my door, they stopped to bless and thank me for the food I sent them. I received it not as my due, but as belonging to my *Master*, who had reached a morsel to them by my hand."

The journal continues, at a later period—

" JUNE 14th, 1777. By a person from Bordentown, we hear twelve expresses came in there to-day from camp. Some of the gondola-men and their wives being sick, and no doctor in town to apply to, they were told Mrs. Morris was a skillful woman, and kept medicines to give to the poor; and notwithstanding their late attempts to shoot my poor boy, they ventured to come to me, and in a very humble manner begged me to come and do something for them. At first I thought they might design to put a trick on me, get me aboard their gondola, and then pillage my house, as they had done some others; but on asking where the sick folks were, I was told they were lodged in the Governor's house. So I went to see them; there were several, both men and women, very ill with a fever; some said, the camp or putrid fever. They were broke out in blotches; and on close examination, it appeared to be the itch fever. I treated them according to art, and they all got well. I thought I had received all my pay when they thankfully acknowledged my kindness; but lo! in a short time afterwards a very rough ill-looking man came to the door and asked for me. When I went to him he drew me aside, and asked if I had any friends in Philadelphia. The question alarmed me, supposing there was some mischief meditated against that poor city; however, I calmly said—'I have an ancient father, some sisters, and other near friends there.'

" 'Well,' said the man, 'do you wish to hear from them, or send any thing by way of refreshment to them? If you do, I will take charge of it, and bring you back any thing you may send for.'

"I was very much surprised, and thought, to be sure, he only wanted to get provisions to take to the gondolas; but when he told me his wife was one of those I had given medicine to, and this was the only thing he could do to pay me for my kindness, my heart leaped with joy, and I set about preparing something for my dear absent friends. A quarter of beef, some veal, fowls and flour, were soon put up; and about midnight the man called and took them aboard his boat. He left them at Robert Hopkins'—at the Point—whence my beloved friends took them to town.

"Two nights afterwards, a loud knocking at our front door greatly alarmed us, and opening the chamber window, we heard a man's voice, saying, 'Come down softly and open the door, but bring no light.'

"There was something mysterious in such a call; but we concluded to go down and set the candle in the kitchen.

"When we got to the front door, we asked, 'Who are you?'

"The man replied, 'A friend; open quickly.' So the door was opened; and who should it be but our honest gondola-man, with a letter, a bushel of salt, a jug of molasses, a bag of rice, some tea, coffee, and sugar, and some cloth for a coat for my poor boys; all sent by my kind sisters!

"How did our hearts and eyes overflow with love to them, and thanks to our Heavenly Father, for such seasonable supplies! May we never forget it! Being now so rich, we thought it our duty to hand out a little to the poor around us, who were mourning for want of salt; so we divided the bushel, and gave a pint to every poor person who came for it—having abundance left for our own use. Indeed, it seemed to us as if our little store was increased by distribution, like the bread broken by our Saviour to the multitude."

L.

~~~~~~~~~

MISCELLANEOUS ANECDOTES.

MANY incidents and scenes of Revolutionary times
are remembered, of the actors in which little is known
beyond what is contained in the anecdotes themselves.
A few of these are subjoined as aiding our general
object of illustrating the spirit and character of the
women of those days. Fragmentary as they are—they
have some interest in this light, and it seems a duty to
preserve them as historical facts, which may possibly
prove of service in future inquiries.

~~~~~~~~~~~~

THE county of Sussex in New Jersey, was noted for
its number of tories. A party of them one night attacked and broke into the house of Mr. Maxwell, the
father of General William Maxwell. Their first assault
was upon the old man, who was eighty years of age ; and
having felled him with repeated blows, so that his skull
was fractured, they left him for dead, and proceeded to
plunder the house. Mrs. Maxwell was compelled to
direct them to the place where her husband's money
was kept, and to send a female domestic to show them

the way. They had determined, when their work should be finished, to make an attack on the house of Captain John Maxwell—the General's brother, who lived about a mile distant, and whom they supposed to have in his possession a large sum of money, he being commissary in the army. But their design of obtaining the spoil was frustrated by the timely information given by the negroes, who, escaping from the old gentleman's house, gave warning to the family of the young officer. John afterwards arrested one of the robbers in the neighborhood, before he had time to change his bloody garments. The others succeeded in effecting their escape.

Some British officers quartered themselves at the house of MRS. DISSOSWAY, situated at the western end of Staten Island, opposite Amboy. Her husband was a prisoner; but her brother, Captain Nat. Randolph, who was in the American army, gave much annoyance to the tories by his frequent incursions. A tory colonel once promised Mrs. Dissosway to procure the release of her husband, on condition of her prevailing upon her brother to stay quietly at home. "And if I could," she replied, with a look of scorn, and drawing up her tall figure to its utmost height, "if I could act so dastardly a part, *think you that General Washington has but one Captain Randolph in his army?*"

The cattle and horses of many of the whig residents on Staten Island having been driven away by the loy-

13

alists—they had no means of attending divine worship. After the establishment of Independence, one winter's day, when several families of those who had suffered during the war, were returning in their sleighs from "meeting," the word was given by Mr. Dissosway to stop before the house of a tory captain. He gave a loud thump with the handle of his whip at the door, and when the captain appeared, said—"I called, sir, to inform you that 'the rebels' have been to church; it is their turn, now, to give thanks!" He then returned to his sleigh and drove on.

AMONG the noble spirits whose heroism has never been known beyond the circle of their personal acquaintance, was Mrs. Jackson, who resided on a farm upon Staten Island. The island, as is known, was a "nest of tories;" and it was thought proper to banish her husband, on account of his zeal in the cause of his country, although he had not joined the army. He was nine months confined in the Provost, and the remainder of two years was on his parole on Long Island and in the vicinity. During his absence the house was for a great part of the time the abode of British officers and soldiers, who made themselves quite at home in the use of every thing. On one occasion a soldier, carrying through the house a tin pail, used for milking, was asked by the mistress what he meant to do with it. "My master wants to bathe his feet," was the insolent reply. "Carry it instantly back," said the resolute lady, authorita-

tively; "not for your master's master shall you touch
what you have no business with!" By the exhibition
of such firmness and spirit she saved herself much
inconvenience.

This lady was in the habit of sending provisions from
time to time, to the American army on the opposite
shore. This she was obliged to do with the utmost
secrecy; and many a time would she set going the
mill which belonged to her husband—to allow the black
man she employed to cross the water unsuspected by
the watchful enemy. At one time having a calf which
she was anxious to send to the suffering American soldiers, she kept it concealed all day under her bed, having muzzled it to prevent its cries.* She sometimes
came to New York, with friends, to visit prisoners in
the Provost. They were received on such occasions at
Whitehall by a gentleman, who, though of whig principles, had been permitted to remain in the city—the
father of one whose genius has rendered his name illustrious. He was in the habit of accompanying the ladies
to the prison, and directed them, when they wished to
convey money to the captives, to drop it silently as they
went past, while he would walk just behind, so as to
screen them from the observation of the stern provost-
marshal.

On one occasion, Mrs. Jackson received intelligence
that one of the American generals was coming to her
house in the night, to surprise and capture the enemy
quartered there. She gave no information to her guests

* These facts were given the writer by the daughter of Mrs. Jackson.

of what awaited them, till there was reason to believe the whig force was just at hand. Then, unwilling to have her house made the scene of a bloody contest, she knocked at each of the doors, crying out, "Run, gentlemen, run! or you are all prisoners!" They waited for no second bidding, and made their escape. Mrs. Jackson used afterwards to give a ludicrous description of their running off—each man with his boots and clothes in his hands.

Mr. Jackson's house was robbed after his return home. A knock was heard at the door one night, and on opening it he felt a pistol pressed against his breast, while a gruff voice bade him be silent, on pain of instant death. His little daughter uttered a terrified scream, and received a violent blow on the forehead with the pistol from the ruffian, which stretched her upon the floor. The house was then stripped of all that could be taken away; and the path of the villains might have been traced next morning by the articles dropped as they carried off the plunder. The family believed this to have been done by tories, whom they found at all times much more cruel and rapacious than the British soldiers.

MARY BOWEN, the sister of Jabez Bowen, Lieutenant Governor of Rhode Island, was celebrated for her charitable efforts in behalf of those who suffered in the war. Through her influence and exertions a petition was addressed to the commandant at Providence for the lives of two soldiers—brothers—who had been com-demned as deserters. The petition was successful, and the reprieve was read when the prisoners were on the scaffold. Miss Bowen was active in collecting charita-ble contributions for clothing for the army, and assisted in making up the material, exerting herself to interest others in the same good work. General La Fayette was one of her visitors, and maintained a correspon-dence with her. Her information was extensive, her manners gentle and pleasing; and she had the respect and affection of all who knew her. Her brother, who resided at Providence, was in the habit of entertaining persons of high distinction. Rochambeau occupied part of his house during his stay in the town.

A GENTLEMAN residing in Charlottesville, to whom application was made for personal recollections of the Baroness de Riedesel, mentions the following instance of female patriotism.

At the time that Tarleton with his corps of cavalry was making a secret and forced march to surprise and capture the Governor and Legislature of Virginia—the latter then holding its session in Charlottesville—several of the members chanced to be at the house of Colonel John Walker, distant some twelve miles from the town. This was directly on the route; and the first intimation the family had of the enemy's approach, was the appear-ance of Tarleton's legion at their doors. Colonel Walker was at the time on service with the troops in

Lower Virginia. Having made prisoners of one or two members of the Legislature, Colonel Tarleton ordered breakfast for himself and his officers and men. Mrs. Walker, who was a staunch whig, knew well that the design of her unwelcome guest was to proceed to Charlottesville, and plunder and destroy the public stores there collected. She delayed as long as possible the preparations for breakfast, for the purpose of enabling the members who had escaped to reach the town, and to remove and secrete such portions of the stores as could be saved. Her patriotic stratagem gained time for this. Tarleton remained but a day or two at Charlottesville, and then hurried back to join the main army under Cornwallis.

Of the same kind was the service rendered by Mrs. Murray, which Thacher has acknowledged in his Journal.

On the retreat from New York, Major General Putnam with his troops, was the last to leave the city. To avoid any parties of the enemy that might be advancing towards it, he made choice of a road along the river, from which, at a certain point, another road would conduct him in a direction to join the American army. It happened that a force of British and Hessians more than twice as large as his own, was advancing on the road at the same time, and but for a fortunate occurrence, would have encountered that of General Putnam, before he could have reached the turn into the other road. In ignorance that an enemy was before them, the British officers halted their troops, and stopped at the house of Robert Murray, a Quaker, and friend to the whig cause. Mrs. Murray treated them with cake and wine, and by means of her refreshments and agreeable conversation, beguiled them to stay a couple of hours—Governor Tryon jesting with her occasionally about her American friends. She might have turned the laugh upon him; for one half hour, it is said, would have enabled the British to secure the road at the turn, and cut off Putnam's retreat. The opportunity was lost—and it became a common saying among the officers, that Mrs. Murray had saved this part of the American army.

THE following record of an instance of female patriotism has appeared in several of the journals. It is relied upon as fact by the friends of the family who reside in the neighborhood where the occurrence took place, and there is no reason to doubt its authenticity. A grand-nephew of the heroine is living near Columbia, South Carolina.

"At the time General Greene retreated before Lord Rawdon from Ninety-Six, when he had passed Broad River, he was very desirous to send an order to General Sumter, then on the Wateree, to join him, that they might attack Rawdon, who had divided his force. But the country to be passed through was for many miles full of blood-thirsty tories, and it was a difficult matter to find a man willing to undertake so dangerous a mission. At length a young girl—Emily Geiger, presented herself to General Greene proposing to act as his messenger; and the General, both surprised and delighted, closed with her proposal. He accordingly wrote a letter and gave it to her, at the same time communicating the contents verbally, to be told to Sumter in case of accident. Emily was young, but as to her person or adventures on the way, we have no further information, except that she was mounted on horseback, upon a side-saddle, and on the second day of her journey was intercepted by **Lord Rawdon**'s scouts. Coming from the direction of Greene's army, and not being able to tell an untruth without blushing, she was shut up; and the officer in command having the modesty not to search her at the time, he sent for an old tory matron as more fitting for the purpose. Emily was not wanting in expedients, and as soon as the door was closed, she ate up the letter, piece by piece. After a while the matron arrived. Upon searching carefully, nothing was to be found of a suspicious nature about the prisoner, and she would disclose nothing. Suspicion being thus allayed, the officer commanding the scouts suffered Emily to depart whither she said she was bound. She took a route somewhat circuitous to avoid further detection, and soon after struck into the road to Sumter's camp, where she arrived in safety. She told her adventure, and delivered Greene's verbal message to Sumter, who in consequence soon after joined the main army at Orangeburg. Emily Geiger afterwards married a rich planter on the Congaree. She has been dead thirty-five years, but it is trusted her name will descend to posterity among those of the patriotic females of the Revolution."

~~~~~~~~~~~~~~~~~~~~~

It is said that the first Governor Griswold, of Connecticut, was once indebted to a happy thought of his wife for his escape from the British, to whom he was extremely obnoxious. He was at home, but expected to set out immediately for Hartford, to meet the legislature, which had commenced its session a day or two previous. The family residence was at Blackhall, opposite Saybrook Point, and situated on the point of land formed by Connecticut River on the east, and Long Island Sound on the south. British ships were lying in the Sound; and as the Governor was known to be at this time in his own mansion, a boat was secretly sent on shore for the purpose of securing his person. Without previous warning, the family were alarmed by seeing a file of marines coming up from the beach to the house. There was no time for flight. Mrs. Griswold bethought herself of a large meat barrel, or tierce, which had been brought in a day or two before and was not yet filled. Quick as thought, she decided that the Governor's proportions—which were by no means slight—must be compressed into this, the only available hiding place. He was obliged to submit to be stowed in the cask and covered. The process occupied but a few moments, and the soldiers presently entered. Mrs. Griswold was of course innocent of all knowledge of her husband's whereabouts, though she told them she well knew the legislature was in session, and that business required his presence at the capital. The house and cellar having been searched without success, the soldiers departed. By the time their boat reached the ship, the Governor on his powerful horse was galloping up the road on his way to Hartford.* Blackhall, in Lyme, Connecticut, is still the residence of the Griswolds.

~~~~~~~~~~~~~~

A MAN named Hubbs, who had served with the bloody tory and renegade Cunningham in South Carolina, was an "outlier" during the war. At one time he proposed, with two confederates, to rob an old man of Quaker habits—Israel Gaunt—who was reputed to be in the possession of money. The three rode up one evening to the house and asked lodging, which was refused. Hubbs rode to the kitchen door—in which Mrs. Gaunt was standing, and asked for water. He sprang in while she turned to get the water, and as she handed it to him she saw his arms. Her husband, informed of this, secured the doors. Hubbs presented his pistol at him; but his deadly purpose was frustrated by the old man's daughter, Hannah. She threw up the weapon, and, being of masculine proportions and strength, grappled with, and threw him on the floor, where she held him, though wounded by his spurs—in spite of his desperate struggles—till he was disabled by

* This traditional anecdote is communicated by a relative of the family, who believe it entirely authentic.

her father's blows. Gaunt was wounded through the window by Hubbs' companions, and another ball grazed his heroic daughter just above the eye; but both escaped without further injury. Hannah afterwards married a man named Mooney. The gentleman who relates the foregoing incident* has often seen her, and describes her as one of the kindest and most benevolent of women. She died about the age of fifty, and her grandson, a worthy and excellent man, is now living in the village of Newberry.

The same company of marauders, with Moultrie, another of Cunningham's gang, visited Andrew Lee's house, at Lee's Ferry, Saluda River, for the purpose of plunder. Moultrie succeeded in effecting an entrance into the house. Lee seized and held him, and they fell together on a bed; when he called to his wife, Nancy, to strike him on the head with an axe. Her first blow, in her agitation, fell on her husband's hand; but she repeated it, and stunned Moultrie, who fell on the floor insensible. Lee, with his negroes and dogs, then drove away the other robbers, and on his return secured Moultrie, who was afterwards hanged in Ninety-Six.

In the collections of the Maine Historical Society is an account of the exertions of the O'Brien family. The

* The Hon. Judge O'Neall of South Carolina. He gives this incident and that of Mrs. Lee's exploit, in his " Random Recollections of Revolutionary Characters and Incidents," published in the Southern Literary Journal, 1838, pp. 104, 105.

wife of one of a party who left Pleasant River settlement, on an expedition, found a horn of powder after
their departure, and knowing their want of it, followed
them twenty miles through the woods—for there were
no roads—to bring it to her husband.   Hazard's Register* gives a notice of Margaret Durham, one of the
early settlers of a portion of Pennsylvania, who shared
largely in the toils and dangers of the war.   When the
thinly-scattered population fled before the savages, she
was overtaken, scalped, and left for dead; but recovered
to be an example of Christian faith and virtue.   The
daughter of a miller in Queens County defended her
father from his brutal assailants at the risk of her life,
when men who witnessed the cruelty dared offer no
assistance.   "The death bed of Mercer was attended
by two females of the Society of Friends, who, like
messengers from heaven, smoothed his pillow, and
cheered his declining hours.   They inhabited the house
to which he was carried, and refusing to fly during the
battle, were there when he was brought, wounded and
dying, to the threshold."

When the wife of General Woodhull, who perished
under the inhuman treatment he received at the hands
of his captors, reached his bed-side, it was only in time
to receive his last sigh.   She distributed the wagon-load
of provisions she had brought, for the relief of the
other American prisoners.†   Rebecca Knapp, who died
recently in Baltimore, was one of those who relieved the

* Vol. IV., page 192.

† Revolutionary Incidents of Queens County, by H. Onderdonk, Jr.

American prisoners in Philadelphia, by carrying them provisions from her own table. Others were associated in the same good work in New York. Mary Elmendorf, who lived in Kingston, Ulster County, studied medicine, that, in the absence of the physicians, who were obliged to be with the army, she might render assistance to the poor around her. Mrs. Speakman, of Philadelphia, daily visited the soldiers who were brought into the city ill of the camp fever, and placed in empty houses—carrying food and medicines, and ministering to their wants. Eleven in one house were restored through her kind attentions.

The journal of Rev. Thomas Andross, who escaped from a prison ship through Long Island, alludes frequently to female kindness and assistance. These prison ships were indeed store houses of pestilence and misery. A large transport—the Whitby—was the first anchored in the Wallabout; she was moored October 20th, 1776, and crowded with American prisoners, whom disease, bad provisions, and deprivation of air and light, soon reduced to a pitiable condition. The sand-beach and ravine near were filled with graves, "scratched along the sandy shore." One of these ships of death was burned the following year—fired, it is said, by the sufferers, who were driven to desperation.* Mr. Andross thus describes the old Jersey, in which he was a prisoner : " Her dark and filthy exterior corresponded with the death and despair reigning within. It is supposed that eleven thousand American seamen perished in her. None came to relieve

* Thompson's History of Long Island

their woes. Once or twice, by order of a stranger on the quarter-deck, a bag of apples was hurled promiscuously into the midst of hundreds of prisoners, crowded as thick as they could stand—and life and limbs were endangered in the struggle. The prisoners were secured between the decks by iron gratings ; and when the ship was to be cleared of water, an armed guard forced them up to the winches, amid a roar of execrations and reproaches—the dim light adding to the horrors of the scene. Thousands died whose names have never been known ; perishing when no eye could witness their fortitude, nor praise their devotion to their country."

A VERY interesting account is given in Dwight's Travels of the capture and escape of General Wadsworth. He had been for many years a member of Congress—and was sent by the legislature of Massachusetts to command in the District of Maine. In February, 1781, he dismissed his troops, and made preparations for his return to Boston. His wife and her friend Miss Fenno, who had accompanied him, shared in the peril, when, by order of the commander of the British fort, an attack was made on the house where the General lodged. It was near midnight, the weather being severely cold, and the ground covered with snow, when the enemy came suddenly upon the sentinel, and forced an entrance into the guard-room. Another party of them at the same instant fired through the windows of Mrs. Wadsworth's apartment; a third forcing their

way through the windows into Miss Fenno's room.
The two terrified women had only time to dress hastily,
when the intruders assailed the barred door of the
General's chamber. He made a brave defence, but at
length, being wounded in the arm, was compelled to
surrender.

With the most admirable self-command, Mrs. Wadsworth and her friend gave no expression to their own
agitated feelings, intent only on relieving those of the
wounded prisoner. The wife wrapped a blanket round
him, and Miss Fenno tied a handkerchief round his arm,
to check the effusion of blood. In this condition, his
strength almost exhausted, he was carried off and the
ladies were left behind in their desolated house. Not a
window had escaped destruction; the doors were broken
down, two of the rooms set on fire, the floors drenched
with blood; and an old soldier, desperately wounded,
was begging for death, that he might be released from
his sufferings. The neighboring inhabitants, who came
to see what had happened, spared no labor—so that the
next day they could be more comfortable; but the
anxiety endured on the General's account could not be
relieved by any kind attentions to themselves.

In about two months, Mrs. Wadsworth and her friend
obtained permission to visit the prisoner, in the gloomy
solitude of his quarters at Bagaduce. Parting from him
at the end of ten days, Miss Fenno contrived to give
him an intimation of the knowledge she had gained that
he was not to be exchanged, by saying in a significant
manner, "General Wadsworth—take care of yourself."

The General soon understood this caution, learning that he was regarded as a prisoner of too much consequence to be trusted with his liberty.   The account of his imprisonment, his remarkable escape, and his adventures wandering through the wilderness, before reaching the settlements on the river St. George, where he found friends—has all the interest of the wildest romance, but would here be out of place.   His wife and Miss Fenno had sailed for Boston before his arrival at Portland. They were overtaken by a violent storm, and barely escaped shipwreck—being obliged to land at Portsmouth. There they had a new source of anxiety.   The wife had left all her specie with her captive husband, and the continental bills had lost their currency.   Without money, and without friends, after meditating on various expedients, she at last remembered that she had one acquaintance in the place.   To him the wanderers applied—receiving assistance which enabled them to return to Boston, where a happy reunion terminated the distresses of the family.   It may be added that General Wadsworth was an ancestor of the distinguished American poet, Henry Wadsworth Longfellow.

IMMEDIATELY before the battle of Bennington, General Stark, with several of his officers, stopped to obtain a draught of milk and water, at the house of Mr. Munro, a loyalist, who chanced to be absent.   One of the officers walked up to Mrs. Munro, and asked where her husband was.   She replied that she did not know;

whereupon he drew his sword, and endeavored to intimidate her into a more satisfactory answer. The General, hearing the commotion, severely reproved the officer for his uncivil behavior to a woman; and the offender went out, apparently much abashed. Mrs. Munro always remembered Stark's words—"Come on, my boys,"—as they marched to battle. The firing continued till late; and after a sleepless night, Mrs. Munro and her sister repaired with the earliest dawn to the battle-field, carrying pails of milk and water—and, wandering among heaps of slain and wounded, relieved the thirst of many sufferers, of whom some—the Hessians —were unable to express their thankfulness, save by the mute eloquence of grateful looks. Towards noon, wagons were sent to convey them to hospitals, and to bring away the dead for burial. This was not the only occasion on which Mrs. Munro was active in relieving distress, nor was her share of hardship and trial a light one.*

A SPIRIT kindred to that of Mrs. Motte was exhibited by Mrs. Borden at a period when American prospects were most clouded. New Jersey being overrun by the British, an officer stationed at Bordentown,† endeavored to intimidate her into using her influence over her husband and son. They were absent in the American army when she was visited at her residence for this pur-

* This fact is mentioned by a descendant of Mrs. Munro.

† Said by Major Garden to be Lord Cornwallis.

pose. The officer promised that if she would induce them to quit the standard they followed and join the royalists—her property should be protected; while in case of refusal, her estate would be ravaged and her elegant mansion destroyed. Mrs, Borden answered by bidding the foe begin the threatened havoc. "The sight of my house in flames"—she said, "would be a treat to me; for I have seen enough to know that you never injure what you have power to keep and enjoy. The application of a torch to my dwelling I should regard as a signal for your departure."

The house was burned in fulfillment of the threat, and the property laid waste; but as the owner had predicted, the retreat of the spoiler quickly followed.

~~~~~~~~~~~~~~

THE spirit exhibited by Mrs. Thomas Heyward, of Charleston, S. C., is as worthy of remembrance. A British order having been issued for a general illumination, in honor of the victory of Guilford, it was remarked that the house occupied by her and her sister showed no light. An officer called to demand the reason of this mark of disrespect to the order. In reply, Mrs. Heyward asked how she could be expected to join in celebrating a victory claimed by the British army, while her husband was a prisoner at St. Augustine? The answer was a peremptory command to illuminate. "Not a single light"—said the lady—"shall with my consent be placed in any window in the house." To the threat that it should be destroyed before midnight, she answered with the same expression of resolute determination. When, on the anniversary of the battle of Charleston, another illumination was ordered in testimony of joy for that event, Mrs. Heyward again refused compliance. Her sister was lying in the last stage of a wasting disease. The indignation of the mob was vented in assaults upon the house with brickbats and other missiles; and in the midst of the clamor and shouting, the invalid expired. The town major afterwards expressed his regret for the indignities, and requested Mrs. Heyward's permission to repair the damages done to the house. She thanked him, but refused, on the ground that the authorities could not thus cause insults to be forgotten, which they should not have permitted to be offered.*

An American soldier, flying from pursuit, sought the protection of Mrs. Richard Shubrick. The British, who followed him, insisted with threats that he should be delivered into their hands. While the other ladies in the house were too much frightened to offer remonstrance, this young and fragile creature withstood the enemy. With a delicacy of frame that bespoke feeble health, she possessed a spirit strong in the hour of trial: and her pale cheek could flush, and her eyes sparkle with scorn for the oppressor. She placed herself resolutely at the door of the apartment in which the fugitive had taken refuge, declaring her determination to defend

* Garden, First Series, p. 227.

it with her life. "To men of honor," she said, "the chamber of a lady should be sacred as a sanctuary!" The officer, struck with admiration at her intrepidity immediately ordered his men to retire.

On another occasion, when a party of Tarleton's dragoons was plundering the house of one of her friends, a sergeant followed the overseer into the room where the ladies were assembled. The old man refused to tell him where the plate was hidden, and the soldier struck him with a sabre ; whereupon Mrs. Shubrick, starting up, threw herself between them, and rebuked the ruffian for his barbarity. She bade him strike *her*, if he gave another blow, for she would protect the aged servant. Her interposition saved him from further injury.*

The family of Dr. Channing, on their way from France to America, not long after the commencement of the war, were attacked by a privateer. During the engagement that ensued, Mrs. Channing remained on deck, handing cartridges, with encouraging speeches to the crew, and assisting the wounded. When the colors of the vessel were struck, she seized the pistols and side-arms of her husband, and flung them into the sea, declaring that they, at least, should not be surrendered to the enemy.

AN anecdote is related of Mrs. Daniel Hall, who was a guest in the house of Mrs. Sarah Reeve Gibbes when

* Garden, First Series, 240.

the British surrounded it.   It is said that having obtained
permission from the authorities then in power, to go to
Johns' Island on a visit to her mother, she was stopped
when going on board by an officer who demanded the
key of her trunk.   She asked him what he wished to
look for.   "For treason—madam," he replied.   "Then,"
retorted Mrs. Hall, "you may be saved the trouble of
search, for you may find enough of it at my tongue's
end."*

⁓⁓⁓⁓⁓⁓⁓⁓⁓⁓⁓

IT is well known that the name of Gustavus Conyngham, the captain of one of the first privateers under the
American flag, was one of terror to the British.   The
print of him exposed in the shops of London, labelled,
"The Arch Rebel," and representing a man of gigantic
frame and ferocious countenance, was one of the expressions indicating the popular fear attached to his name.
He was repeatedly captured by the enemy, and treated
with barbarous severity, being only saved from death
by the resolution of Congress that his execution should
be avenged by that of certain royalist officers then in
custody.   While he was a prisoner in irons on board
one of their vessels, his wife made an eloquent and
touching appeal in his behalf, in a letter to General
Washington, which was laid before Congress.   "To
have lost a beloved and worthy husband in battle," she
says, "would have been a light affliction;" but her
courage failed at the thought of the suffering, despair,

* Garden's Revolutionary Anecdotes.

and ignominious death that awaited him. The interposition she besought was granted, and saved the prisoner's life.

A letter written from Antigua, published in the Pennsylvania Register, gives an account of Mrs. Conyngham s romantic introduction to the noted hero who was afterwards her husband. She was, with two other ladies, at sea, and shared the common fear of meeting with some American privateer—" the Revenge" in particular—cruising near the West India Islands. The Captain was pacing the quarter-deck with a glass in his hand, and was pressed with many questions as to the danger by his fair passengers, who had heard dreadful accounts of the cruelty of the Americans. Suddenly a cry from aloft—"A sail! a sail!" caused general confusion. "The captain hastened up the shrouds, gave orders to the man at the helm, and remained some minutes watching the approaching suspicious stranger; then coming on deck, said that ' the vessel looked d—d rakish; he had no doubt it was a privateer, probably the Revenge—the terror of those seas.' The ladies were in tears, and withdrew to the cabin half fainting from apprehension." There was no prospect of escape; the sail gradually drew near; a gun was fired, and the pursued vessel lay to. A boat put off from the stranger, and two officers and several men were soon upon her deck. The spokesman wore a blue roundabout and trowsers, and was well armed; he was about twenty-five, of a light and active figure; his sunburnt face showed much intelligence, and was, withal, interesting from a shade of melancholy. He made some inquiries concerning the vessel, cargo, and passengers, and on being informed there were ladies in the cabin, colored, and observed to his lieutenant—that he would have to go and say to them, the passengers were not prisoners, but guests. The lieutenant replied that he had not "confidence enough to speak to them," and the other went into the cabin. The fears of the ladies were soon dispelled, and the youngest asked the officer, with much naiveté, if he was really a pirate. " I am captain of an American privateer," he answered, " and he, I trust, cannot be a pirate." " Are you the captain of 'the Revenge?'" " I am." " Is it possible you are the man represented to be a bloody and ferocious pirate, whose chief delight is in scenes of carnage?" " I am that person of whom these nursery tales have been told ; whose picture is hung up to frighten children. I have suffered much from British prisons and from British calumny ; but my sufferings will never make me forget the courtesy due to ladies."

During the few days the vessels were together, the chivalrous spirit of Conyngham, and his kindness towards the passengers, won their esteem, and they listened with pleasure to the lieutenant's account of his gallant achievements on the seas. The beautiful Miss Anne ——, who chatted with him in so sprightly a manner, was, a day or two afterwards, with her two companions, put on board a vessel bound to one of the islands. When the writer of the letter saw her again at L'Orient, some time afterwards, she was the wife of the far-famed captain of "the Revenge."

~~~~~~~~~~

THE case of Sir Charles Asgill, a young officer of the British Guards, selected by lot for execution in retaliation for the murder of Captain Huddy, was made the ground-work of a French tragedy by Sauvigny, represented in Paris, in 1789. The story of his imprisonment—the sufferings of his mother and family while the doom hung over him—her appeal to the King and Queen of France—their intercession, and the final relenting of Congress—is one of deep and touching interest. It is included, with the letters of Lady Asgill, in many of the books on the Revolution.

END OF VOL. II.